The Invisible Landscape

The Invisible Landscape

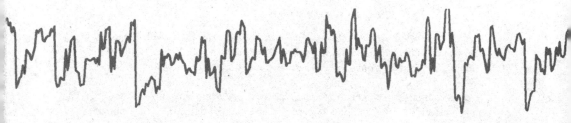

Mind,

Hallucinogens,

and the I Ching

Terence McKenna and
Dennis McKenna

HarperOne
An Imprint of HarperCollins*Publishers*

HarperOne

To inquire about Time Wave software in both Macintosh and DOS versions please contact Blue Water Publishing at 1-800-366-0264. fax# (503) 538-8485.

or write:
P.O. Box 726
Newberg, OR 97132

HarperCollins Web site: http://www.harpercollins.com
HarperCollins®, 📖®, and HarperOne™ are trademarks of HarperCollins Publishers.

FIRST PUBLISHED IN 1975 BY THE SEABURY PRESS
FIRST HARPERCOLLINS EDITION PUBLISHED IN 1993

Interior design by Margery Cantor and Jaime Robles

Library of Congress Cataloging-in-Publication Data
McKenna, Terence K., 1946–
    The Invisible landscape : mind, hallucinogesn, and the I ching /
Terence McKenna and Dennis McKenna.—1st HarperCollins ed.
        p. cm.
    Includes bibliographical references and index.
    ISBN: 978–0–06–250635–1
    1. I ching. 2. Mind and body. 3. Shamanism. I. Oeric, O. N. II. Title.
    BF161.M47   1994
    133—dc20   93–5195

23 24 25 26 27 LBC 40 39 38 37 36

In Memory of our dear Mother

THUS WERE THE stars of heaven created like a golden chain
To bind the Body of Man to heaven from falling into the Abyss.
Each took his station and his course began with sorrow & care.

In sevens & tens & fifties, hundreds, thousands, number'd all
According to their various powers, subordinate to Urizen
And to his sons in their degrees & to his beauteous daughters,
Travelling in silent majesty along their order'd ways
In right lined paths outmeasur'd by proportions of number, weight
And measure, mathematic motions wondrous along the deep,
In fiery pyramid, or Cube, or unornamented pillar square
Of fire, far shining, travelling along even to its destin'd end;
Then falling down a terrible space, recovering in winter dire
Its wasted strength, it back returns upon a nether course,
Till fir'd with ardour fresh recruited in its humble season,
It rises up on high all summer, till its wearied course
Turns into autumn. Such the period of many worlds.
Others triangular, right angled course maintain. Others obtuse
Acute, Scalene, in simple paths; others move
In intricate ways, biquadrate, Trapeziums, Rhombs, Rhomboids,
Parallelograms triple & quadruple, polygonic,
In their amazing hard subdu'd course in the vast deep.

Contents

PART ONE: Mind, Molecules, and Magic 1

PART TWO: Time, Change, and Becoming 119

List of Figures and Tables

Foreword to the 1994 edition

When I was researching my history of the psychedelic movement, I pursued many odd and forgotten books. Most were easily obtained, either from libraries or used bookstores. One, however, proved elusive. Written by two brothers, Dennis and Terence McKenna, it was called *The Invisible Landscape,* and it had great posthumous word of mouth. "Now there's a truly heavy book," the owner of one bookstore devoted to mysticism and consciousness told me when I queried him about it. "Haven't seen one in years."

Which is about how long it took me to find my copy. In Boston. My cry of wild exultation lifting heads all over the bookstore.

The bibliophiles among you will appreciate the keen anticipation I felt as I carried it to a nearby cafe and cracked it open and discovered that, indeed, this was a truly heavy book.

Dense. Technical. Fascinating. Infuriating. Marvelously weird.

Mixed in with theories drawn from the study of schizophrenia, molecular biology, and ethnobotany were pungent disquisitions on shamanism and psychedelic philosophy. Plus what seemed to be a story about an encounter with an insectoid intelligence who had curious things to say about the nature of time. The closest thing I could compare it to was an alchemical text published in the classic period—the seventeenth century—before the bonds linking science and magic were severed, when it was still possible to have a scientist magician on the order of Isaac Newton.

Since that first reading, I have met the authors of *The Invisible Landscape.* Though I have never seen them together, I'm told they're one of the great brother acts on the planet. Dennis is the scientific McKenna—the one with the doctorate in psychopharmacology—slow-spoken, factual. Terence is the quicksilver poet-philosopher McKenna. He's what I imagine George Bernard Shaw might have been like if Shaw had been born in the American West in the 1940s and educated at Berkeley in the psychedelic '60s.

Cast your mind back to that milieu as you begin this book. Back to those few months when there was a steep plunge into novelty, as Terence McKenna might say, that carried the most restless minds of the Baby Boom with it. Back to when the possibility that the world could be remade sparkled in the sunshine of what will seem to be, as it recedes into history, a time of perpetual summer—the summer of love, of Woodstock, of massive spring marches through cherry-blossomed Washington to levitate the Pentagon.

Our appetite for simplicity has caused us to compress the chaos of the '60s into one monolithic "Youth Revolt." But there were two philosophies then among the revolutionaries on how the world might be remade. One path, endorsed by the political activists, advocated a traditional Western strategy: seizing political power and using that vantage to raise consciousness and save the world. The other path proposed an attack on consciousness itself using a controversial and soon outlawed family of psychochemicals—the psychedelics.

Hippies and activists. Could a society heal its social ills without first addressing its own internal flaws? As Tim Leary, perhaps the most celebrated spokesman of this second option, put it: "If all the Negroes and left-wing college students in the world had Cadillacs and full control of society, they would still be involved in an anthill social system unless they opened themselves up."

Opened up.

There in a nutshell was the problem vis-à-vis a psychedelic politics: these substances opened up much too much. They were a doorway into a universe of strange and sometimes terrifying information. These were not facile tools; rather, they were an invitation to explorers, and a percentage of the Baby Boom's best and brightest responded by turning into mind wanderers, seeking adventure in the unclaimed real estate of the imagination.

Such was the case with our two authors, who were convinced that the future of the species could best be secured through a transformation of consciousness.

> We believed that the widespread use of psychedelic drugs in modern society was somehow rooted to the intuition that exploration and reassimilation of so-called magical dimensions was the next valid step in humanity's collective search for liberation.

They focused their work on the psychedelic dimethyltryptamine, or DMT. They were curious about DMT's apparent stimulation of the language centers of the brain. Not only was glossolalia (speaking in tongues) common, but sometimes one encountered dancing molecular forms that seemed to be made out of visible language.

Is it any wonder they were entranced?

One day, the McKennas came across a description of the shamanic usage of the tryptamine-containing plant *ayahuasca* in an anthropological monograph about a tribe in the upper Amazon Basin. According to the Jivero shamans, *ayahuasca* induced a state of consciousness in which a fluorescent violet substance was generated, and this substance allowed them to work their magic.

From this aperçu an expedition grew.

It took years for the journey to jell, but in 1971, joined by three friends, the McKennas embarked on a trek up the Amazon to investigate the shamanic usage of such shamanic power plants as *ayahuasca*.

> None of us was yet twenty-five years old. We had been drawn together through the political turmoil that had characterized our years shared in Berkeley.... We had sorted through the ideological options, and had decided to put all of our chips on the psychedelic experience as the shortest path to the millennium, which our politics had inflamed us to hope for.

I'm giving nothing away by telling you that things didn't work out as planned, that the little expedition never even reached its target village, that it was sidetracked, that they discovered instead a strange mushroom, the ingestion of which provoked the events that *The Invisible Landscape* attempts to explain. They embarked upon a serious lark and ended up stumbling across the alien, the mysterious, the other. Deep in the forest. A long, long way from civilization.

The complete telling of this story, which strikes me as one of the archetypal stories of the Baby Boom generation, is contained in Terence McKenna's *True Hallucinations,* a book that was composed in the fullness of time, years after the occurrence of the events it describes. The McKennas' initial response, however, is in the book you now hold in your hands.

In his preface to the German edition of *The Invisible Landscape,* Dennis McKenna says:

> The book was written in dead earnest by two individuals struggling to come to grips with a deluge of ideas triggered by a very personal and idiosyncratic experience. No one is more aware than myself that certain passages read like the musings of a naive and scientifically untutored student.... Even though the passage of nearly twenty years since these ideas were first committed to paper have lent a certain perspective, and have made me less willing to insist on the veracity of these concepts as revealed truth, it is still not an admission that is easily made.

Revealed truth. What happened to the McKennas up the Amazon was one of those sudden, shattering discontinuities that sever the recipient from normal time, normal experience, and usually force a complete rewriting of one's life. Time is separated into those things that occurred before the revelation and those things that have come after—the aftershocks.

The Invisible Landscape is the McKennas' first attempt to wrestle with this revelation using the handholds of Western science and philosophy. They may seem to use these disciplines in an uncharacteristic and perhaps "naive" way, but what strikes me more is the ingenious and sometimes brilliantly intuitive application of these methods by two kids who were only in their early twenties.

Nowadays, whenever some fossil starts giving me that Allan-Bloom-*Closing-of-the-American-Mind*-it's-all-the-fault-of-the-sixties'-generation rap, I plan to hand him *The Invisible Landscape* and suggest he chew through a few chapters before we chat further about declining standards.

What these fossils would find is a book divided into three sections. The first is Dennis McKenna's attempt to understand the psychedelic effects of the mushroom revelation in neurobiological terms. Dennis was interested in the cellular and molecular changes that accompanied the altered state, assuming that the dozens of techniques humans used to promote these states were just different ways of triggering the same organic process. Just different roads to the top of the same mountain.

The second part of the book is Terence's attempt both to understand the mushroom revelation and to assess whether it possibly could be true. A taste of the text is in order here.

> We could feel the presence of some invisible hyperspatial entity, an ally, which seemed to be observing and sometimes exerting influence on the situation to keep us moving gently toward an experimental resolution of the ideas we were generating. Because of the alien nature of the tryptamine trance, its seeming accentuation of themes alien, insectile, and futuristic, and because of previous experiences with tryptamine in which insectile hallucinatory transformations of human beings were observed, we were led to speculate that the role of the presence was somehow like that of an anthropologist, come to give humanity the keys to galactarian citizenship.

This strange insectoid intelligence gently directed our authors to study the King Wen sequence of the *I Ching*, which just happens to be the oldest sequence in that ancient divinatory tool. What they found there (maybe I am giving away too much of the mystery now) was a pattern, a rhythm, a rhythm moving through time, maybe the key to time itself—a rhythm that danced its way through the millennia toward an omega point that the McKennas calculated to be the year 2012.

Which brings us to the third part of the book, the computer program that describes the mathematics from which the McKennas derive this conclusion. In the long years between the first and second editions of *The Invisible Landscape,* our authors have turned their mathematical model into a computer program that runs on most PCs. The first time Terence demonstrated the Timewave Zero software for me, he said something like, "My God, man, what if it's true? And even if it isn't, you've still got a great computer game."

Perhaps you're beginning to see what I mean when I call this book dense, technical, fascinating, infuriating. Marvelously weird.

Jay Stevens
Weathersfield Bow, Vermont

Preface to the 1994 edition

Someone encountering this book for the first time is certain to find that many, if not most, of the ideas and concepts discussed are extremely peculiar. The speculations in it are so radically outside the mainstream of modern scientific and philosophical thought that you may wonder whether this book is really meant as a sort of parody of serious scientific discourse. Let me hasten to reassure the baffled: The book you hold in your hands was written in dead earnest by two individuals struggling to come to grips with a deluge of ideas triggered by a very personal and idiosyncratic experience. No one is more aware than myself that certain passages read like the musings of a scientifically untutored student, while others are perhaps more indicative of the associations of an unhinged mind.

Indeed, it must be admitted that both operative modes played a role in the fashioning of the speculations which this work sets forth. Even though the passage of nearly twenty years since these ideas were first committed to paper have lent a certain perspective, and have made me less willing to insist on the veracity of these concepts as revealed truth, it is still not an admission that is easily made. I would like to think that those years have brought with them some small degree of intellectual maturity, and perhaps a certain humility. The writing of a book which purports to explain all and everything, as this one does, is a task best left to the young, for whom such pedestrian considerations as scientific rigor and credibility are mere impediments.

Having acquired considerable formal training in both the theory and practice of science in the interim, I now realize that even that vaunted discipline may remain forever incapable of satisfactorily accounting for the simplest, most basic elements of everyday existence: our experience of life, of mind, of being in the world. Science, by its very nature, is rendered uncomfortable when faced with such questions, because it is intrinsically suited to the examination of parts rather than wholes. Scientific scrutiny can unlock the minutest details of each piece of the puzzle, but more poetic sensibilities must be called on to appreciate what it is to *be* a brain/mind/body experiencing the marvelous totality of being in all of its blooming, buzzing confusion.

It is in this respect that psychedelic drugs have been a major conundrum for science, and are likely to remain so for some time. For it is in the phenomenon of the psychedelic experience that the irrefutable, self-evident qualities of the mind come up hard against the reductionist models of the molecular neurobiologist. While it seems clear that the modalities of the psychedelic state must be rooted in neuronal pharmacodynamics, explanatory paradigms couched in terms of receptor selectivities, structure/activity relationships, agonist/antagonist interactions, activation of limbic substructures, etc., all somehow fail to do justice to the transcendent, transformative reality that becomes manifest when one actually consumes a psychedelic drug.

One possible approach to the resolution of this dilemma might be termed the way of the shaman: one dispenses with all attempts at reductionist analysis and simply accepts the experience on its own terms, perhaps as a divine revelation from a source outside the self—a god within a plant, for instance. Indeed, the psychedelic experience is so profound and overwhelming that even scientifically sophisticated individuals can easily succumb to the misperception that "the trip is in the drug." The alternative response, which might be characterized as the way of the alchemist, is to become utterly obsessional in the seeking of reductive explanations, and to construct wildly elaborate models in an attempt to integrate the irreducible reality of what is experienced into some scientific or, more often, quasi-scientific paradigm. This book tries, unsuccessfully perhaps, to steer a middle course between these two approaches.

Nevertheless, though there is much within this work that I would no longer attempt to defend as scientifically valid, there is also much food for thought. The intuition that led Terence and me to write *The Invisible Landscape* was that the key to the brain/mind problem and perhaps many other questions of considerable ontological significance for our species lies in a thorough understanding of the psychedelic experience, from its molecular mechanisms to its historical and evolutionary implications. That original intuition has remained a valid working hypothesis to this day, and in fact has been the stimulus, at least in our lives, for most of our subsequent intellectual development. In that time we have partially revised our interpretations of the precipitating causes and consequences of our experiences, have acquired new information, and have examined alternative hypotheses ranging from the pharmacological to the mythical; but always driving the searching and questioning has been the desire to understand the nature of the psychedelic experience. We are, if anything, less assured of the success of our quest today than when this book was written, but remain convinced that any model of the brain/mind that does *not* reconcile the observations of neurobiology with the *fact* of the psychedelic state, as it is experienced, is doomed to remain scientifically incomplete and philosophically unsatisfying.

Psychedelic drugs have always been and remain the most useful molecular probes available to science for exploring the relationship between the subjective experience of mind and neurobiological processes. Given the validity of this statement—and I suggest that no neuroscientist with personal knowledge of the psychedelic state would contest it—one cannot fail to be puzzled by science's curious neglect of psychedelic research over the last two decades. While it is true that in this era of government-supported science, budgetary constraints and research priorities can influence which scientific problems are investigated and which are allowed to languish, one suspects that more than benign neglect is behind the hiatus in psychedelic research. Despite its pretensions to objectivity, science, like any other human institution, places a certain vested interest in its own self-preservation; thus it is likely to be less than enthusiastic, if not openly hostile, toward any investigative strategy that could potentially call its most basic assumptions into question. Psychedelic drugs exert their influence at the brain/mind/body interface, and are clearly well within that shadowy and forbidden territory where cognition itself originates. Is it any wonder that science hesitates to rip that veil aside and illuminate those shadows with the cold light of reason—knowing that reason itself may become the ultimate sacrifice for such audacity? It may be that the psychedelic experience cannot be understood using only the reductionist models of science, and that only by a conscious unification of the reductionist, analytical methods of science with the holistic, nonanalytical approach of the shaman can we hope to understand, appreciate, and apply the lessons learned from such experiences. This book is a first, faltering, step in that direction.

I am pleased that Terence and I again have the opportunity to make it available for public scrutiny, even though it is a very different work from the one I would write today, given the necessary time and freedom from more immediate and pressing concerns. I urge that it be read with this thought in mind: While there is much within these covers that would have to be rejected in the light of new knowledge, there is also much that is more supported by current scientific knowledge than it was nearly twenty years ago. Examples that could be cited include the possible holographic nature of neural organization, retrograde axoplasmic transport, the possible role of superconductivity and other quantum mechanical processes in living systems, the intercalation of drug molecules into nucleic acids, and the importance of oscillatory processes in regulating the functions of nucleic acids and proteins. While none of these has actually been incorporated into conventional scientific dogma, they are all active areas of experimental investigation.

Scientific progress, and human understanding generally, is a self-refining, exponentially accelerating process. The past two decades have witnessed advances in scientific understanding that were scarcely imagined when this book was written. It seems virtually certain that science and human thinking will experience an even more radical transformation over the next two decades. Ironically, the speculations in this book may resemble the result of that scientific and noetic (r)evolution more than the unquestioned paradigms of current scientific knowledge.

Dennis J. McKenna
December 1988

Acknowledgments to the 1975 edition

The authors wish to express their grateful appreciation to the many friends who aided this project. In South America we were assisted by Mr. Michael Laski and Ms. Sarah Hartley and by the Naval del Sur de Colombia, whose vessels often were our only means of transportation. The Witoto people of La Chorrera and the Mission of La Chorrera were most hospitable, the former providing invaluable access to local psychoactive plants. Drs. Horatio and Isabella Calle of the Universidad Nacional, Bogotá, provided valuable information on the endemic tryptamines of Colombian Amazonas. Thanks to the Octavio Luna family, who placed their country home at our disposal for a portion of the time during which the manuscript was written. Thanks especially to Luis Eduardo Luna, whose support and enthusiasm for these ideas helped greatly in their clarification.

Dr. Wolfram Eberhard kindly read and criticized chapter 8. Special thanks to Richard Brzustowitz and Professor Erich Jantsch, both of whom made many valuable suggestions and were most instrumental in helping us secure publication. Ron Curry made several suggestions we have used in the *I Ching* graph.

We especially acknowledge the contribution made by Erica Nietfeld. She was a willing listener in the thousands of situations in which these ideas unfolded and gave very generously of her energy in helping type and order these pages.

Last, we wish to thank sincerely our editor, Dr. Justus George Lawler of The Seabury Press. He has been most kind and patient throughout the preparation of the manuscript. Friends too numerous to mention participated in the years of conversation out of which these pages were forged. To them, to Michael Malcolm, Elizabeth Hutchinson, Kevin Mahoney, William Cole, Ernest and Barbara Waugh, John Parker, Jr., William Patrick Watson, Martin Inn, Massayasu Takayama, Mark Skolnick, Ralph Abraham, and all the others, many thanks.

Acknowledgments to the 1994 edition

I wish to express thanks and appreciation to all the people who helped to make a new edition of *The Invisible Landscape* possible. Deep and special thanks to Dan Levy, who pursued this project over several years and through a number of jobs. Thanks also to my literary agents in New York, John Brockman and Katinka Matson. For mathematics and programming contributions, I owe a great debt to Peter Meyer, who translated my mathematical intuitions into C and thus defined the core algorithm of the Timewave theory; to Billy Smith for Hypercard implementation of the Timewave on the Macintosh; and to Peter Broadwell, who was the first to implement the Timewave in a PC environment.

Peter Meyer especially has been a devoted explorer of the mathematics and metaphysics behind the Timewave. His company, Dolphin Software of Berkeley, California, has been very helpful by developing and marketing the software that supports my mathematical ideas. Thanks also to Klaus Scharff of Bergisch-Gladbach, Germany, for his mathematical insights.

Sincere thanks to my close friend Rupert Sheldrake, a theoretical biologist and scientific heretic, whose ideas concerning morphogenetic fields and formative causation were instrumental in shaping my own conceptions of the Timewave and of the conservation of novelty as a universal principle.

Over the years, I have given numerous seminars and weekend teaching retreats on these subjects at New York's The Open Center, at Chicago's Oasis, and at the Rim Institute in Payson, Arizona. Especially important were the five-day sessions at Esalen Institute in Big Sur, California, in 1988 and 1991. For the time I spent at Esalen as a scholar in residence, from 1988 until 1992, during which discussion of these ideas was prominent, I'd like to give special thanks to Esalen and to its programming director, Nancy Lunney. To all those who attended my seminars and lectures over the years I also give my thanks and appreciation.

At Harper San Francisco, I was supported by publishers Clayton Carlson and Tom Grady, and by my editor, Caroline Pincus. Thanks to Jaime Robles for the new illustrations, which have taken difficult concepts and made them very clear. The general look and feel of the book is due to designer Margery Cantor. And once again, it was my great good fortune to have Leslie Rossman as my publicist. Every author should be so blessed. To all of you and to all the people unknown to me who worked to make this book available once again I offer sincere thanks and appreciation.

Finally I want to thank my brother and coauthor, Dennis McKenna, for his continued devotion to these themes and ideas throughout the many years that have passed since the original experiment at La Chorrera. His evolution into a research scientist with a distinguished record of scientific discovery and publication has been a great source of satisfaction to me.

Terence McKenna

Introduction to the 1994 edition

It has been eighteen years since the original 1975 publication of *The Invisible Landscape*. And it will be about nineteen years until the denouement that will surely be the acid test for this series of psychedelically inspired speculations. I have long struggled to maintain a suspended judgment on these matters, yet I'm also aware that if nothing at all comes of this extraordinary intellectual adventure, it will be a rather ironic comment on the idea that nature does nothing in vain.

I believe that *The Invisible Landscape* remains our magnum opus, and that it is monumental in its ambition to build a new system that integrates all nature—animate, inanimate, social, and psychological—into one mathematically coherent web of interconnected and evolving resonances.

The 1975 edition was small and its readership widely scattered. I hope the evolution of scientific thinking and the new resurgence of interest in shamanism and the use of psychotropic plants will contribute to an intellectual climate in which the ideas of *The Invisible Landscape* will be fairly examined and considered by a wider audience. My faith that the ideas explored here will be found to have an extraordinary explanatory and persuasive power remains unshaken. As for Truth, I will argue today—as I did in 1971 at La Chorrera—that these ideas are, in Wittgenstein's wonderful phrase, "True enough."

Terence McKenna
Opihihale, Hawaii
November 1993

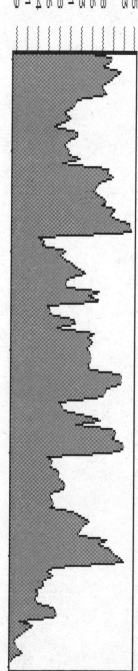

Part One

Mind,

Molecules,

and

Magic

Introduction

The search for liberation, a paradisiacal state of freedom that mythology insists is the ahistorical root of the historical process, has always been the raison d'être of the human species' conscious pilgrimage through time. In the name of drawing near to this liberation, humankind has built and then partially rejected an endless procession of societies, governments, philosophies, and religions. The understanding of what form this liberation might take has been in a constant state of refinement, often, if not always, evolving at cross purposes to itself, creating again and again situations wherein systems in violent competition, and seemingly antithetical to each other, sought the same goal—a goal always reducible to this complex idea, liberation. Systems as divergent as Buddhism and Marxism, National Socialism and Christianity, have all claimed possession of a set of concepts that would in some sense "free" their practitioners. The entire human experience, individual and collective, can be described as the pursuit of that which frees.

It has not been a search without success; it may be said that although progress is erratic, nevertheless each successive age has expanded our understanding of the nature of being and freedom. Monotheism, as it developed in the West, freed early humans from the nearly complete domination of consciousness by the pan-vitalistic animism seen everywhere resident in Nature. The coming of Christianity freed its adherents from the fear of a wrathful and paternalistic god. Similarly, the modern era offered freedom from the dogmatic stasis of late medieval Catholicism. It may be argued that each of these events, rather than advancing humans along the path toward liberation, had quite the opposite effect, and, in fact, each step down the path of history has led deeper into time and away from the paradise *in illo tempore*. However, viewed objectively, the historical process may be seen as the expansion of cross-cultural contacts between various peoples and a resultant sharing of a continuously growing pool of information, ideas, and myths. This body of inherited and shared information represents our collective understanding of the nature of our species' conscious journey through time. As such, each new epoch, each new religion or philosophy, however much it may appear to erode the search for liberation in its own right, as an addition to the racial collectivity of conscious information, represents advance. Although our entire being is caught up in the pursuit of liberation, we share no collective understanding of what this liberation might be. The search is reflected on all levels within our species and is intensely present in each of us as individuals. Whether Marxist or mystic, each of us pursues those threads of thought that seem, subject to our own uniqueness, to be fruitful in leading to this liberation.

The personal response to this situation by the authors of this book has been to follow the "nostalgia for paradise" through a survey of the ideas associated with shamanism and pharmacology, with frequent forays into apparently distant fields.

During 1970 our thinking coalesced to a point where we felt that a basic reconstitution of culture, while theoretically possible through an archaic holo-cybernetic revolution, was practically impossible, given the intransigence of power elites and the lack of direction evinced by putative revolutionaries. Our interest then centered upon primitive societies where a connection with the timeless world of the unconscious is maintained through the office of the shaman, the technician of the sacred. We believed that the widespread use of psychedelic drugs in modern society was somehow rooted to the intuition that exploration and reassimilation of so-called magical dimensions was the next valid step in humanity's collective search for liberation. Our studies centered upon tribal peoples who had a highly refined tradition of shamanism and the use of psychotropic substances. Practical experience indicated that entry into the "separate reality" or the "nonordinary reality" of the shamanic cosmology was most easily achieved through the use of hallucinogenic tryptamines. To investigate this assumption, we organized, early in 1971, an expedition to the Upper Amazon Basin to locate sources of organic tryptamines and to explore their possible relevance to the search for liberation into eschatological time.

Our intuition was that the physical interaction of mind and brain, and its potential for manipulation through hallucinogenic drugs, might provide a situation where new and radical experimental approaches could shed light on problems still largely unelucidated, problems such as the relation of metabolism to mind and the molecular nature of memory and recall. We hoped to create a model of mind and its parameters that would be neither reductionist nor exclusive of paranormal phenomena. Indeed, in the institution of shamanism we felt that the normal and the paranormal were somehow merged, and in the shamanic world, physical manipulation of psychic space via hallucinogens is raised to the level of "science"—more precisely of a folk science. We assumed that the merging of the normal and the paranormal and the use of hallucinogens were directly related. Unlike most researchers, we did not seek to reduce the paranormal aspects of the shaman's world to mere psychologisms; instead, we set out with the open-ended premise that in matters as mysterious as the nature of mind, surprises might well be in store. We sought to experience shamanic phenomena on whatever level of existential validity they could present themselves. We were not wrong in anticipating that what we would encounter would leave our own culture-bound categories severely strained. This book attempts to present the assumptions that led us to the Amazon and to describe our research there.

We assumed that mind and life are rooted in a bioelectronic field phenomenon, since a corpse is similar to a living body except for the latter's bioelectronic continuum of energy exchange and metabolism. We hoped to understand the mechanics of the mutual interrelatedness of mind and the organic matrix at formative submolecular junctures. If, as we postulate, mind and its contents, both conscious and unconscious, reside somewhere in the structure or dynamics of the genetic matrix, then it would be useful to seek a means of enhancing access to those portions of the genetic apparatus where the "unconscious" mind, both personal and collective, may be seated. As is common knowledge, numerous techniques of "mind expansion," from drugs to yoga, have been devised to make unconscious portions of the mind available for conscious contemplation. Nearly all of these seem to involve the induction of some biophysical alteration of the condition of the organism, and it is likely that the change at the cellular and molecular level is the same whatever the technique employed. If, indeed, some molecular mechanism is capable of unlocking the realms of the personal and collective unconscious, then the understanding and application of such a process would be of tremendous benefit in the search for human liberation. Our own understanding of our Amazon experiences is that they seem, however cryptically, to argue strongly that the liberation whose attainment is the very motivation of conscious life is a more tangible thing than we had thought possible.

It will be useful, for purposes of clarification, to divide the work in which we were engaged at La Chorrera into three categories, which can then be discussed independently of each other—though certainly in our own subjective experience, during the experiment and since, these categories have tended to migrate toward each other, leading, as we anticipated, to an understanding that seems to hover at the very edge of language while being clearly rooted in the sphere of cognition. We have thought it reasonable to attempt to discuss this work on three levels, made only as distinct as is necessary for its comprehension, and understanding further that in our subjective experience, these levels were not distinct at all. These categories may be thought of as (1) the actual biophysical experiment, (2) the subjective psychological experience triggered by the experiment, and (3) the continuum graphs of the evolution of change in space-time that are the objective content derived from our attempts to investigate the bioelectronic constellation of mind. These graphs seem to imply a possible ecological crisis within the community of species that may make access to the shamanic dimension a fact of historical "fatedness" of unique importance for humankind.

Before these categories can be usefully discussed, some of the principles and methodological assumptions that provided an investigative set of tools for these shamanic researches will be discussed.

Any sort of investigative procedure, whether it be the analysis of the physical world or the exploration of interior realms, is accomplished through the application of some methodology, which in turn is founded on philosophical premises. More often than not, the philosophical assumptions entailed in the practice of science are not made explicit; the hypothesis and experimental procedures and results are presented without articulating the philosophical bias underlying them. Our investigations are concerned with explicating the nature of mind, ideas, and consciousness concepts, which, by their very elusiveness, demand the construction of philosophical postulates. The chapters in Part One are devoted to an exposition of the philosophical and operational biases that influenced and guided our investigations. Chapter 1 focuses on the traditional figure of the shaman as he is found in primitive societies, while chapter 2 presents a comparison of the shaman and the schizophrenic. The shaman and the schizophrenic both seem to possess a greater access to unconscious processes than the "normal" individual. While the schizophrenic is spontaneously inundated and often overwhelmed by these processes, the shaman, through the practice of his "techniques of ecstasy," is able to integrate them into consciousness and to maintain access to them without suffering personality disintegration. If some fundamentally similar molecular process is responsible for the release of unconscious contents in each case, then the figure of the shaman is worthy of close study for his ability to trigger and control this process.

Because the temptation to treat the concept of mind in vague and ill-defined terms is a powerful one, chapters 3 and 4 attempt to delineate our understanding of the nature of mind. Chapter 3 itself deals with some methodological and philosophical assumptions of science that must be made explicit if science is to address the complex phenomenon of mind. An alternative metaphysic, consistent with a quantum mechanical understanding of mind at its primary levels, is advanced as the basis for a scientific methodology able to pursue an experimental and empirical investigation of mind. The ontological premises outlined in chapter 3 do not arise *de novo* from the substratum of individualistic speculation; on the contrary, they are based on the process-oriented "organismic" philosophical tradition that finds its most eloquent expression in the thought of Alfred North Whitehead. The metaphysical and philosophical concepts presented in this chapter will, accordingly, closely reflect some central themes of Whitehead's thought. Chapter 4 finds in the properties of holography new principles of organization that provide useful models for understanding the structure of both brain and mind. Chapter 5 enlarges upon the discussion of brain-mind organization and advances a tentative hypothesis of neurotransmitter and drug activity that attempts to explain how higher cortical experience could be modulated at the molecular level. Chapter 6 describes the procedures and results of our experimental attempt to expand the scope of consciousness through manipulation of the biophysical state of the human organism. The final chapter in Part One deals with our personal and subjective reaction to the experiment at La Chorrera.

Chapter 1

The Figure of the Shaman

Of all the diverse religious institutions that humans have elaborated since before the beginning of recorded history, that of shamanism is one of the most singular and is probably one of the most archaic as well. The shaman is something of a maverick among religious practitioners. While shamanism occurs in virtually every culture on the planet, manifesting itself in religious traditions both ancient and modern, both "primitive" and sophisticated, the shaman remains eminently individualistic, idiosyncratic, and enigmatic, standing ever apart from organized ecclesiastical institutions while still performing important functions for the psychic and religious life of the culture. Comparable, but not identical, with such similar idiosyncratic practitioners as medicine men and sorcerers, the shaman is the possessor of techniques of proven efficacy and of powers bordering on the paranormal, the complete understanding of which still eludes modern psychology. It is this complex and fascinating figure of the shaman that we want to analyze from a standpoint at once sympathetic, interpretative, and psychological, with a view to answering the following questions: (1) What are the traditional aspects of shamanism as it is encountered in primitive cultures? (2) What is the nature of the shamanic personality and abilities, and what is the psychological role of the shaman in the society at large? And (3) Are there institutions analogous to shamanism in modern society?

The vocation of shaman is found in nearly all archaic cultures, from the Australian aborigines to the Jivaro Indians of central Ecuador and Peru to the Yakut tribes of Siberia. It is believed to have originated among these Siberian peoples, though its diffusion into other cultures must have taken place very early in prehistory for, along with sorcerers, magicians, and priests, shamanism can be counted among the oldest of professions.

The word "shaman" is derived from the Tungusic term *saman*, derived in its turn from the Pali *samana*, indicating a possibly Southern (Buddhist) influence among these northern peoples (Eliade 1964, p. 4951). Eliade distinguishes the shaman from other types of religious and magical practitioners primarily on the basis of his religious function and techniques: ". . . he is believed to cure, like all doctors, and to perform miracles of the fakir, like all magicians, whether primitive or modern. But beyond this, he is a psychopomp, and he may also be priest, mystic, and poet." He further defines the shaman as a manipulator of the sacred, whose main function is to induce ecstasy in a society where ecstasy is the prime religious experience. Thus, the shaman is a master of ecstasy, and the art of shamanizing is a technique of ecstasy (Eliade 1964, p. 4).

In archaic societies, a person (either man or woman) may become a shaman in primarily one of two ways: hereditary transmission or spontaneous election. In either case, the novice shaman must undergo an initiatory ordeal before he can attain the status of a full shaman. The initiation generally has two aspects: an ecstatic aspect, which takes place in dreams or trance, and a traditional aspect, in which the shaman is given instruction in certain techniques, such as the use and significance of the shamanic costume and drum, the secret "spirit language," the names of the helping spirits, techniques of curing, the uses of medicinal plants, and so on, by an elder master shaman. These traditional techniques of shamanism are not invariably transmitted by an elder shaman but may be imparted to the neophyte directly through the spirits that come to him during his initiatory ecstasy. Lack of a public ritual in no way implies that such traditional instruction is neglected.

The ecstatic part of the shaman's initiation is harder to analyze, for it depends on a certain receptivity to states of trance and ecstasy on the part of the novice: He may be moody, somewhat frail and sickly, predisposed to solitude, and may perhaps have fits of epilepsy or catatonia, or some other psychological aberrance (though not always, as some writers on the subject have asserted [cf. Eliade 1964, pp. 23ff. and below]). In any case, his psychological predisposition to ecstasy forms only the starting point for his initiation: The novice, after a history of psychosomatic illness or psychological aberration that may be more or less intense, will at last begin to undergo initiatory sickness and trance; he will lie as though dead or in deep sleep for days on end. During this time, he is approached in dreams by his helping spirits and may receive instructions from them. Invariably during this prolonged trance the novice will undergo an episode of mystical death and resurrection: He may see himself reduced to a skeleton and then clothed with new flesh; or he may see himself boiled in a caldron, devoured by the spirits, and then made whole again; or he may imagine himself being operated on by the spirits, his organs removed and replaced with "magical stones," and then sewn up again.

Although the particular motifs may vary between cultures and even individuals, the general symbolism is clear: The novice shaman undergoes a symbolic death and resurrection, which is understood as a radical transformation into a superhuman condition. Henceforth, the shaman enjoys access to the supernatural plane; he is a master of ecstasy, can travel in the spirit-realm at will, can cure and divine, can touch red-hot iron with impunity, and so on. In short, the shaman is transformed from a profane into a sacred state of being. Not only has he effected his own cure through this mystical transmutation, he is now invested with the power of the sacred, and hence can cure others as well. It is of the first order of importance to remember this, that the shaman is not merely a sick man, or a madman; he is a sick man who has healed himself, who is cured, and who must shamanize to remain cured. Lommel (1967) gives the following description of a shamanic initiation in Siberia:

> The Tungus say of their shamans: "Before a man becomes a shaman he is sick for a long time. His understanding becomes confused. The shamanistic ancestors of his clan come, hack him to bits, tear him apart, cut his flesh in pieces, drink his blood. They cut off his head and throw it in the oven, in which various iron appurtenances of his costume are made red-hot and then forged. This cutting up is carried out somewhere in the upper world by the shaman ancestors. He alone receives the gift of shamanhood who has shaman ancestors in his clan, who pass it on from generation to generation; and only when these have cut up his body and examined his bones can he begin to shamanize." (p. 65)

We have noted that the function of shamanic initiation in the primitive society is to effect the transformation of the shaman from a profane, human condition to a superhuman, sacred one. But while the shaman may carry out activities such as divining and prophesying, and occasionally sorcery, these are not his major functions, and often fall within the province of other types of practitioners. The shaman's primary functions are those of healer and psychopomp. This is related to the specific nature of the shamanic ecstasy; not all forms of mystical ecstasy are shamanic, for this, like initiation, has its own peculiar nature. The shamanic ecstasy is one in which the shaman is supposed to leave his physical body and journey to the Center of the World, which connects the earthly realm with the celestial world above and the infernal regions below. This *axis mundi* may be symbolized as a tree, mountain, tent pole, ladder, liana, or something similar; the shaman is able to make the journey and return safely because he is a master of ecstasy and possesses the guidance of helping spirits along the way. His main functions thus become either guiding the soul of a deceased person to its home in the infernal or celestial realms or journeying to those realms for the purpose of retrieving the soul of a sick person (which has wandered off by itself or been stolen by the spirits while the patient was asleep), returning with it, and restoring it to the patient's body. The shaman thus fulfills his functions by being able to travel in the supernatural realm, and he is enabled to do this because he is a master of ecstasy.

From the description of the shaman's duties in the community, we can draw some obvious conclusions and make some further hermeneutical speculations as to the shamanic function within the cultural context. The curing function of shamanism, as well as such secondary functions as divination and prophecy, show clearly that the shaman, like all magical practitioners, helps a primitive culture to come to terms with environmental forces that are both nurturing and threatening. Thus, through the shamanic propitiation of the spirits, good crops or fruitful hunting can be assured; drought, epidemic, or other natural disasters can be averted. On the deeper level of collective psychology, we can perceive several functions of the shaman that would not be articulated by the members of a given society, but that, nevertheless, are intrinsic to the shamanic function. Lommel (1967) says of the social role of the shaman:

> . . . primitive man is quite exceptionally susceptible to various
> forms of mental disorder. Psychoses, neuroses, hallucinations,
> mass hysteria and the like are of very frequent occurrence. The
> shaman can cure these states—but only when he has overcome
> them in himself. . . . the shaman is the center, the brain and the
> soul of a (primitive) community. He is, so to speak, the regulator
> of the soul of a group or tribe, and his function is to adjust, avert,
> and heal defects, vacillations, disturbances of this soul. Looked at
> biologically, the whole life of primitive people is more strongly
> influenced by the subconscious than seems to be the case among
> ourselves. It is clear that in this situation the position of the sha-
> man is one of paramount importance. (p. 73)

The shaman is able to act as an intermediary between the society and the supernatural, or to put it in Jungian terms, he is an intermediary to the collective unconscious. Through the office of the shaman, the society at large is brought into close and frequent encounter with the numinous archetypal symbols of the collective unconscious. These symbols retain their numinosity, immediacy, and reality for the society through their constant reaffirmation in shamanic ritual and through the shaman's epic narration of mythical scenarios and his artistic production. The shaman does more, however, than just *recite* the myths or express the religious symbolism in making ritual artifacts; the shaman *lives* the myth. By virtue of his superhuman, transformed state, he enacts the role of the mythical hero: He can fly through the air, talk to the gods, see everywhere, understand the animals, and perform other feats characteristic of a semidivine entity. Thus, the shaman is the exemplar in the present epoch, which is regarded by primitives as a profane, historical time, of the condition supposed to have been accessible to all humans *before* the fall (cf. Eliade 1961, chapter 2). In his ecstasy the shaman reenters that mythical, paradisiacal condition that existed before the fall and thus reasserts, for the entire culture, the reality of that mythical time. Thus, the validity of the archetypal motifs, which presumably describe the human condition in the paradisiacal era, is reaffirmed.

The shamanic function also includes a psychoanalytic capability. That the shaman can cure illnesses of a psychological or psychosomatic nature is well established. "The shaman is undoubtedly, perhaps essentially, a doctor—but the factual medical knowledge of the primitives is very small; the shaman's medical function seems to be confined to psychological, perhaps psychoanalytical techniques, and his successes fall mainly within the psychological domain" (Lommel 1967, p. 25). By what exact mechanism he is able to do this is not completely understood. It is as though the shaman, in his capacity of ecstatic psychopomp, practices a participation therapy of the most sophisticated type; by means of his ecstatic capacity, the shaman "plunges" into the collective unconscious and restores the patient's self-identity (equivalent to "finding his soul") by taking onto himself the unconscious contents that have inundated the patient through the principle of transference (cf. Jung 1954). Because this is accomplished in the context of ritual, which is real and numinous to the participants, the shaman's task is doubtless somewhat easier than that of a modern psychoanalyst who is often faced with a demythologized, rationally hardened personality.

The shaman, then, acts as a doctor of the soul, both the individual and the collective soul, and he is also a real and living exemplar of the primordial, mythical human condition, and in being so maintains the reality and immediacy of the sacred. He is able to carry out these functions because he is master of the techniques of ecstasy, and it is by virtue of this that he maintains his suprahuman state.

It is clear that the practice of shamanism, to a greater extent than other religious offices, depends on the unique personality of the shaman. This must account in part for the great diversity of preinitiatory traits that constitute a shamanic election as well as the diversity in methods of shamanizing, in the means employed to produce ecstasy, and in the motifs of the shaman's journey, not only in different cultures but between individuals as well. With this in mind, let us lift the shaman out of his cultural context for a moment and focus on the characteristics of his psychological makeup.

An item of the first order in addressing ourselves to this psychological examination of the phenomenon is the question of the psychopathological nature of the shamanic personality. There are, as we have noted, certain cases where the symptoms leading to shamanic initiation can be traced to a condition of mental illness, epilepsy, or catatonia; however, this is by no means true for all such cases, as some have claimed. Initiation can also be triggered by an encounter with a magical animal, the finding of a magical stone or other object, or an ordeal in the wilderness.

Eliade (1967) masterfully points out where such theories have gone astray:

> The problem, in our view, has been wrongly stated. In the first
> place, it is not correct to say that shamans are, or must *always* be,
> neuropaths; on the contrary, a great many of them are perfectly
> sound in mind. Moreover, those who had previously been ill have
> *become shamans just because they succeeded in getting well* [italics
> his]. Very often, when the vocation reveals itself in the course
> of an illness or an attack of epilepsy, the initiation is also a cure.
> The acquisition of the shamanic gifts indeed presupposes the reso-
> lution of the psychic crisis brought on by the first signs of this
> vocation. The initiation is manifested by—among other things—
> a new psychic integration. (p. 77)

And, similarly, Nadel (1946) states:

> And here it is important to stress that neither epilepsy nor insan-
> ity, nor yet other minor mental derangements, are in themselves
> regarded as symptoms of spirit possession. They are diseases,
> abnormal disorders, not supernatural qualification. No shaman
> is, in everyday life, an abnormal individual, a neurotic or a para-
> noiac; if he were, he would be classed as a lunatic, not respected as
> a priest. Nor finally can shamanism be correlated with incipient or
> latent abnormality; I recorded no case of a shaman whose profes-
> sional hysteria deteriorated into serious mental disorders. (p. 36)

From these comments, it is apparent that shamanism is not an institution designed to capitalize on psychological aberrations.

We shall return to the question of the stability of the shamanic personality in the next chapter, where we will consider the similarities between the self-cure of the shaman and the attempt to resolve a life-crisis that characterizes essential schizophrenia.

Let us now consider the shamanic trance itself. All of the shaman's functions, his ability to cure, divine, converse with the spirits, and travel in the supernatural realm, depend on his ecstasy; were he unable to attain ecstasy at will, he could not be a true shaman. Thus, the human will employ certain means for achieving ecstasy, which may be frenzied and prolonged drumming, dancing, and chanting, sleep deprivation, fasting, and so on. These techniques are not dissimilar to the self-flagellation and asceticism practiced by certain Christian mystics. In addition to these techniques and often in conjunction with them, the shaman will employ certain narcotic plants, such as the drinking of tobacco juice or the inhalation of hashish smoke. While Eliade (1964, pp. 220f., 223, 400f., 477) asserts that the use of narcotic substances as an aid to ecstasy invariably indicates a decadence or vulgarization of the shamanic tradition, there is reason to doubt this (cf. Wasson 1971, pp. 326–334). On the contrary, the use of narcotic plants as an adjunct to shamanism is widespread and occurs in every region of the globe where the plants occur. The important role of the hallucinogenic mushroom *Amanita muscaria* in Siberian shamanism has been exhaustively documented by Wasson, and the incredibly complete narcotic technology of New World Indians has been examined by Schultes (Schultes and Hofmann 1973) at length. From this evidence it appears that the narcotic experience and the shamanic experience are, in very numerous cases, one and the same, though the narcotic experience must be molded and directed by the symbolic motifs of ritual to give it its peculiarly shamanic quality.

It is our contention, to be amplified in later chapters, that the presence of psychoactive substances is a primary requirement for all true shamanism, and that where such substances are not exogenously available as plants, they must be endogenously available, either through metabolic predisposition to their synthesis, as may occur in schizophrenia, or through the various techniques of shamanism: dancing, drumming, singing, and the confrontation of situations of stress and isolation. Where these alkaloids are not present, shamanism becomes ritual alone, and its effectiveness suffers accordingly. We hope to show that because of the biophysical roles these compounds play at a molecular level, they are the operational and physical keys allowing access to the powers claimed by the shaman.

One of the most interesting, and least understood, aspects of the shamanic personality centers upon the question of paranormal powers; the shaman is supposed to be a "master of fire and psychic heat," is thought to be clairvoyant, clairaudiant, and telepathic. Further instances are given by Eliade (1967):

> From among the best-observed cases, let us recall those of clairvoyance and thought-reading among the shamans of Tonga, recorded by Shirokogorov; some strange cases of prophetic clairvoyance in dreams among the Pygmies, as well as cases of the discovery of thieves with the aid of a magic mirror; some very concrete instances concerning the results of the chase, also aided by a mirror; examples of the understanding, among these same Pygmies, of unknown languages; cases of clairvoyance among the Zulus; and lastly—attested by a number of authors, and by documents that guarantee its authenticity—the collective ceremony of firewalking in Fiji. (p. 87f.)

There is herein a fruitful and untapped subject for parapsychology. The actual occurrence of such phenomena, in at least some instances, is beyond question and suggests that the radical reorganization of the psychic faculties, which shamanic initiation is supposed to produce, does have some validity beyond the merely symbolical; the shaman actually *is* superhuman in some little-understood manner. Our later speculations will center on a possible biophysical mechanism for this transformation. What is interesting, and also supports the assertion that these phenomena are real, is their essential similarity to paranormal powers encountered in other religious traditions. Such motifs as magical flight, psychic heat, and immunity to hot coals, for instance, are found in the yogic techniques of Buddhism and Hinduism (Eliade 1967, pp. 89ff.). The ability to perform such magical feats, in both the shamanic and the yogic traditions, simply reconfirms the ontological mode associated with such practitioners; they have transcended the human condition and now participate in the condition of the "spirits."

Let us now focus our attention on a more speculative question: whether there are, or could be, institutions in modern society that draw their models from shamanism. There appears to be occurring in modern life a progressive alienation from the numinous archetypal contents of the collective unconscious, which has engendered a gradually encroaching sense of collective despair and anxiety. The archetypal motifs of the Western religious tradition seem to have lost their effectiveness for the larger portion of civilized humanity or, at best, have been depotentiated to the level of a "merely psychological" reality. Western humans have lost their sense of unity with the cosmos and with the transcendent mystery within themselves. Modern science has given us a picture of human beings as accidental products of random evolutionary processes in a universe that is itself without purpose or meaning. This alienation of modern humans from the numinous ground of their beings has engendered the existentialist ethic and the contemporary preoccupation with the immediate historical situation. Humans are regarded as leading a wholly profane existence within a wholly profane time, that is, within history; the reality of the sacred is denied or reduced to the level of psychology.

In non-Western cultures, in "primitive" cultures particularly, humans are not conscious of living in historical time, but regard themselves as inhabiting a numinous sacral time (cf. Eliade 1959). If these humans are conscious of history at all, it is of a mythical, paradigmatic history, a paradisiacal epoch that lies beyond the attritional influence of profane time. From the point of view of religious symbolism, this preoccupation of modern humanity with its historical and existential situation springs from an unconscious sense of its impending end.

It is in this unenviable position, then, that we find the modern temper: anguished by the imminence of death, yet trapped in profane, historical time and thus able to regard death only as nothingness; the saving presence of a sacred, transcendent mode of being is absent from the contemporary worldview. Thus modern humans stand today at the very edge of the abyss of death and nothingness, and it is precisely here that one can perceive a useful role for a modern shamanism. Again there is a need for a doctor of the soul, a figure who can bring humankind into close and fruitful confrontation with the collective unconscious, the creative matrix of all that we are and have ever been.

Naturally, the modern shaman will have to search for means of fulfilling his psychopompic functions, which are different from the relatively straightforward ritualistic techniques of his predecessor. One of the most potentially effective of such means lies in his artistic and poetic capacities; the soul of modern humanity is still open to influence by aesthetic means. Hence one of the first places we should look for signs of a modern shamanism is in the artistic sphere. The shamanic role of the artist in modern cultures extends not only to his work, but to his very life. Through manipulation of his physical medium, the artist seeks to express his personal vision of reality—a vision arising from the roots of the unconscious and not dependent upon public consensus, in fact, often actively opposed to it. More than that, the artist exemplifies in his life a freedom that is similar to the superhuman freedom of the shaman.

Although it is not too difficult to recognize the role of the artist in the modern world as being in some sense shamanic, it is perhaps more difficult to understand our second nomination for a contemporary counterpart to the shamanic practitioner, the scientific researcher. Eliade (1967) has pointed out that scientists are the creators and keepers of a new mythology of matter. Indeed, the scientist who charts the unexplored levels of organization to be found in nature, from the bizarre, paradoxical realms of quantum physics to the staggering vastness of the metagalaxy, has much in common with the shaman who journeys through the magical topography of the spirit-world.

One area of modern life that does not appear to be shamanic, but that might profitably model itself after shamanism, is psychoanalysis. A modern "soul doctor" might well achieve better results if he or she could model therapy after a psychopompic journey through the collective unconscious. The exact techniques would, of course, have to be adapted to modern patients, but where the unconscious is concerned, all people are "primitive." One approach to such a shamanic psychoanalysis could be through the controlled and judicious use of psychotropic drugs; knowledge of both the promises and dangers of such agents has increased tremendously in recent years, as has understanding of the role they play in shamanism. A combination of knowledge and wisdom in applying their properties could very well give an effective and harmless "technique of ecstasy" that could be usefully employed in psychoanalysis (cf. Naranjo 1973).

With this we conclude our preliminary discussion of shamanism. The background that we have laid down, our discussion of the shaman's traditional role in archaic societies, our examination of his singular personality, abilities, and techniques have been skeletal at best. Our speculation on shamanism and modern society is likewise incomplete and intentionally so; we sought only to make the point that the numinous motifs of shamanism can have a relevance to modern humans, and doubtless there are instances of this that have not been mentioned. If we are to draw a conclusion as to how we can profit from the study of shamanism, it is this: Perhaps, through understanding the fascinating and alien figure of the shaman, we can draw somewhat nearer to that numinous, archetypal, *living* mystery that dwells within each of us.

Chapter 2

Shamans and Schizophrenia

The question of just how much of the human experience of the supernatural stems from mental aberrance or experiences during trance or intoxication has intrigued anthropologists and psychologists for a number of years. In the preceding chapter we discussed the characteristics of shamanism, one of the most archaic of religious technologies. We now want to show that significant similarities exist between shamanic election and initiation and the effort at psychic reorganization that characterizes some forms of schizophrenia. If, as we proposed earlier, the mind and its buried unconscious contents have their origin at some submolecular interface, then it is reasonable to suggest that a similar biophysical release mechanism is responsible for the irruption of these contents in both shamanism and schizophrenia. Comparison of the two syndromes could be useful for what it might reveal, not only about the processes that trigger access to such unconscious material but also about the means of *controlling* these processes. Whereas schizophrenia may or may not result in eventual control of the nonordinary experience and psychic reintegration, in shamanism this step is, nevertheless, a *sine qua non.*

The primary difficulty in formulating any definition of mental aberrance in general and schizophrenia in particular is that any such definition will necessarily reflect the cultural bias out of which it is formed. Behavior considered abnormal or pathological in one culture may be quite congruent with the norms of another. Belief in witchcraft might be indicative of paranoid delusion in one culture but might represent a prevailing view in another.

For our purposes, abnormal behavior can be defined as behavior differing from the accepted cultural standard as a result of an *inner* conflict or crisis in the life of the individual, regardless of the standard of normative behavior in the society in which the life-crisis occurs. One of the basic distinctions between normal and abnormal behavior lies not in the outward manifestations of the conflict, but in differing cultural attitudes toward the life-crisis and its resolution.

The term "schizophrenia" is used to denote a number of heterogeneous, but related, disorders usually characterized by withdrawal from the environment and preoccupation with interior processes, attended by a resultant disintegration of the personality. An early term for schizophrenia was *Dementia Praecox,* meaning an intense pathological state beginning early in life. In 1896 the psychologist Kraepelin classified schizophrenia into three subtypes and ascribed organic, endogenous causes to each type. Later, a fourth type, known as simple schizophrenia, was added to this classification and its cause adduced to be a crisis in an individual's life situation.

Boisen (1936) lists the following subtypes of schizophrenia (in Boisen's terms, *dementia praecox*), first noting that ". . . findings have indicated that it is important to distinguish dementia praecox as a *way of life* from dementia praecox as an *attempt at reorganization*" [italics his] (p. 314): (1) Simple schizophrenia, represented by the individual who drifts off into a world of fantasy and easy pleasure-taking without putting up any resistance. This type of schizophrenia is classed as denoting a way of life. (2) Paranoic schizophrenia, characterized by an individual's inability to admit defeat or error and a resulting distortion of beliefs to save the conception of the individual's relation to the external world on which his psychic structure is based. This type also represents a way of life. (3) Catatonic schizophrenia represents a desperate attempt at reorganization following upon an awareness of danger. Catatonic disturbances often take on the form of stupor or excitement and may be looked on as more severe forms of the anxiety neurosis. They bear a close relationship to certain types of religious conversion experiences. (4) Hebephrenic schizophrenia represents the terminal stage of the drifting reaction or demoralization that may follow upon an unsuccessful attempt at reorganization. Speech tends to lose logical sequence, and the individual becomes silly, uninhibited, and indecent and tends to have bizarre ideas.

Silverman (1967) lists as clinical symptoms of schizophrenia: (1) an unmistakable change in personality, (2) autism—nonreality-oriented ideation, (3) disturbances of perception, (4) disturbances of thinking, (5) profound emotional upheavals, and (6) bizarre forms of behavior. He makes four classifications of significance for our study under the general heading of schizophrenia, based on Sullivan's classification (Silverman 1967). The first is "process schizophrenia," in which the personality is poorly integrated; there is continuous and prolonged development of schizophrenic symptoms, and prognosis is poor. It is ". . . the congeries of signs and symptoms pertaining to an organic, degenerative disease usually of insidious development" (Sullivan 1953). "Reactive schizophrenia," on the other hand, ". . . is primarily a disorder of living . . . the person concerned becomes schizophrenic—as one episode in his career among others—for situational reasons and more or less abruptly" (Sullivan 1953). Under the reactive schizophrenic category, Silverman differentiates between "essential schizophrenia," in which ". . . the profoundest of emotional upheavals and . . . religious and magical ideation unfold under conditions of marked environmental detachment," and "paranoid schizophrenia," in which ". . . the patient, caught up in the spread of meaning, magic, and transcendental forces, suddenly 'understands' it all as the work of some other concrete person or persons . . . attention is thereafter focused primarily upon environmental events and people." Silverman goes on to say of essential types that they ". . . evidence an overtly indifferent orientation to unfamiliar stimuli, a reduced attentiveness to the environment, and a tendency to attenuate the experienced intensity of environmental stimulation," whereas he characterizes the paranoid type as one who is "overtly responsive to unfamiliar stimulation, extensively scans the environment . . . and evidences a tendency to augment the experienced intensity of environmental input" (Silverman 1967, pp. 22–23).

Both the shamanic initiation and the inwardly directed essential form of schizophrenia reflect an attempt at psychic reorganization as a means of resolving an inner conflict or crisis in the life of the individual. The non-paranoid type of schizophrenia bears the most favorable prognosis for an eventual working through of the inner conflict, resulting in a reintegrated, "healed" personality:

> It is as if the paranoid schizophrenic, unable to comprehend or tolerate the stark terrors of his inner world, prematurely redirects his attention to the outside world. In this type of abortive crisis solution, the inner chaos is not, so to speak, worked through or is not capable of being worked through. Since the working through of the inner-world experience turns out to be a primary concern . . . (both for the shaman and for the schizophrenic), the paranoid schizophrenic resolution is considered to be an incomplete one, and the essential, nonparanoid schizophrenic form is therefore regarded as more comparable to that of the shaman, the "healed madman." (Silverman 1967)

The onset of essential schizophrenia usually begins with the magnification of some unresolved conflict in the individual's life, perhaps a poor sexual adjustment or deficiencies in social relationships, which is apt to give rise to intense feelings of impotence, failure, or personal incompetence to the extent that self-concern may so overwhelm the personality that the schizophrenic becomes aware of little else. The schizophrenic syndrome may end at this point if the individual is successful in attaining some sort of personality reorganization and resolution of the precipitating conflict.

The patient may then return to normal, sometimes improved but often with a seriously damaged self-esteem.

More often, however, the sense of estrangement and isolation is followed by an ever more marked narrowing of attention to the external environment, increased absorption in interior fantasy, and withdrawal from the outside world. "Sustained constriction of the field of attention under these conditions also results in a state of self-initiated sensory deprivation, with consequent inevitable difficulty in the differentiation of fantasy and non-fantasy, between hallucination and perception" (Silverman 1967, p. 24). In this and later stages, auditory and tactile hallucinations may manifest themselves; the patient often hears voices or engages in conversation with imaginary companions and also may experience distortions of body-image, the sensation of dying or of the body being cut up, disintegrating, or melting. Often the patient falls under the compulsion to obey the imperative of the "voices" and may engage in irrational, sometimes symbolic and ritualistic, actions or gestures (Boisen 1942). This stage is tantamount to the stage that Silverman terms "fusing of higher and lower referential process," in which

> the already unstable and weakened "psychological self" is disorganized by this drastically altered environment and is inundated by lower order referential processes such as occur in dreams or revery. Owing to the depths of the emotional stirring that triggered the whole process, the world comes to be experienced as filled with supernatural forces and profound but unimaginable meaning. (Silverman 1967, p. 24)

In Boisen's (1942) words:

> It is known as the "inspiration" or the "automatism," and may be defined as the idea or thought process which after a period of incubation darts suddenly into consciousness . . . they seem to him entirely different from anything he had ever thought or dreamed before. He assumes therefore that they must come from a superhuman source. (p. 25)

The fifth stage—what Silverman calls the "cognitive reorganization"— occurs when the schizophrenic succeeds in reintegrating his personality and assimilating the new unconscious contents to which he has gained access. This stage constitutes the main difference between essential and paranoid schizophrenia, in that it is conspicuously lacking in the latter. It may be said to represent a "cure," not in the sense that the schizophrenic henceforth returns to "normal" and is no longer bothered by autonomous unconscious contents, but rather in that he manages to integrate these contents into the sphere of consciousness and learns to cope with the "expanded reality" in which he now must live. This stage may develop to any point, from a very marginal adjustment accompanied by constant relapses to an extremely pronounced state of mental acuity in which awareness, sensitivity, and creative capacity are likely to be many times greater than in "normal" individuals, as if entire areas of the brain, previously inaccessible, had been opened up by the transforming experience. The schizophrenic who has managed successfully to complete this final adjustment is in every sense superior, for he is truly a "healed madman," one who not only has crossed over to the other side but has returned and hence possesses access to both spheres of reality.

Up to this point we have examined the phenomenon of schizophrenia in its successive stages, from its onset to its resolution. We must now search for correlations between this most severe of mental aberrances and the motifs encountered in shamanism, the revered and respected "archaic techniques of ecstasy" that occupy a central position in the religious life of tribal peoples.

The criteria that define the vocation of shaman are many and varied throughout the world, and it is certainly untrue that every shaman must be a schizoid personality. We have observed that the shaman is usually considered a "healed one" and that he gains shamanic status because he has healed himself; but the crisis for which he works out a resolution is not always a mental disorder and, in some cases where it is, it is not always a schizophrenic type of aberrance. The shaman's "call" or election may arise from a purely physical malady, the spirits making their desire that he become a shaman known to him during a feverish delirium. Still other forms of shamanic election may arise from an accident in the external world, such as being struck by lightning or being bitten by a snake. In instances where mental aberrance is a factor in shamanic vocation, a predisposition to epileptic or cataleptic seizures, to hysteria or anxiety, may be the underlying cause rather than schizophrenia. But whatever the underlying cause of the shaman's election, it is important to constantly keep in mind that it is the ability to *cure* that is the real basis of the shamanic status:

> . . . we must also consider the fact that the shamanic initiation proper includes not only an ecstatic experience but . . . a course of theoretical and practical instruction. . . . Whether they still are or are not subject to real attacks of epilepsy or hysteria, shamans, sorcerers, and medicine men in general cannot be regarded as merely sick; their psychopathic experience has a theoretical content, for if they have cured themselves and are able to cure others, it is, among other things, because they know the mechanism, or rather, the *theory* of illness. (Eliade 1964, p. 32)

In a significant number of cases, however, it is possible to discover important similarities between certain elements of shamanic initiation and the motifs associated with progressive schizophrenic disintegration. Now let's return once again to the stages of essential schizophrenic onset, this time to uncover similarities between these stages and those associated with the shamanic election and initiation.

The onset of schizophrenia usually arises at the time of some basic life-crisis, when the individual is likely to experience feelings of guilt, impotence, or incompetence in a life situation culturally acknowledged as crucial. We find that this is also true in many cases of shamanism; in addition to being introverted and of a nervous constitution since childhood, the future shaman often receives his vocational call through accident, sickness, familial misfortune, or similar mishap. Thus, we may infer that in cultures where the shamanic institution exists, an individual may choose to restructure his life and become a shaman as a means of resolving a life-crisis.

The second stage of schizophrenic withdrawal is manifested by a sense of isolation and estrangement from ordinary cultural concerns, which may be followed or accompanied by a pathological fixation on certain ideas, events, or objects purportedly imbued with some sort of supernatural significance. This is also found in shamanism; initiatory seclusion of the shamanic candidate is common among many tribes, and this is symbolic of the shaman's psychic isolation, for ". . . the medicine man stands apart from the world of the profane precisely because he has more direct relations with the sacred and manipulates its manifestations more effectively" (Eliade 1964, p. 31). In this and later stages, the schizophrenic or shaman may develop a fixed ideation on a narrow circle of significant ideas, "omens," or objects, often becoming so intense as to result in sleep loss or autohypnosis. The boundaries between sleeping and waking break down, and the novice shaman lives in a twilight world of hypnagogic fantasy and half-waking reverie.

> The principle behind the induction of autohypnosis is one of perceptual fixation, and some of its behavioral manifestations are present in the pathological staring of schizophrenics or novice shamans or in the total attentiveness of certain shamans to their frenzied, prolonged drum-beating or whistling. (Silverman 1967, p. 26)

This acute constriction of the field of attention brings about a state of self-initiated sensory deprivation. Experiments with sensory deprivation at McGill University (Nordland, in Edsman 1967, pp. 170ff.) have shown that in this state, visual and auditory hallucinations and perceptual distortions are common, with subjects often hearing voices, seeing imaginary people, and having sensations of body-image distortion. All of these manifestations can be found to a marked degree in shamanism. The shaman is said to "make a journey," during which he is spoken to by the spirits, who give him curing instructions and make their wishes known for certain kinds of propitiatory sacrifices; they may also appear to him in the form of visions or apparitions. Motifs of death and rebirth, often involving bodily dismemberment and reassimilation, are common in shamanism, as Eliade (1964) illustrates:

> . . . both spontaneous vocation and the quest for initiation involve . . . a more or less symbolical ritual of mystical death, sometimes suggested by a dismemberment of the body and renewal of the organs . . . equivalent to re-entering the womb of this primordial life, that is, to a complete renewal, to a mystical rebirth. (pp. 53, 63ff.)

In both schizophrenia and shamanism, this is followed by a fusion of lower referential processes with higher, so that the mind is inundated by a flood of archaic imagery that seems to come from outside sources; in shamanism, this stage is typical of the fully manifested trance.

> The fact that they are entirely different from anything previously experienced lends support to the assumption that they have come

from the realm of the supernatural. One feels oneself to be
dwelling among the mysterious and the uncanny. Ideas of world
catastrophe, of cosmic importance, and of mission abound.
Words, thoughts, and dreams can easily be seen to reside in external objects. Causal relationships are perceived against a background of magic and animism. (Silverman 1967, p. 28)

The difference between the shaman and the schizophrenic must be
sought in the degree of cultural acceptance of this lower-order referential
content. The altered perception of reality into which this newly opened
region of cognition plunges the schizophrenic has, in modern societies, no
cultural validity.

The last stage in the progression, that of "cognitive reorganization" to
cope with the altered perception in which the individual now lives, is for
the shaman and for the schizophrenic much the same thing—the arduous
task of learning to use the altered perception to good advantage, for creative endeavor and increased sensitivity. An important difference, however, is that in our culture the schizophrenic is forced to work out his
adjustment without the benefit of culturally sanctioned attitudes of acceptance for the expanded reality that he now inhabits, whereas in primitive
society not only is the shaman in possession of an elaborate body of traditional teachings regarding his illness, but his adjustment is made much
easier by virtue of his accepted and respected social position.

The shaman must indeed be possessed of a superior flexibility and constitution, for not only must he attend to the needs of his patients in this
world but he must also satisfy his spirits in the other. He is the technician
of the numinous par excellence, and his vocation is a demanding one,
consisting as it does of maintaining a constant equilibrium between ordinary reality and the supernatural realm. The shaman's psychic life is not
unlike the unnaturally dexterous dances he performs at the height of his
ecstasy; it is a constant balancing act, as though he were a psychic tight-
rope walker on the razor's edge between the external world and the bizarre, magical, often terrifying "world within."

However, one of the major differences between shamans and schizophrenics appears to lie in the cultural attitudes with which they are regarded, and this disparity is perhaps deserving of some comment.
Lommel (1967) says of shamanism as a possible cure technique:

The way out of the situation lies in shamanizing; that is to say, the
mental sickness can be healed only if the sufferer accepts the often

unwanted and feared office of shaman, which the spirits are forcing upon him. We gain the impression that early man has found an almost unfailing way of curing mental disease, that a certain "psychic constitution" makes escape from a pathological state possible. (p. 53)

The suggestion that we wish to infer from Lommel's observation is that perhaps, in literate cultures, the schizophrenic is the victim of a culturally misdirected attitude. It seems reasonable to suggest that in our culture the schizophrenic provides a necessary pipeline to the collective unconscious, just as the shaman does in tribal societies. The spiritual atrophying of contemporary culture may be due in large measure to its loss of sensitivity to processes in the collective unconscious. A reinstitution of the shamanic role in modern society might prevent its total estrangement from the collective unconscious, which remains the fountainhead of all human cultures, archaic or modern.

Chapter 3

Organismic Thought

The progress of science is, like all other creative activities of human intelligence, a groping toward pattern—toward the accumulation of assigned pattern for the coordination of observed details and toward the uncovering of novel pattern and the consequent introduction of novel details. This tendency toward synthesis, toward the apprehension of ever more complex and inclusive orders of pattern, appears to be a fundamental quality of human thought. It is characteristic of aesthetics, philosophy, and religion, as well as of science. Understanding consists of the assimilation of patterns encountered in the external world, and insofar as understanding progresses, it is the assimilation of novel forms of pattern and the modification of previously perceived patterns that such novel patterns introduce. One of the chief resistances to this progressive penetration of understanding is the dogmatic tendency to adhere to orthodox modes of assigned pattern when confronted with novel details that call for a reordering of understanding. In the case of science, one can point to the persistence, in our conceptual models, of the Newtonian doctrine of concrete material entities possessing the properties of simple location; whereas the order of pattern revealed by quantum physics allows for neither concrete endurance nor simple location at its most basic levels. On the opposite end of the scale, one can point to the doctrine of relativity, which has shown that space and time must be regarded as properties of each other, yet one generally continues to characterize space in terms of the relationships of Euclidean geometry on any scale short of the cosmic. Still another example can be cited in the scientific assumption of the sufficiency of purely physicochemical properties to explain the fact of living organisms and, by extension, the fact of mind.

To carry on its empirical investigations, science must embark on this methodological license of abstracting certain sets of facts from the totality of patterned relationships of which those facts are a part. As long as these assumptions are understood for what they are, as a set of ad hoc hypotheses employed for the purpose of characterizing a given phenomenon, that is, purely for the sake of methodological convenience, then science encounters no difficulty. It is when science proclaims the adequacy of a given order of pattern to characterize *all* levels of organization that it runs into philosophical difficulties, for then it extends the methodological abstractions used to characterize a phenomenon to sets of phenomena that may in actuality exhibit patterns of a quite different order. It is to the philosophical consequences of this methodological inconsistency of science that this chapter is addressed. We intend to examine in some detail the philosophical problems raised by scientific methodology; we will attempt finally to tentatively suggest the fundamentals of a metaphysics that is consistent not only with the pursuit of scientific abstraction but also with the apprehension of the world as it impinges on us as living, sensing, minded organisms.

Alfred North Whitehead, in *Science and the Modern World* (1967, p. 7), states: "Every philosophy is tinged with the coloring of some secret imaginative background, which never emerges explicitly into its chains of reasoning." For science this intuitive speculation consists in its assumption of the knowability of the world, in its belief that every event can be correlated with its antecedents in a definite manner exemplifying general principles. This assumption, that in nature there is a secret, and that that secret can be unveiled, forms the unconscious metaphysical assumption behind all research. This scientific faith was not the creation of science itself but was inherited from the insistence of Greek and Scholastic philosophy on the rational order of nature, on the belief that nature conducts itself according to inexorable, orderly laws. This view in Greek cosmology is found in the conception that all things in nature tend toward a definite and proper end; while in Scholastic philosophy, it is reflected in the instinctive tone of faith centered upon the rationality and scrutability of God. Every detail of nature was conceived as supervised and ordered; the search into nature could only vindicate the faith of centuries. Though the tacit philosophical creed of science is embodied in these antecedent rational traditions, the way was paved for the rise of science itself by a turn away from theoretical contemplation toward an interest in nature for its own sake, the observation of concrete, irreducible facts. In this aspect, modern science arose out of a reaction *against* the abstract rationalism of Scholasticism. What could not be demonstrated, what was not apparent to observation, was inadmissible as evidence in the scientific worldview. And yet the belief that the diversity of irreducible and stubborn facts was harmonizable into an intelligible, rational order arose not as a result of empirical observation, but out of faith in the order of nature.

In the light of these mixed origins of modern science—its instinctive belief in the rationality of nature, coupled with its insistence on the observation of irreducible facts—it is interesting to consider the role of induction in science. When one observes, one also selects; a pure observation deals only with a particular set of conditions giving rise to a particular phenomenon. When one extrapolates the particular observation to the whole set of phenomena exemplifying similar conditions, this is induction. An entire class of phenomena has been characterized on the basis of a limited sampling of such phenomena. By this process of induction, science thus arrives at a formulation of general conditions that characterize not only the particular entity or occasion under investigation but also any other real or theorized occasion or entity that satisfies the postulated general conditions. This process of framing abstract postulates that bear a reference to no particular occasion or entity (and, in consequence, enters into the description of *all* such occasions) reaches its height in mathematics. The characterization of number, for example, "five," does not depend on whether you are referring to five apples or five minutes; it can be impartially applied to either, regardless of the intrinsic differences of apples and minutes. Pure mathematics exists in the realm of pure abstraction; all it asserts is that reason insists that if any entities whatsoever have any relations that satisfy such-and-such purely abstract conditions, then they must have other relations that satisfy other purely abstract conditions.

To the extent that science seeks to explain the mechanism of physical phenomena with mathematically expressible laws, it reduces the data of concrete observation in particular events to the status of pure abstractions. The abstractions existed antecedently to the physical phenomena they were found to describe. The complex of ideas surrounding the periodic functions had to be worked out, as pure mathematical theory, before their relations to such physical phenomena as the motion of a pendulum, the movements of the planets, and the physical properties of a vibrating string could be discerned. The point is that as mathematics became more abstract, it acquired an ever-increasing practical application to diverse concrete phenomena. Thus, abstraction, characterized by numerical operations, became the dominant conceptual mode used to describe concrete facts.

In the process of induction, one extrapolates given characteristics of a particular past; one does not extrapolate general laws except on the basis of an assumed rationality of nature. The introduction of mathematics into the scheme supplies the nature of the data to be searched for in observation, namely, measurable quantities. In physics, this emphasis on measurable elements reached its satisfaction in the Newtonian concepts of mass and force. Mass was conceived as a constant property inherent in all material bodies in measurable amounts, whether that body was at rest or

in motion, and that remained inherent in the body from one moment to
the next, for as long as the body endured. Force was defined as mass times
acceleration, and hence refers primarily to bodies in motion. It is important for our purposes to note that there is in these laws the tacit assumption of the self-identity of a material body in both space and time; a body
is the same body whether it is at point A or point B or any point between
them. Similarly, the body remains fully itself in its transitions through
time and at any instant, however short, of time. The material is said to
have the property of simple location; that is, it can be said to be definitely
here in space and *here* in time, without reference to any other region of
space or time. But this notion raises difficulties for induction, for if in the
location of configurations of matter through a stretch of time there is no
inherent reference to any other times, past or future, it immediately follows that nature at any period does not refer to nature at any other period.
Accordingly, induction is not based on anything that is inherent in nature.
The order of nature cannot be justified by the mere observation of nature,
for there is nothing in the present fact that inherently refers to either the
past or the future.

This doctrine of simple location has a further consequence for science
in that it explains physical phenomena in terms of the interaction of material entities in space. To the scientific mind of the seventeenth century,
physical phenomena, including the phenomenon of a living organism,
were understood as a manifestation of the interaction of material entities;
the world consisted of physical bodies having mass, location, and locomotion, such entities having these properties as essential qualities. But other
qualities exist, which normally enter into observations of a phenomenon,
but which are suppressed by the purely physical description that admits
only of mass, location, and motion. We refer to such secondary qualities
as color, or roundness, or scent, or texture. These qualities were not considered inherent in the entities themselves, but as arising out of our apprehension of phenomena and having no existence apart from apprehension.
Such qualities were in fact considered to be products of the mind alone:

> . . . But the mind in apprehending also experiences sensations
> which, properly speaking, are qualities of the mind alone. These
> sensations are projected by the mind so as to clothe appropriate
> bodies in external nature. Thus the bodies are perceived as
> with qualities which in reality do not belong to them, qualities
> which in fact are purely the offspring of the mind. Thus nature

gets credit which should in truth be reserved for ourselves: the rose for its scent: the nightingale for his song: the sun for his radiance. The poets are entirely mistaken. They should address their lyrics to themselves, and should turn them into odes of self-congratulation on the excellency of the human mind. Nature is a dull affair, soundless, scentless, colourless; merely the hurrying of material, endlessly, meaninglessly.

However you disguise it, this is the practical outcome of the characteristic scientific philosophy which closed the seventeenth century. (Whitehead 1967, p. 54)

This abstraction of the secondary qualities from the primary ones of physical bodies had the unfortunate effect of creating a dualism between mind and nature. Nature became identified with matter and its movement, whereas mind, believing, suffering, perceiving, but not interfering, was conceived as existing apart from the external nature that it observed, described, and measured. Yet to the extent that mind is in nature, it is a product of nature. Mind is a quality proceeding from living organisms, and organisms are regarded by mechanist science as arising from the blind interactions of undirected matter; both life and mind become in this view simply the outcome of the random interactions of matter over a vast scale of time. Any apparent "meaning" to this process, any type of evolutionary advancement or value or purpose, is simply a projection of the observer; in itself, nature is intrinsically blind, without purpose, meaning, or value. This was the philosophical paradox that modern science, based on inductive abstraction, led itself into: confronted with a universe both lifeless and devoid of mind, how to explain the apparent intelligibility of nature and the fact of living organisms.

The preceding discussion has tried to point out that in science certain axiomatic, a priori assumptions accompany any exercise of scientific methodologies. Though we have by no means exhausted the list of such assumptions, we have hopefully pointed to some of the major ones: the implicit faith in the knowability and the rationality of nature, a legacy to science of Greek metaphysics and medieval Scholasticism; the utilization by science of the inductive method, and the twofold assumption of this use—that observation of representative concrete phenomena can lead to the formulation of abstract, general laws, and the assumption of the relevance of past events to present and future events; the assumption of the sufficiency of interactions of material entities having simple location in giving rise to nature, and proceeding from this assumption, the exclusion of mind as a causative factor in the universe, and the consequent exclusion of value and teleology from nature. That science makes these assumptions in the exercise of its methodology is not our criticism; they are necessary for the pragmatic practice of science. In the absence of such self-imposed limitation, the practice of science would be impossible. Our criticism is that these assumptions are not made explicitly, with the understanding that, of course, they are philosophically arguable; they are made merely in the service of methodological convenience. Instead, in the greater number of cases, no attempt at philosophical justification is made; the tacit assumptions of science are left unstated, to be inferred by the philosopher. Because the methods of science work, because they can produce results, science feels no need to concern itself with philosophy.

The progress of science in recent years, that is, primarily since the turn of the century, has unlocked vast new areas to human understanding. It has revealed novel orders of pattern in nature that not only went undetected and unsuspected by the science of an earlier day but also have necessitated almost the complete restructuring of the scientific worldview. We have in mind such discoveries as relativity, with its non-Euclidean topology, and quantum theory, with its notion of the discontinuous nature of matter and energy. Yet, in the face of these novel orders of pattern, whose explication was spearheaded by scientific methodology itself, other areas of science, not concerned directly with investigating such areas, have continued to carry the burden of outmoded, false conceptions as intrinsic components of their epistemological equipment.

In the following section of this chapter, let us focus attention on one area of classical scientific assumption, the notion of materialism, and see in what ways this notion finds itself in need of revision in the light of modern quantum theory. Then let us apply our revised concepts to those two stumbling blocks of classical materialism, organism and mind, to see if we have come any distance toward framing a set of epistemological principles that are both supportive of scientific investigation and truer to our everyday apprehension of the world.

One approach to the quantum theory can be found in the assumption that an electron does not continuously traverse its path in space, but instead appears at discrete positions in space for successive durations of time:

> It is as though an automobile, moving at the average rate of thirty
> miles an hour along a road, did not traverse the road continuously;

but appeared successively at the successive milestones, remaining for two minutes at each milestone . . .

But now a problem is handed over to the philosophers. This discontinuous existence in space, thus assigned to electrons, is very unlike the continuous existence of material entities which we habitually assume as obvious. The electron seems to be borrowing the character which some people have assigned to the Mahatmas of Tibet. These electrons, with the correlative protons, are now conceived as being the fundamental entities out of which the material bodies of ordinary experience are composed. Accordingly, if this explanation is allowed, we have to revise all our notions of the ultimate character of material existence. For when we penetrate to these final entities, this startling discontinuity of spatial existence discloses itself. (Whitehead 1967, pp. 34–35)

The problem can be overcome if we accord to matter the same vibratory character that we apply to light and sound. The adoption of this vibratory picture of matter is going to necessitate the drastic revision of our ideas of simple location. One recalls that a unit of matter having simple location does not require a given period of time in which to manifest its essential identity—it is fully itself even if the period of its endurance is subdivided indefinitely. Similarly, subdividing the space of the material entity does divide the volume, but its elements are conceived to retain their essential spatial continuity. Note that in this view the passage of time is conceived of as accidental, rather than essential; that is, the passage of time has nothing to do with the character of the material. If we adopt the vibratory description of matter urged by quantum theory, time becomes of the essence of the material. In an analogous way, as a note of music is nothing at any instant, but requires its whole period in which to manifest itself, so the vibratory entity of a primordial unit of matter requires a definite period of time, however small, for the expression of its essential nature. Another consequence arises as well: Quantum theory tells us that the electron, the basic unit of matter, does not have continuous spatial existence, but discrete points of manifestation (quanta) in space. Now, at first sight, this view seems much less in congruence with our everyday experience than the old classical notion of simple location in space. After all, we perceive all around us objects that seem to have continuity both in space and in time; are we then to believe that such apparently solid entities are actually vibratory processes? That such a view is actually more true to experience, in that it opens the way to explain those other commonsense elements of experience, organisms and minds, we will try to show next. However, one feature of the quantum view can be immediately pointed out; that is, that matter ceases to have simple location, mass, and locomotion as "primary" qualities; these become as referent to the synthesis of a perceiver as such "secondary" qualities as color, texture, or noisiness. Thus, either matter no more has primary qualities than it does secondary qualities and is in itself without quality, or the secondary qualities are just as "real" as the primary ones and are there to be perceived by the mind.

Thus, in the quantum view, the notion of material entities having form, a discrete and fixed spatial configuration, and endurance, a continuous sustenance through time, yields to the notion of process, a dynamical act of continuously evolving *becoming*. Material entities assume the character of an event; apart from process, there is no being. A thing is what it is by virtue of the serial unfolding of pattern through time; if one attempts to isolate an object at a single, nontemporal instant, apart from the instants preceding and following it, the object loses its essential identity. The object requires a self-defined, indivisible epoch for its realization; its reality is defined by the unity of the various processes that enter into its makeup. It is the process of unfoldment of the various components of an entity, gathered into a prehensive unity, that we experience as the sense object; it is not the components themselves that we experience as the sense object, but our unified prehension of these unfolding components. Thus, nature becomes a structure of evolving processes, and space and time the locus of the unification of these processes into sense objects. It is ridiculous, therefore, to ask if color is less "real" than, say, spatial location; color is one ingredient in the process of realization; it enters into the unified prehension of an event, and apart from prehension, there is no realization.

There is a further consequence derivative of this notion of nature as a unity of processes. This is that the modal ingression (realization) of an event into space-time bears a relation to past events, to contemporary events, and to future events. An event in itself is a unity of processes, but in combination with other events, past or present or future or all three, the event becomes one process in the unity of a still larger event. Thus the mode of ingression of any given event is subject to the influence of its antecedents, its contemporaries, and its descendants, which are in turn influenced by still other events, and so on. The unity of process that is an event therefore incorporates the influence of all events; each event mirrors within itself every other event. Insofar as a given event is considered apart from other events, which participate in its unity in making it just that event and no other, our understanding of the event remains incomplete. The total unity of an event can only be understood with reference to the totality of process, that is, to the whole of nature. Thus, in this view, a way is cleared not only for the implicit reference to past events to be found in the formulation of scientific laws but for our own psychological unity of memory, immediate realization, and anticipation.

Let us see if this definition of an entity as an evolving process can shed light on the problem of organisms. One recalls that an entity is a unity of processes requiring a given, indivisible span of time, or epoch, for its realization. The duration of an epoch can vary for different entities, depending on the complexity and number of processes entering into their realization. An electron or a mu-meson require a very short epoch for their realization, on the order of picoseconds; a mayfly requires a somewhat longer epoch, on the order of forty-eight hours; a human or an elephant require an epoch of fifty to a hundred years for their realization, while a universe requires an epoch on the order of tens of billions of years. The point is that each of these entities requires its full epoch to realize itself as a unified totality of process. Its full identity as a realized actuality depends on its full epoch of evolving becoming. It is nothing at any one of its instants; it is itself only when taken in its unified totality of successive instants.

Thus, identity, for any actual entity, consists of a unity of ongoing process, a unity that incorporates into its present aspect conditioning influences of its past and the anticipation of its future. In a living organism, this immediate experience of ongoing process becomes identifiable with its notion of self; that is, its awareness of itself, its "selfhood," becomes synonymous with its experience of dynamical process. To clarify this, let us state what the selfhood of an organism does not consist of. Selfhood does not consist of its identification with the material bodily components, for its material components are continually being effaced and replaced with others by the process of metabolism:

> . . . the material parts of which the organism consists at a given
> instant are to the penetrating observer only temporary, passing
> contents whose joint material identity does not co-incide with the
> identity of the whole which they enter and leave, and which sus-
> tains its own identity by the very act of foreign matter passing
> through its spatial system, the living *form*. It is never the same
> materially and yet persists as its same self by not remaining the

same matter. Once it really becomes the same with the sameness of its material contents—if any two "time slices" of it become, as to their individual contents, identical with each other and with the slices between them—it ceases to live; it dies . . . (H. Jonas 1966, pp. 75-76)

We see, then, that for the organism not only does identity persist in material change but it depends on this material flux. This is what is meant by the statement that its selfhood is derived from its experience of itself as a process. Its self-awareness does not apply to a material structure, but to an event-structure. The event-structure, the process in question, is the persistence and development of bodily form in the face of material flux. For in the case of living organisms, form is not determined by material substrate:

. . . viewed from the dynamic identity of the living form, the reverse holds: the changing material contents are states of its en-during identity, their multiplicity marking the range of its effec-tive unity. In fact, instead of saying that the living form is a region of transit for matter, it would be truer to say that the material contents in their succession are phases of transit for the self-continuation of the form. (Jonas 1966, p. 80)

Thus, the selfhood of the organism is identified with the dynamical persistence of form, a process.

It can be seen, then, that organisms exhibit an outward orientation to-ward a twofold transcendent horizon: toward the horizon of the outer world as the source of material for the sustenance of its form and toward the horizon of the future into which it is ever on the verge of extending by its existence as a continuous process of becoming. But life also must be characterized by an internal horizon, a self-integrating identity of the whole, spanning the succession of ever-vanishing substrata. There is no way of inferring this internal horizon from external characterization alone; it must derive from our own immediate experience of the organic mode of being. But it is the only way by which the self-integrative persistence of a metabolizing organism can be explained. The mode of realization of an inorganic entity can be explained by its external relations alone, but the persisting self-identity calls for forms of process transcending mere exter-nal relations.

Thus, the self-integrative persistence of the special form of process that is an organism is characterized by an internal horizon that is indicative of its possessing the quality of mind. Therefore, any view of the organismic process that strives for completeness must take account of mind as a factor entering into the process. If, then, mind is an element of the total process comprising an organism, is it possible to explain the fact of organisms without reference to the influence of mind? This amounts to saying, does mind enter into the organism as a causative element in its existence, or is this merely attributable to physical interactions? One can see that since the states of mind do enter into the total plan of the organism, it follows that it affects each subordinate component of the process, until the smallest subordinate components, for instance electrons, are affected:

> Thus an electron within a living body is different from an electron outside it, by reason of the plan of the body; the electron blindly runs either within or without the body; but it runs within the body in accordance with its character within the body; that is to say, in accordance with the general plan of the body, and this plan includes the mental state. (Whitehead 1967, p. 79)

We have been examining heretofore some of the methodological assumptions of science and have found, particularly with reference to the classical notion of material, that many of these assumptions have a limited application. The notion of material entities having simple location and indefinite temporal divisibility, while apparently congruous with (some) aspects of our daily experience, turns out to have the character of an abstraction when our observations focus on the minutest levels of submolecular organization. We have found the characterization of material entities as vibratory epochal processes to be more consistent with the discoveries of quantum mechanics and have found that this model also opens the way to the explanation of organisms and mind.

Perhaps we have arrived, then, at a point where we can suggest a basic reformulation of the metaphysical basis of science. This suggestion is, first, that science consider the *event* as the ultimate unit of natural occurrence, and second, that in seeking to analyze the component elements of an event, it should look for primary organisms rather than material parts. For there is in nature virtually nothing that exhibits the classical attributes of a material; nature is a process of processes, and processes within processes. Accordingly, the analysis of nature should concern itself with the analysis of aggregate processes into primary processes. Biology is concerned with the larger processes that are organisms, whereas physics concerns the smaller processes, which are likewise organisms, in that they experience a reference to things past, immediate, and future. For the primary organisms, we observe this relation as a factor in its external aspects; for ourselves, we observe it as an element of our psychological field of awareness. But if we experience, in experiencing ourselves as process, our essential relatedness to other processes in other times and places, are we justified in denying this experience to other, primary organisms? Is it not more affirmative to assume that, in some sense, a primary organism, being a dynamical process, is "aware," or experiences itself as process and, to the extent that it does, possesses itself an internal horizon? Of course, this question can never be resolved by science, focusing as it does only on the external aspects of a process. It seems reasonable, however, to postulate an element of mind, that is, an internal horizon, as basically intrinsic to even the simplest primary organism. This postulate allows for the reintroduction of value and teleology into nature. Clearly, nature appears to our common sense to have purpose and value; it seems to evolve from simple to more complex, from primitive to more advanced, from less conscious to more conscious. Indeed, it appears to have direction, and it seems to have purpose, which guides it in that direction. Yet, we are asked by science, in the face of all evidence, all reason, and all intuition, to regard nature as purposeless, meaningless, and valueless. If we admit mind as an aspect of even the most primary organism, however, this vast complexity suddenly takes on an added meaning; a new and deeper sublimity replaces that sense of baffling futility and waste with which a blind universe confronts us.

Chapter 4

Toward a Holographic Theory of Mind

*A philosophy of life comprises the philosophy of the organism and the philoso-
phy of mind. This is itself a first proposition of the philosophy of life, in fact
its hypothesis, which it must make good in the course of its execution. For the
statement of scope expresses no less than the contention that the organic even
in its lowest form prefigures mind, and that mind even on its highest reaches
remains part of the organic.* (Jonas 1966, p. 1)

The central, in some ways the final, question in any philosophy of organisms, which seeks to be complete, is the question of mind. Any thorough
explication of the phenomenon of life must face squarely the problem of
the existence of mind and must explain its qualities adequately in terms
that do not beg the question; that is, it cannot seek to understand the
nature of mind in physicochemical, reductionist terms. The insufficiency
of such an approach will inevitably betray itself, for just as the operations
of organisms cannot be reduced to the physicochemical properties of the
matter that composes them because they impose boundary conditions on
the incorporated matter in such a way that the operation of the material
organic system as a whole transcends the boundaries of physics and chemistry, so the same holds for mind on the next hierarchical level of organization. It exhibits qualities peculiar to itself, such that it is not simply
reducible to events occurring in the organic matrix from which it arises, although it certainly includes those events in the conditions of its organization and functioning. This amounts to saying that mind is more than the
sum of its parts, just as the fact of a living organism is more than the sum
of its atoms and molecules and their interactions; in each case, an adequate
explanation must have recourse to a more comprehensive hierarchical level
of organization than the physicochemical level, in the case of organism,
and than the organic level, in the case of mind. The existence of an organism or of a mind imposes boundary conditions on the next lower level of
organization. Organisms and minds incorporate and yet transcend such
lower levels (M. Polanyi 1968).

The hierarchical structuring of organisms and minds implies that mind
cannot be *totally* explained through organic structure, having as it does
principles of organization that transcend the organic level; still, a problem
remains to be dealt with, that of the nature of the relationship between

mind and its physical matrix, a brain. That the organization of the mind does partially reflect the physical organization of the brain can be seen by anyone willing to accept the evidence of experimental neurophysiology. The questions still to be answered are: What is the nature of the physical interface of brain and mind? Where is this interface found in the neural structure? and How does the organization of the brain reflect the organization of the mind? In recent years, neurophysiology has come a considerable distance toward answering these questions, particularly through its discovery of the apparently holographic nature of brain-mind organization. In this chapter, we intend to examine this holographic principle of neural organization by outlining the state of empirical discoveries to date in this area of research. Finally, we will venture some philosophical speculations intended to suggest that the holographic structure of mind may simply reflect, on one hierarchical level, a principle of organization present at all levels in nature.

Holography is a young science whose enormous potential is only now beginning to be explored, although its principles were first discovered accidentally, in 1947, by Dr. Dennis Gabor in trying to design improvements for the electron microscope. It was not until the advent of lasers, which provided a coherent, concentrated light source, that the technology became available that could implement the principles (cf. Pennington 1968, pp. 40–49). Conventional holography is a technique for making lensless, three-dimensional photographs, whose basis is fairly simple. A low-intensity laser beam is passed through a semiopaque mirror, causing part of the beam to pass through the mirror and illuminate the object to be photographed. This light is then reflected from the object onto a photographic plate in front of the object. Simultaneously, the other part of the beam is reflected off a series of mirrors such that it falls on the photographic plate at an angle to the beam reflected from the object (see fig. 1). This convergence of the two beams of coherent light creates an interference pattern that is recorded on the photographic plate. The image that is recorded on the photographic plate, which is called the *hologram* (Gr. *Holos,* whole), bears little resemblance to the object photographed; it is merely a record of the interference pattern of the two intersecting beams. When this hologram is reilluminated using a single, unsplit laser beam, however, a unique phenomenon occurs: Floating in empty space just beyond the illuminated hologram is a fully three-dimensional replica of the object originally photographed. Such a holographic image does not merely give the illusion of three-dimensionality; it is as three-dimensional

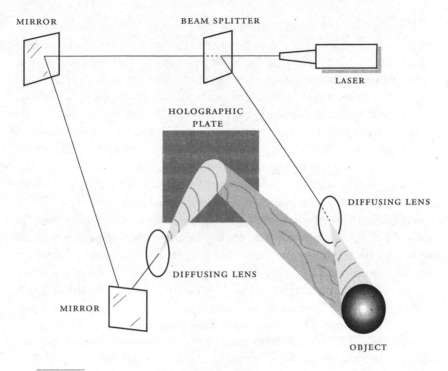

MIRROR · BEAM SPLITTER · LASER · HOLOGRAPHIC PLATE · DIFFUSING LENS · DIFFUSING LENS · MIRROR · OBJECT

FIGURE I *How a Hologram is Made*

as the original object, can be viewed from any angle, will exhibit parallax with other objects or holograms, and can be photographed with a conventional camera. It is, in fact, indistinguishable from its original model by vision alone and can only be so distinguished by passing one's hand or other material object through the image to reveal that it is composed of what in physics is called a *standing waveform,* an apparently motionless arrangement of photons.

Holograms exhibit several other unique properties of particular relevance to our discussion to follow. For instance, what are called "volume" holograms have an as yet untapped potential for information storage. An image can be recorded onto the hologram in the conventional manner described; the plate can then be tilted slightly with respect to its recording laser beams and the image of a second object reexposed onto the same plate without disrupting the previously recorded image. The hologram can then be decoded at angle 1 to yield an image of the first object, or at angle 2 to yield the second object. A large number of separate objects can thus be coded into a single hologram and "replayed" by illuminating the hologram from the proper angles.

Another peculiar quality of holograms is that because the hologram records a set of interference patterns, this pattern is distributed equally and ubiquitously throughout the holographic plate, such that any part of it embodies the whole image. In a conventional photograph, each point from the scene corresponds to one point in the photograph; in a hologram, each point is diffused to many points in the holographic plate. Thus, one can take a hologram and tear it in half and then shine a laser on one of the halves; the resulting image will be a reconstruction of the entire object; if one then tears it into quarters and illuminates one of the quarters, the result is still the same: The total image can be reconstructed from any fragment of the hologram, right down to the very smallest "chip" of the plate. In theory, a fragment of a hologram will yield a total image of the object without significant loss of resolution unless the fragment is so small as to approach the size of the wavelength of the illuminating beam. In practice, however, the coarseness of the photographic emulsion will cause a loss of detail considerably before this level is reached, so that while a total image can be reconstructed from even a very small chip of a hologram, if the chip is too minute, the image will be lacking in detail. Only the details will be lost, however; the essence of the entire message will remain to the last. Similarly, if the hologram is "layered" (two or more images are recorded in the same hologram), each one of the images will be preserved intact throughout each part of the hologram matrix.

We can thus distinguish two features of holography that make it unique as an information storage device: The first is that any one of its parts is equal to the sum of its parts, because the message is reduplicated ubiquitously throughout every part of the hologram. If we had to formulate this into a geometrical axiom, we would say that all points are cotangent. The second feature is that the hologram records the "essence" of an object, and thus, repeated superimposition of essences supplies the details, the particularities, of the object when the total hologram is illuminated.

To understand the applicability of holographic principles to the organization of the brain, it is necessary to talk about memory. One of the paradoxes of memory storage is that a person is born with practically all the neurons that he or she will ever possess; whereas growth of normal tissue is caused by cell division, the nerve cells do not divide, and, moreover, will not regenerate if damaged, although the axon of a nerve cell can regenerate provided the cell body containing the nucleus is undamaged. The problem facing scientists investigating memory and learning has been one of understanding how the brain can store memories and learned information with apparently no alteration of neural organization; how can new information be stored in the brain in the absence of nerve-cell reproduction? The problem has been a baffling one for scientists searching for *engrams,* or memory traces, some evidence of a neural reorganization corresponding to a stored input of information.

This paradox was partially resolved by Karl Lashley (cf. Lashley 1950, pp. 454–482) when he demonstrated that under certain conditions of prolonged or repeated stimulation, the nerve cell can multiply its production of nerve fibers, thus creating new synaptic junctions without actual reproduction of the cells. This can occur in the following manner: The nerve cells ordinarily are surrounded and prevented from growing new fibers by encasing cells called *glia.* It has been found (Pribram 1971a, p. 471), however, that electrical stimulation of a nerve synapse triggers the production of specific molecules of RNA, which have been found to cause (or at least to be correlated with) heightened metabolic activity of the glial cells, thus encouraging them to divide; the tip of the neuron fiber is then free to grow between the daughter glial cells to form new contacts with the neurons beyond it. In this way, the synaptic microstructure can be modified by experience; an interrelated set of such modified neuronal synapses can constitute the neural engram, the encoded memory trace. The result of this process is that the brain develops a kind of neural model of the environment, a spatiotemporal pattern of organization against which inputs are constantly matched.

One aspect of the neuronal storage process had still to be understood. Granted that an input of new information elicited the production of a new set of neural junctions, which when restimulated decoded itself as a memory or learned behavior, the question yet remained as to whether there was a one-for-one correspondence between each part of the memory or perception, or was the memory and/or perception distributed equally throughout every part of the synaptic microstructure? In other words, does one nerve cell, for instance, comprise some fragment of the total experience, one "bit" of information that will be lost to the whole if that nerve cell is damaged? Or does each and every part of the synaptic engram simultaneously contain all "bits" of the whole experience? Experiments performed by Lashley, in which large areas of the cerebrum of rats were destroyed without significantly impairing learning or recognition, indicate that the latter case is the truer one. Lashley found that, while intensity of recall was in proportion to the mass of the brain, nothing short of removal of the entire cerebrum could interrupt recall altogether. Thus he was led to postulate the principles of mass action and equipotentiality in his theory of memory: Intensity of recall depends on the total mass of the brain, but memory is recorded ubiquitously throughout the cerebrum. Here, at last, we begin to gain a glimpse of the relevance of holography in neural organization. As in a hologram, the meaning—stored memory or learned information—appears to be stored ubiquitously throughout the cerebral matrix rather than to be caused by the interrelationship of separate parts. This is the implication, at least, of experiments in which the disruption of the electrical field of the brain, using aluminum hydroxide cream, failed to impair pattern discrimination, while surgical removal of large sections failed to impair memory, learning, or recognition (Pribram 1971b, p. 47f.).

These experiments appear to demonstrate that memories and learned behavior have multiple representation in the cortex; in other words, the information is stored redundantly in the neural matrix so that removal or disruption of part of the cortex will not distort the message stored in another part. Redundant storage, however, is still not equivalent to holographic storage. The redundant system can be compared to a stack of several hundred photocopies of the same message; when part of the stack is removed, the message still resides in the rest of the stack. Ablation of the cortex is analogous to removing part of the stack of pages. If, however, we took the stack of photocopies, threw them up in the air, tore some into fragments, and glued them back together at random, the conventional message, even though redundant, would be disrupted; but if we had performed this operation on a stack of holograms, no amount of random shuffling, tearing, and repasting would disrupt the message, because the entire message resides in each of the parts and does not depend on the relationship between parts. If the brain truly is capable of storing information in a holographic fashion, not only would it be unaffected by cortical ablation, but it should not be disrupted by a random rearrangement of its anatomy. Experiments involving just such an anatomical "shuffle" of parts were carried out by Dr. Paul Pietsch, using cortical sections from salamanders. The theory was that such shuffling of cortical parts would not disrupt normal salamander behavior if the holographic theory were true:

> In more than 700 operations, I rotated, reversed, added, subtracted, and scrambled brain parts. I shuffled. I reshuffled. I sliced, lengthened, deviated, shortened, opposed, transposed, juxtaposed, and flipped. I spliced front to back with lengths of spinal cord, or medulla, with other pieces of brain turned inside out. But nothing short of dispatching the brain to the slopbucket—nothing expunged feeding! . . . The experiments had subjected the holo-

graphic theory to a severe test. As the theory predicted, scrambling the brain's anatomy did not scramble its programs. Meaning was contained within the parts, not spread out among their relationships. If I wanted to change behavior, I had to supply not a new anatomy, but new information. (Pietsch 1972, pp. 46, 48)

The clincher to these encouraging results came when Pietsch transplanted the brain of a tadpole to the cranium of a salamander. While the salamander is a traditional predator on the tubifex worm, the tadpole is symbiotic to it, using its sucker mouth to remove algae from the flanks of the tubifex without harming it. Pietsch found that the salamander with the transplanted tadpole brain mimicked the tadpole, and in more than eighteen hundred trials, the salamander did not once attack the tubifex: The transplanted herbivorous brain had carried its holographic set of peaceful behavior patterns right into the salamander's cranium. Vindication of the holographic theory of information storage was complete.

Two questions remain to be answered. Granting that the cerebrum can store information in a manner analogous to holographic storage, then what mechanism in the brain can function in the role of the interference pattern set up by the two encoding laser beams in normal holography, and what mechanism functions in the role of the single "decoding" beam used for retrieval of the holographic image?

The key to answering the first question lies in the understanding that holography does not depend on the physical presence of light waves. Holograms have been constructed from sound waves and even infrared waves. R. W. Rodieck (cf. Pribram 1969, p. 77) has shown that the mathematical equations describing the holographic process match exactly what the brain does with information, and computer simulations of holographic storage have been carried out on the basis of the equations (convolutional integrals and Fourier transformations) alone. It is not the presence of physical waves, as such, that is needed for making a hologram, but rather an interference pattern, a ratio of harmonic relationships:

The question remains: how can interference effects be produced in the brain? One can imagine that when nerve impulses arrive at synapses (the junction between two nerve cells), they produce electrical events on the other side of the synapse that take the form of momentary standing wave fronts. Typically the junctions made by a nerve fiber number in the dozens, if not hundreds. The patterns set up by arriving nerve impulses presumably form a

microstructure of wave forms that can interact with similar microstructures arising in overlapping junctional contacts. These other
microstructures are derived from the spontaneous changes in
electrical potential that ceaselessly occur in nerve tissue, and from
other sources within the brain. Immediate cross-correlations
result, and these can add in turn to produce new patterns of nerve
impulses.

   The hypothesis presented here is that the totality of this process
has a more or less lasting effect on protein molecules and perhaps
other macromolecules at the synaptic junctions and can serve as a
neural hologram from which, given the appropriate input, an
image can be reconstructed. (Pribram 1969, p. 77)

The long-known "functional" areas of the brain, such as Broca's area
(speech cortex), the visual cortex at the back of the brain, or the auditory
cortex at the sides, may function as the mechanism for "reconstruction" of
a stored neural hologram to yield a memory, perception, or thought. These
areas are known to have a function in various modes of behavior and perception, and for many years it was thought that they were storage sites relating to specific functions such as speech, vision, hearing, and so on. In
the holographic theory, these centers would act not to store information,
but rather as "processing" stations for the encoding and recalling of programs from the holographic storage areas of the cerebral cortex. Thus,
these functional centers could operate in the role of the "reconstructing"
laser beam; whether the memory or perception was experienced visually,
auditorily, tactually, or as some combination would depend on what centers were activated in reconstruction, a process that would be equivalent to
using lasers of different wavelengths in reconstruction.

What kind of neural mechanism plays the role of the coherent
light source to make and display holograms? Perhaps a kind of
coherence results from the anatomical fact that the retina and
visual cortex are linked by many thousands of fibers arranged in
parallel pathways. Or it could be that the nerve cells in the visual
channel achieve coherence by rhythmic firing. Still another possibility is that coherence results from the operation of the variety
of detectors that respond to such simple stimuli as the tilt of a line
and movement . . . (Pribram 1969, p. 77)

It is not possible to outline entirely the present state of experimental and theoretical evidence centering on holographic neural organization. Many areas of uncertainty still exist in current research that, it is to be hoped, will yield to scientific understanding in the near future. One such area is "split-brain" research, focusing on investigating the brain's operation when the *corpus callosum,* the intermediary pathway between the left and right cerebral hemispheres, has been severed. Certain results of this research suggest that each hemisphere records only specific kinds of information, a finding that would tend to contradict the holographic theory of ubiquitous storage; other theorists suggest that this may only indicate unequal *access* to information in the right hemisphere, rather than unequal storage. A definitive answer awaits further research. There is no doubt that other objections could be leveled at the holographic theory that have not been met by us as laypersons. It seems clear, however, that the principles of neural organization do bear some significant similarities to holography, although it would of course be presumptuous to claim that holography explains *all* aspects of brain organization. No such claim is made here; we seek only to provide a basic understanding of the (probably) fundamental role played by holographic structuring in the present picture of neural organization. The interested reader should examine Karl Pribram's *Languages of the Brain* (1971) for the current status of holographic theories of brain function.

Let us now turn to the more philosophical and speculative aspect of this theory of mind. Granted that holography reflects in part the structure and organization of the brain, and granted also that the brain and its structure will in part reflect the nature of the mind arising from it, it follows therefore that the mind itself must in some sense be holographically structured. The questions we must ask then are: (1) In what sense is the mind holographically structured, and (2) why should it be so structured?

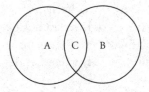

FIGURE 2

Let us illustrate the first question with a diagram representing mind-world interaction. We can represent this interaction by two overlapping circles, or realms, which we designate as A and B (fig. 2). Circle A represents the physical world. Circle B represents the mind; this is the seat of thoughts, will, creativity: in short, circle B comprises the experiencing self, which, through the brain-body liaison, makes its causal presence felt in the external world. We can think of circle B as existing in the temporal dimension; it is a process developing through time, much in the way that a piece of music develops through the temporal process of being played. The realm where the two circles overlap, which we call C, forms the region of interface between the physical world and the mind. Realm C corresponds to the brain-body system; it forms the pathway by which the mind receives information (perception), and also the mechanism by which it responds to its perceptions. The comparison to holography that this suggests can be made through analogy; the brain-body system represented by realm C is comparable to the physical apparatus necessary for generating a hologram; the brain in this analogy is equivalent to the exposed holographic plate; the body, with its afferent and efferent pathways, acts as the laser system, both receiving (perceiving) information and encoding this information into the neural holographic plate. Realm B, in this analogy, the realm of states of consciousness, is then comparable to the actual holographic image, the standing wave form of ongoing awareness. Circle A, which includes external reality and the subjectively experienced state of the body, forms the "subject," which becomes encoded through receptors and afferent pathways into the neural holographic plate, where it is then "reconstructed" as part of realm B, that part of realm B representing its "model" of the external world. So far, this analogy lacks the notion of temporal flux. The interactions between the mind and the body, and through the body with the external world, consist of dynamic processes. The analogy with holography is more accurate if we think of the process as a holographic movie rather than as a static, frozen image. In this dynamic version, the neural hologram (the brain) is continually exposed and reexposed to the changing environment, thus encoding a constantly shifting set of interference patterns that are "read out" as a temporally unfolding hologram, that is, the mind, with its constantly shifting "model" of reality and associated thoughts, memories, images, and reflections.

The holographic capacity of the mind for ubiquitous storage of information can be seen most readily in the phenomenon of imagination. We can imagine all of the universe or any part of it and thus can say that the mind "contains" all of the physical world, that is, that the mind is a hologram of external reality. This concept has been anticipated by the alchemists in their notion of man as microcosm, and also in the symbol of the alchemical monad (cf. Jung 1952, pp. 103–104, 370), a synonym for the *Lapis Philosophorum,* that part in which the whole may be found. Reference might also be made to the central axiom of Hermeticism, the Hellenistic philosophical system that is the forerunner of alchemy: "What is here is everywhere; what is not here is nowhere" (cf. Jung 1952). This is a formula for a holographic matrix.

The complex symbol systems of alchemy are but one example of a property that seems to characterize mind in general; that is, its tendency to construct symbolic totality metaphors. The constructs of the mind are, by and large, couched in symbols; even "raw" sensory data is seldom experienced without symbolic interpretations, associations, and judgments. This tendency of the mind to symbolize, to organize experience into meaningful, coherent pattern is indicative of its ceaseless effort to somehow "encompass" reality, to construct a suitable model of self and world. This quality of mind is seen best of all, however, in the dynamics of unconscious processes, in dreams, vision, and trance; indeed, the individuation process in Jungian psychology represents an attempt by the unconscious to construct a totality symbol that both encompasses and defines the self and the world in relation to the self. Jung has shown in numerous works (cf. 1952, 1959) the important role played by mandala symbolism as a means for expressing the underlying order of psychic unity and totality. This property of symmetrical, mandalic organization is found universally in all artifacts of human thought, from the most abstract metaphysical systems to the commonest objects of everyday use, and it, indeed, appears to be intrinsic to the organization of the psyche. May not this proclivity of the mind to elaborate symbolic totality metaphors be reflective of the holographic structure of the psyche?

The unformed archetypes of the collective unconscious may be the holographic substrate of the species' mind. Each individual mind-brain is then like a fragment of the total hologram; but, in accordance with holographic principles, each fragment contains the whole. It will be remembered that each part of a hologram can reconstruct an entire image, but that the details of the image will deteriorate in proportion to its fragmentation, while the overstructure will remain. Out of this feature of holography arises the quality of individual point of view and, in fact, individuality itself. If each mind is a holographic medium, then each is contiguous with every other, because of the ubiquitous distribution of information in a hologram. Each individual mind would thus be a representation of the "essence" of reality, but the details could not be resolved until the fragments of the collective hologram were joined.

We have seen that the construction of an immaterial corpuscular stand-ing waveform image from the physical substrate of the holographic plate is closely analogous to the generation of the mind from the holographic cerebral substrate. We will mention some other qualities of a hologram that indicate its suitability as a model of mind. One example is the recon-struction of a hologram using nonvisible light; this is perfectly possible and in the mind would constitute an unconscious content. Another inter-esting quality of holograms is that they can be constructed using laser beams reflected from *two* objects, which then interfere on the holographic plate; when the hologram is then reilluminated using *one* beam, both ob-jects appear. Thus we can say that holographic matrices have the property of associative recall.

The list of examples could be extended; however, these should illustrate our point—that the mind itself, as well as the brain from which it arises, does, to some extent, exhibit holographic qualities. Let us now venture to speculate how and why this might be so.

Confronted with certain holographic qualities as a feature of both mind and brain, it seems reasonable to ask whether holographic principles are found on other levels of organization. We can find this most appar-ently in the organismic realm, in the fact of the ubiquity and redundancy of DNA. We refer to the fact that DNA seems to store information holo-graphically, in that the nucleotide sequence of the molecule is identical in every cell of a given organism. The DNA from one cell theoretically con-tains all the information necessary to regenerate the entire organism. It is due to the presence of certain "inductors" (notably RNA) that DNA makes some cells into skin, others into nerves, and still others into mus-cles, and so on. Thus, on the organismic level, also, we note the ubiquity of genetic information, but also that each cell "reads" only some part of the DNA-hologram, though the entire message is there.

When we descend to an even more basic level of organization, the atomic level, the holographic metaphor is not so readily apparent. We are essentially asking whether a holographic structure underlies the nature of external reality itself. If this could be shown, it would explain why holo-graphic structure is reflected in the organization of DNA, the brain, and mind. We find that we have been preceded in our speculations by Leib-niz, in his concept of the cosmic Monad (cf. Leibniz 1890, pp. 218ff). Leibniz argues that the universe is a plenum, and that it is composed of a "simple substance" that is everywhere and alike in all its parts, and that it is by virtue of the affectations and interactions between these parts, or monads, that distinctness and particularity arise:

... Each monad, its nature being representative, nothing can limit it to representing only a part of things; although it may be true that this representation is but confused as regards the detail of the whole universe, and can be distinct only in the case of a small part of things, that is to say, in the case of those which are nearest or largest in relation to each of the monads—otherwise each monad would be a divinity. It is not in the object, but only in the modification of the knowledge of the object that monads are limited. They all tend confusedly toward the infinite, toward the whole, but they are limited, and distinguished by their degrees of distinct perceptions ... (Leibniz 1890, pp. 223, 226–228)

Leibniz is saying that each monad is identical to every other monad, differing only by its "perspective," its relation to the whole, that is, to other monads, each of which mirrors every other. A similar idea is encountered in Whitehead's concept of the "extensive continuum," which he characterizes as a "relational complex in which all potential objectifications find their niche." This extensive continuum can be conceived as the set of all possible relationships, both actual and potential, both of all actual and of all potential entities. The extensive continuum therefore "... expresses the solidarity of all possible standpoints throughout the whole process of the world. It is not a fact prior to the world; it is the first determination of order—that is, of real potentiality—arising out of the general character of the world" (Whitehead 1967, p. 82). The extensive continuum can thus be viewed as a holographic matrix of all potentiality. Only a finite number of potentialities ever become realized as "actual entities," in the same way that a holographic plate in which multiple images have been stored at different orientations can be "decoded" at some angles, but not at others:

In the mere continuum there are contrary potentialities; in the actual world there are definite atomic actualities determining one coherent system of real divisions throughout the region of actuality. Each actual entity in its relationship to other actual entities is in this sense somewhere in the continuum, and arises out of the data provided by this standpoint. But in another sense it is everywhere throughout the continuum; for its constitution includes the objectifications of the actual world and thereby includes the continuum; also the potential objectifications of itself contribute to the real potentialities whose solidarity the continuum expresses.

> Thus the continuum is present in each actual entity, and each
> actual entity pervades the continuum. (Whitehead 1967, p. 83)

Quantum theory gives a view of the underlying substructure of reality that is quite consistent with the holographically structured metaphysical models of Leibniz and Whitehead. The particulate concept of matter has been superseded by the idea that the atom is both wave and particle, both continuum and actual entity. Bohr was the first to show that the electron, the basic subunit of matter, could not be considered to have a spatiotemporal location (around the nucleus of an atom, for example), but instead had to be mathematically approached as a "cloud" of probability: The free electron possesses a "mass" coincident with the entire universe, and its occurrence at a given space-time locus is a function of extreme possibility, not of definable position. This quantum concept of the electron is strikingly reminiscent of the Leibnizian monad, that is both "here" and "everywhere" at once. Under the quantum theory, each quantum of matter is both wave and particle and pervades the universe; there is no solid matter as such, but only probability densities in the continuum, interference patterns created by the interaction of quanta that, to the synthesizing perceptual mechanism in the brain-mind, appear as objects—"actual entities" —rocks, tables, people, stars, and so on. Thus, a holographic image of reality is reconstructed by the brain-mind from the underlying substrate of concrescences of probability. Note the similarity here to the potentiality of Whitehead's extensive continuum.

Would such a model of a holographic extensive continuum be inconsistent with the theory of relativity? If "all points reflect every other point," and if "all points are cotangent," as implied by a holographic theory of a quantum-monad, then how can the relativity of space-time be preserved? The objection is overcome if we postulate that space-time exists within each monad (quantum); thus, each wave-particle would have relativistic effects operating within it. A collection of such quanta (a galaxy, for instance) would also have relativistic effects, resulting from the superimposition of the space-time events occurring in each of its monadic parts. Remember that in a holographic monadology not only does each part mirror the whole but the whole (or any fragment thereof) mirrors each part; thus, we would expect relativistic effects on all levels, from the quantum to the cosmic.

> The example of hierarchical cosmic sub-structures (Wilson 1969)
> shows that levels may be distinguished by a characteristic time or
> frequency, which is to say that each level is temporally closed. This

suggests that the properties of space and time are closure properties of structures, bringing to mind the basic idea of Leibniz that space and time have no independent existence, but derive from the nature of structures. Einstein's equivalence of dynamics and geometry contained in his field equations (e.g., matter and density determines spatial curvature) is also consistent with Leibniz's view and a departure from the Newtonian idea that all structure exists within an independent framework of space and time. It may then be that from the various closures and partial closures of structures and systems, we infer the descriptions we call space and time . . . (Whyte et al. 1969, p. 55)

We can see that while relativity would operate in each monad, and in the universe *as* monad, the extensive continuum of potentiality would exist outside of space-time in a fifth Einsteinian dimension. Space-time, and the relativistic effects arising therefrom, would exist as properties of actual entities existing in the extensive continuum, but the continuum itself, underlying the configurations of three dimensions, would exhibit the quality of simultaneity, as, in some sense, the holographic matrix of potentiality would make all times "simultaneous."

Let us now summarize the factual and speculative ground we have covered in our holographic theory of mind. We began by noting the special qualities of holography and went on to illustrate that the organization of the brain seems to be in part holographic. We have introduced evidence which suggests that the mind itself is holographic in quality and to that extent reflects its neural substrate. We have speculated that this holographic structure of the mind may proceed from the fact that holographic principles operate on many structural levels; the ubiquity and redundancy of DNA in organisms was mentioned as an illustration of this. We found that holographic principles might also be applied to the structure of reality itself by virtue of the quantum nature of matter, whose wave-particle qualities suggest a holographic monad. Finally, we saw that such a holographic model of reality did not violate the laws of relativity if it were postulated that the monadic substrate existed in a fifth Einsteinian dimension, that is, a fourth spatial dimension. We are not prepared to assert the "truth" of our speculations over other models of reality, recognizing that all such models are ultimately constructs of the human mind, each no "truer" than any other. Nevertheless, a holographic picture of mind and of external reality has enhanced our understanding of both.

Chapter 5

Models of Drug Activity

In recent years great strides have been made toward the elucidation of the neurophysiological and neurochemical processes underlying the phenomenon of consciousness. The Cartesian dualism of strict separation of mind and body has come to be recognized for what it is, at worst a dogmatic presumption without any empirical basis, at best a methodological expedient (cf. chapter 3). Most physiologists have graduated to a view of the organism as a complex, integrated system, not reducible to merely the sum of the physicochemical processes taking place within it. The primary feature of organisms is, after all, *organization*—the complex spatiotemporal ordering of processes on the molecular and physiological level that makes the organism an integrated whole rather than a disorganized "mush" of proteins (cf. Sinnot 1950, p. 21). The next logical step in the recognition of the principle of organization as a fundamental constituent of living things is its extension to the problem of consciousness in higher organisms:

> Interpreted in terms of the present hypothesis, therefore, the
> whole conscious life of human beings, rich in ideas, in inspiration,
> in intellectual subtleties, in imagination and emotion, is simply
> the manifestation of an organized biological system raised to its
> loftiest levels. Upon this the outer world impinges as a series of
> sensations, real or imagined, and out of it come actions, either
> actual physical responses or the more subtle ones of the mind.
> What takes place between these events is, at bottom, the regula-
> tory activity of the protoplasmic system. In its lowliest expression
> this appears as regulatory control of growth and function. This
> merges imperceptibly into instinct, and from these simplest of
> psychic phenomena gradually emerge the complex mental activi-
> ties of the higher animals and finally the enormously rich and
> varied life of the mind and spirit of human beings. At no point
> is there a sudden break, a radical innovation. The complex has
> come from the simple by a gradual process of evolutionary pro-
> gression. The basic phenomenon from which all this ultimately
> arises, the fact that living things are organized systems, is the
> fundamental problem still unanswered. Upon its solution will
> depend our understanding not only of biology and psychology
> but of the whole of man. (Sinnot 1950, p. 721)

In some branches of biology, notably the neurosciences, this fundamental interdependence of mental phenomena and physiochemical processes has already achieved the status of a truism.

The relationship between electrochemical events occurring in the brain and consciousness is made nowhere more clear than in the study of the influence of psychotropic drugs, and in particular the hallucinogens, on the phenomenology of consciousness. The alteration of mental function that hallucinogens can elicit illustrates that our apprehension of "reality" is largely determined by chemical and physiological parameters. It is only through an "accident" of evolution that our nervous systems—and the version of reality that they provide us—have come to be structured as they are. This profound interdependence of mind and the molecular configuration of its neural substrate appear to be a direct repudiation of the existential proposition that nature is "mute."

In recent years great progress has been made in the elucidation of the molecular and biochemical mechanisms of nervous functioning, and the interaction of these mechanisms with hallucinogenic and other psychotropic drugs. Yet, for all the progress, the central question remains unanswered. This question, framed in its simplest terms, might be phrased thus: What qualities characterize the physical interface between molecules and mind?

To date, only tentative theoretical and speculative steps have been taken toward answering this question. In this chapter we intend to present our own hypothetical model for drug and neurotransmitter activity; it is first necessary, however, to acquaint the reader with some fraction of the hypotheses and experimental findings currently extant. We will first discuss the problems of drug action from the biochemical standpoint; here we will focus on the questions of structural relationships between hallucinogens and neurotransmitters, their metabolic uptake by the nervous system, their enzymatic fates and possible endogenous origins in certain kinds of enzymatic dysfunctions, and related considerations. Second, we will consider the problem of drug action at the receptor site and will discuss problems involved with this study and current theoretical models. Last, we will present our own theoretical model, using the preceding information as a basis for hypothesis.

Neurotransmitters are chemicals that mediate the propagation of nerve signals across the synapse. They are released at the presynaptic nerve terminal and cross the synaptic gap to react with a receptor on the surface of a postsynaptic nerve (or other excitable postjunctional cell), and they may either stimulate or inhibit the firing of the postjunctional cell. Only two substances, acetylcholine and norepinephrine, have been definitively shown to function as neurotransmitters, but other likely candidates include serotonin (5-hydroxytryptamine or 5HT), dopamine, epinephrine, and histamine, among others. A neurotransmitter substance should conform to three major criteria: Nerves should be able to produce the chemical, the chemical should be released when nerves are stimulated and react with a postjunctional receptor to produce a specific biological response, and some enzymatic or other mechanism should be available to rapidly terminate the action of the transmitter (Axelrod 1974).

The structural configurations of a large number of hallucinogens have been elucidated, and the similarity of these to certain neurohumoral factors has been noted:

> When the structural types in figure 3 are compared, it is striking to see how often indole structures appear, and always in the form of tryptamine derivatives. These may be tryptamines without any substitution in the indole nucleus or with hydroxy- methoxy- or phosphoryloxy-groups in the phenol ring of the indole; or else the tryptamine residue forms part of a polycyclic ring system, as in the case of the beta-carboline and lysergic acid derivatives and of ibogaine. The most specific and most potent hallucinogens, such as LSD (d-lysergic acid diethylamide) and psilocybin, belong to the tryptamine type.
>
> Since they are tryptamine derivatives, the indolic hallucinogens are structurally related to the neurohumoral factor serotonin (5-hydroxytryptamine). Serotonin is widely distributed in warm-blooded animals. It accumulates in the brain, where it plays a role in the biochemistry of nervous regulations. Consequently, it seems that certain tryptamine structures which occur so frequently in hallucinogens, as well as in the neurohormone serotonin, may be biochemically important in the metabolism of psychic functions . . .
>
> A chemical relationship similar to that between the tryptaminelike hallucinogens and serotonin exists between the phenylethylamine derivative mescaline and the neurohormone norepinephrine. (Schultes and Hofmann 1973, pp. 17–20)

FIGURE 3

Structural Types of Principal Hallucinogens

(Examples only)

I. Phenylethylamine derivatives related to Norepinephrine

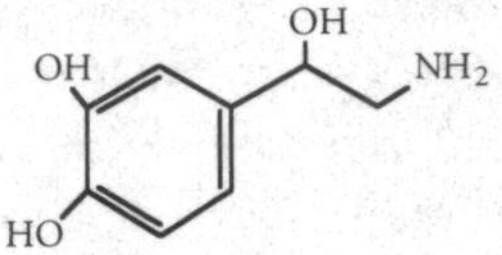

NOREPINEPHRINE
(neurotransmitter)

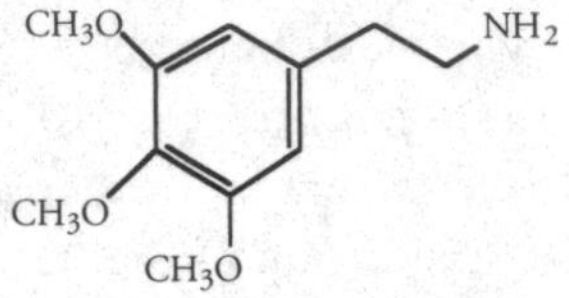

MESCALINE
(alkaloid of peyote and other cacti)

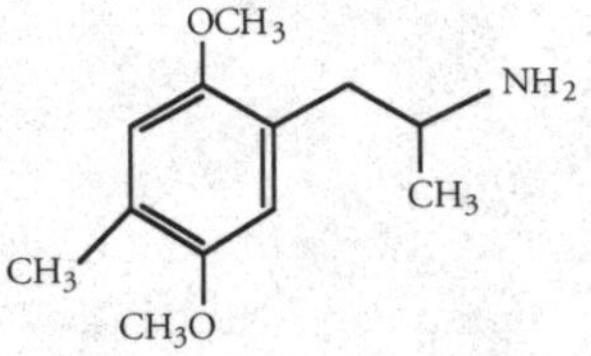

DOM, A.K.A. STP
(synthetic)

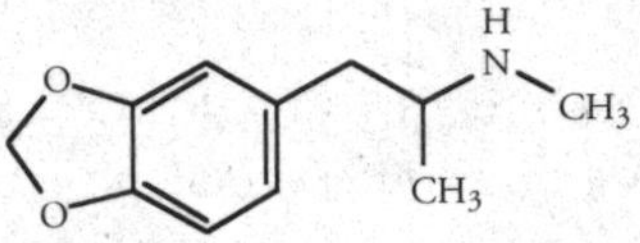

MDMA
(synthetic)

II. Indole derivatives related to Serotonin
   a. simple tryptamine derivatives

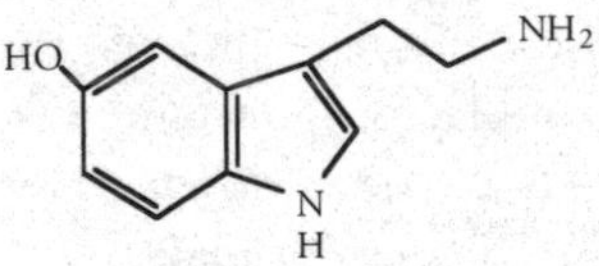

SEROTONIN
(5-Hydroxytryptamine;
neurotransmitter)

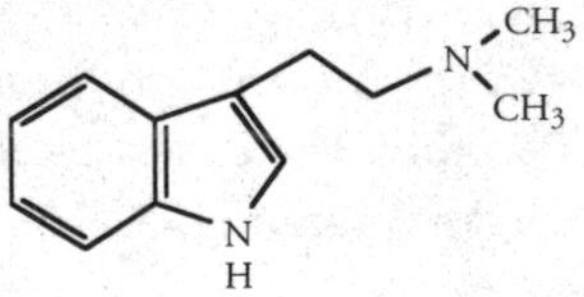

DMT
(N, N-Dimethyltryptamine)

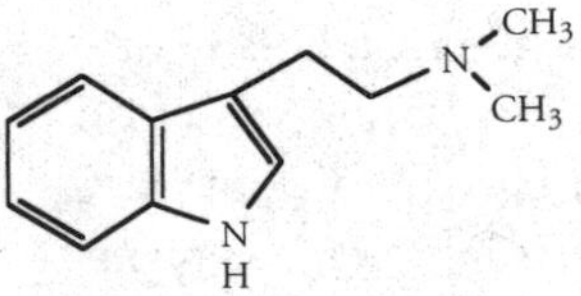

5-MeO-DMT (5-Methoxy-N,
N-Dimethyltryptamine)

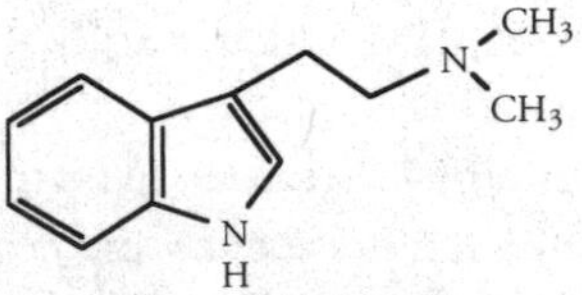

PSILOCIN (4-Hydroxy-N,
N-Dimethyltryptamine)

II. Indole derivatives related to Serotonin

b. tricyclic indole derivatives (ß-carbolines)

HARMINE

TETRAHYDRO-HARMINE

HARMALINE

c. complex indole derivatives

IBOGAINE
from Tabernanthe iboga

LSD-25
(semisynthetic)

In view of the structural analogies between neurohormones and the hallucinogens, it is not surprising that many studies have shown an interaction between drugs and neurotransmitters. There are still problems in finally delineating these interactions, since a drug will often exhibit a variety of interactions; thus, while the following passage illustrates that there is an interaction with serotonin and NE mechanisms, these are by no means the sole types of action that can occur:

> To the already formidable list of complications in the interpretation of the effects of these compounds, Kopin now proceeded to add some others. If there are no transmitters on which these drugs can act, and as there are three possible modes of interaction (potentiation, inhibition, or both, with no net effect) there may be as many as 3n possible modes of interaction produced by the drug. To this one must add the quantitative consideration that drugs often have one effect at one dose level, and the opposite at another; action on different brain areas must be considered; the fact that there may be more than one type of receptor of a molecule will also be a determinant.

The effect of a drug may depend on its action at multiple sites. For example, for effect X to materialize, the drug must inhibit 5HT synapses, potentiate NE synapses, and have no effect on histamine synapses. For effect Y, it may be necessary to inhibit histamine and NE synapses and have no effect on 5HT synapses, etc. (Smythies, in Schmitt et al. 1971, p. 32)

The technical problems inherent in the study of chemical transmission at the synapse have proved virtually insurmountable in the case of the central nervous system. The result has been that experimental investigations have concentrated on the role of the neurotransmitter acetylcholine (Mandell and Spooner 1968) in the peripheral nervous system. Hence, many of the theoretical models for neurotransmitter function in the central nervous system have been drawn from studies conducted on acetylcholine in the peripheral nervous system.

Any similar investigations of the synaptic events in the central nervous system are complicated by several factors:

The technical problems involved with any attempt to use analogously systematic research approaches to a potential transmitter in the central nervous system are great. Peripheral synapses can be isolated by microdissection, they can remain functional in an isolated profusion experimental situation for hours, and their activation can be manifested by clearly defined and measurable phenomena (such as the miniature end-plate potential or the contraction of smooth muscle). The central nervous system has little in the way of focal synaptic regions. The dendrites and the cell bodies of central neurons are densely covered with synapses, many of which may be of a chemically heterogenous nature. In addition, the extra-neuronal space is packed with a tangle of glia, closely approximating the membranous surfaces of nerve cells and possibly intrinsically important to their function. This makes the isolated, chemical manipulation of central synapses extremely difficult. (Mandell and Spooner 1968, p. 1443)

Because of these complications, most of our evidence for norepinephrine and serotonin as the primary central synaptic transmitters is at best of an indirect nature. Data that seem to indicate that these compounds act as neurotransmitters in the central nervous system include observations of regional differences in the distribution of these compounds in the brain, a distribution of synthesizing and degradative enzymes that closely parallels the distribution of the amine, high levels of these amines and of enzymes related to their synthesis in the subcellular fractions associated with synaptic vesicles, and high levels of degradative enzymes in the subcellular fractions associated with synaptic structures (cf. Mandell and Spooner 1968).

A diagrammatic model of the probable actions of a neurotransmitter at the synapse is shown in figure 4. Drugs could alter neurotransmitter function by influencing one or more of these steps. Current theories as to the possible nature of the interaction of hallucinogenic drugs with serotonin and NE functions have tended to favor the concept that they function as "false" transmitters and can be bound into the receptor site in place of the endogenous neurotransmitters:

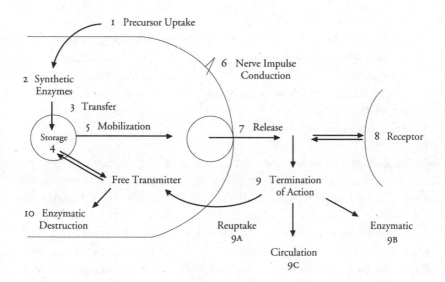

FIGURE 4

Actions of Neurotransmitters at the Synapse: (1) Uptake of precursor; (2) Synthesis of transmitter by possibly several steps; (3) Transfer of transmitter; (4) Storage of transmitter; (5) Mobilization of transmitter; (6) Nerve impulse conduction; (7) Release of transmitter; (8) By some action on the receptor site; (9) Termination of action of transmitter, (a) Reuptake, (b) Enzymatic, (c) Diffusion; (10) Enzymatic destruction of the transmitter in the nerve ending. (Smythies, in Schmitt et al. 1971, p. 27)

The false transmitter replaces the NE in the storage granules so that less NE is released, because a constant number of molecules are released by nerve impulse. False transmitters can compete for neuronal uptake of NE. Thus the NE that is released will be potentiated; blockage of uptake potentiates the action of the catecholamine. On the other hand, the false transmitter might interact with the receptor, preventing the NE from activating it and thereby depressing the effect of the released physiologic transmitter. Finally, the false transmitter itself may activate the receptor, but usually not as efficiently as NE. In other words, a single substance can, through at least six different mechanisms, alter the effectiveness of the nerve impulse.

The reaction of these compounds may be understood if looked at from the standpoint of the amine group. The amine group has a potential for interacting with a wide variety of receptor sites. As groups are added to the molecule, it becomes more difficult for the molecule to interact with these various receptor sites. If one has the phenylethylamine structure only, it will fit, perhaps, only NE and 5HT; it will not fit the histamine site. If a methoxy group is added, this may make it more difficult for it to fit the adrenergic receptor, and it now reacts almost purely with the serotonergic receptor. The chemical manipulation therefore changes the balance of the interaction of the compound with various receptor sites. (Symthies, in Schmitt et al. 1971, pp. 29, 67)

A good deal can be learned about the actions of both neurotransmitters and hallucinogenic drugs by studying the enzymatic mechanisms functioning in their metabolism. Studies of this nature have shown clearly that enzymes are present in the brain that are capable of synthesizing endogenous hallucinogenic compounds. Among the most important of these are phenol-O-methyl transferase, which can O-methylate tyramine to form the potentially psychotomimetic substance paramethoxyphenylethylamine; N-methyl transferase, first isolated from rabbit lung, can synthesize dimethyltryptamine and bufotenin from tryptamine and serotonin, and hydroxy-indole O-methyl transferase, an enzyme of the pineal gland, which can O-methylate N-acetylserotonin to form melatonia, and bufotenin to form 5-methoxy-N,N-dimethyltrypamine. In addition, the hallucinogenic substance 6-methoxyletrahydroharman has been found to be identical with the pineal hormone adrenoglomerulotropine. A potential precursor for this, 6-methoxyharmalan, has been found to derive from metatonin:

> Of much interest is the recent discovery of substances closely
> related to the harmala alkaloids in animals. One of these is
> adrenoglomerulotropine, a hormone of the pineal body, the chem-
> ical identity of which has been indicated as 2,3,4,9-tetrahydro-
> 6-methoxy-1-methyl-1H-pyrido (3,4,6) indole. This substance is
> identical to 6-methoxytetrahydroharman which has been shown
> to be formed *in vivo* from 5-methoxy tryptamine and acetalde-
> hyde. 6-methoxytetrahydroharman is an isomer of tetrahydro-
> harmine, one of the alkaloids in *Banisteriopsis,* and in the African
> *Leptactinia densiflora.* One more substance, 6-methoxyharmalan,
> has been shown to derive, at least *in vitro,* from melatonin, which
> results from the methylation of acetylserotonin. The enzyme
> which makes this possible, hydroxyindole O-methyl transferase,
> has only been found in the pineal body. (Naranjo, in Efron et al.
> 1967, p. 385)

In view of the natural occurrence in the brain of hallucinogenic compounds, such as 6-methoxyharmalan, and of enzymes capable of originating similar compounds, it is not surprising that many researchers have
looked for enzymatic dysfunctions underlying certain types of mental disease, such as schizophrenia (cf. Snyder et al. 1974).

It seems unlikely that the biochemical causes of abnormal behavior can
be elucidated in the absence of any definitive understanding of the role
played by neurotransmitters (and possibly endogenous psychotomimetics)
and their related enzyme systems in the regulation of normal behavior.
Snyder (1974) makes the interesting speculation that methylated tryptamines, enzymatically derived from serotonin substrates, may function in
monitoring people's levels of internal and external perception. Little is
known about the function of serotonin itself in the modulation of perceptions or mentation, but the following passage suggests that it might
function in a variety of ways:

> Elkes also suggested that the 5HT system in the brain might
> represent an ancient evolutionary system. Serotonin was widely
> distributed through animal and even plant life (i.e., vertebrates,
> molluscs, the sea anemone, and hairs of the white nettle). Can

it be that in some way the older biological function of 5HT could
be related to light and that a piece of (originally) light-sensitive
enzymatic machinery was in some way internalized and built into
some primitive nervous nets (the myenteric plexus, the pineal,
the raphe nuclei)? It is also well to remember that some powerful
plant growth hormones, the auxins, were indoles. Could the
indoles be growth regulators in the CNS? (Smythies, in Schmitt et
al. 1971, p. 26)

The speculation that 5HT function may be related to a light-sensitive
mechanism takes on added significance if considered together with current
data on the function of the pineal gland. The human pineal contains more
serotonin by weight than any neural structure of any mammalian species.
It contains the highest levels of the enzyme tryptophan hydroxylase, which
is essential in the synthesis of serotonin from tryptophan. The pineal also is
the only organ containing the enzyme HIOMT, which converts serotonin
to melatonin. We have already noted that the pineal contains the hallucinogenic compound 6-methoxyharmalan.

The pineal is one of the least understood of the brain organs; until recently, it was thought to be a phylogenetic relic left over from some reptil-
ian ancestor as a nonfunctional "third eye." It is now generally recognized
as a functional endocrine gland. The pineal's probable evolutionary deri-
vation from a primitive "third eye" is supported by the fact that it is
known to receive a variety of environmental inputs and to respond to this
input by circadian fluctuations in its enzyme activity, including the activity of HIOMT and hence the production of melatonin:

The pineal gland is now known to receive two main types of input,
photic and olfactory, and to emit two main types of output, anti-
gonadal and melatonin.

First and most important, the pineal gland receives sense from
the retina. This is not the sense of sight as we know it. It is a
description of intensity, type, and timing of light, and perhaps
of other characteristics of light of which we are consciously
unaware . . .

Next, there is input from that area which once was known as
the rhinencephalon, the smell brain, and which now in the United
States goes by the name of the limbic system or visceral brain . . .
(Wiener 1968, p. 915)

Evidence also exists that indicates that the pineal is sensitive to other kinds of input in addition to photic and olfactory, including temperature, sound, long wavelength light, and X rays (Wiener 1968, pp. 923, 931).

Pineal output appears to be regulated by an antagonistic relationship between the pineal and the pituitary. They affect many of the same target organs, including melanocytes, gonads, brain, thyroid, thymus, and adrenal cortex, and both glands influence growth of body and of tumors, carbohydrate and fat metabolism, diuresis, and blood pressure (Wiener 1968). In general, the pineal tends to have an inhibitory effect on pituitary hormones. This pineal-pituitary antagonism extends particularly to an interaction between pineal melatonin and pituitary MSH (melanocyte stimulating hormone). The only known functions of these hormones are on pigment cells (melanocytes); melatonin lightens skin pigment cells by concentrating pigment granules, while MSH darkens pigment cells by dispersing the granules through the cytoplasm of the cell. Although melatonin is the most powerful skin-lightening substance known, its precursor, serotonin, does not have any skin-lightening effect in doses up to 4,000 micrograms (Wiener 1968). These two pigment-affecting hormones have been regarded by some as a phytogenetic "fossil" without any particular function in humans. Wiener (1968), however, has proposed the bold hypothesis that the melanocytes may function as a source of pheromones, that is, exohormones or external chemical messengers (ECM), substances released by an organism into the environment to affect the behavior of other organisms:

> All pituitary and pineal hormones that we know, except for MSH and melatonin, exert some trophic or antitrophic effect on other secretory cells. The MSH-melatonin pair, on the other hand, seem to act largely on pigmented cells of the skin periphery, not to regulate production of any known chemical messengers, but to push and pull pigment granules around the cell, and that in frogs rather than in man . . .
>
> The pigment cell makes no important hormone that acts on its owner's body. But it is located at the surface of the skin. Could it be making a hormone that acts on someone else's body, an exohormone rather than an endohormone? (Wiener 1968, p. 932)

His hypothesis is interesting and suggests the related speculation that the neurotransmitterlike hallucinogens found in the plant kingdom may similarly act as pheromones (or, more accurately, allomones) when they interact with a mammalian nervous system. Indeed, it seems reasonable to speculate that neurotransmitter-type molecules may not only function in nervous systems but also as carriers of certain kinds of information from the environment to the organism, and from the organism to other organisms. We will return to this speculation, and to the question of pineal function, after we have presented our own theoretical model for drug action at the receptor sites.

Up to this point, we have been discussing, in broad terms, some of the current thinking regarding possible modes of action for hallucinogenic drugs. The probable function of neurotransmitters was outlined. The structural analogies between many of the hallucinogens and CNS transmitters were noted; the parallels between the localization of neurotransmitters and the regional uptake of hallucinogens, and their possible function as false transmitters, was also mentioned. Next, we reviewed the evidence that enzymatic pathways exist in the brain that could be capable of producing endogenous psychotomimetic substances from neurotransmitter substrates. Finally, we pointed out that there is likely an important, if little understood, relationship between the pineal and pituitary glands in the regulation of many of these precursor substances, that the pineal gland has been shown to respond to a variety of external stimuli, and that it may play a role in the production of exohormones or ECM. The bulk of the points we have reviewed up to now represents little that is unorthodox in the current state of neurophysiological theory, and our primary purpose has been to provide an informational background for what follows. We must now focus our attention on the more specific question of the sequence of molecular events at the synapse, and the possible influence on these events of hallucinogenic compounds.

In the first section of this chapter, we reviewed some of the data relating to the probable functions of neurotransmitters in the central nervous system and some of the ways in which these functions might be altered by hallucinogenic drugs. In the course of our discussion, we noted that detailed experimental investigations of these problems are hampered by a host of formidable technical problems. The problems associated with the study of the neurotransmitters, however, appear minimal when compared with those encountered in any attempt to characterize the molecular nature of the receptor site. While a good deal is known about the molecular configuration of the neurotransmitters, and that of drugs that interact with them, this has provided little in the way of clues as to the molecular specifications of the receptor site. Structure-activity studies can lead to tentative deductions at best, since a drug's action may be influenced by factors other than its interaction with a receptor site. The receptor site is generally assumed to be located in protein, lipoprotein, or glycoprotein present in the membrane, and the neurotransmitter binding into the receptor site is thought to induce some conformational change in the macromolecule that opens the ionic channel. Unfortunately, this cannot reveal much about the specific chemical nature of the receptor because of the wide variety of groups present in proteins, lipids, or carbohydrates with which amines can interact. The problem would be lessened if something were known on independent grounds about the chemical nature of the receptor site (Smythies 1970).

Recent evidence indicating the presence of RNA in synaptosonal membrane (Morgan and Austin 1968) has cast doubt on the assumption that the receptor site must be located in protein, lipid, or polysaccharide, and Smythies has proposed the hypothesis that RNA or ribonucleoprotein present in the membrane may function as a primary receptor site. According to the model elaborated by Smythies, the possible functional significance of serotonin, or one of its structurally analogous derivatives, binding to a nucleic acid site in the membrane is that RNA may act as a channel for the passage of charged ions (and, perhaps, amines themselves) through the membrane. The intercalated compounds would affect the torsion of the RNA helix, causing it to act as a regulatory "shutter" mechanism, perhaps involving charge-transfer complexes:

> Segments of helical RNA may be arranged perpendicular to the surface and running through it from side to side: Each segment will provide two helically wound "half tubes" connecting the interior of the cell with the exterior. The long RNA molecule would thus run a convoluted course through the membrane. The "half tubes" could be converted into full tubes or channels by running flexible molecules with right basic bonding groups (such as polyamines like spermine) between the phosphate groups on adjacent turns of the helix. Thus the RNA molecule will compose one potential large tube subdivided into two smaller tubes separated by a "shutter"—that is, the hydrogen bonded base pairs. If the base pairs were disrupted, the base pairs could fly apart and open up the full lumen of the tube. The maximum length of RNA required to cross an average membrane would be about two coils. The channel could also consist of an RNA "shutter" of shorter

length leading to a protein channel. Now, as Hofmann and Ladik (1961) have shown, nucleic acids have certain very interesting properties in an electrical field. Normally they are insulators, but if they are located in an electrical field parallel to their own length and a powerful electron donor or acceptor intercalates at one end, the entire molecule can become a conductor by means of a migration of pi electrons in the electrical field. The resulting charge-transfer can polarize the base pairs and disrupt the hydrogen bonds joining them so that they come apart and the double helix unwinds. In our model the electrical field is provided by the resting potential of the neuronal membrane and the electron donor is 5HT. If this intercalates between the first base pairs on the outer end of the helical RNA, the helix could open up thus opening the internal "shutter" in the channel making it large enough to transmit hydrated Na+ or K+ ions depending on the length of the holding polyamine stays. The flow of ions will depolarize the membrane, the RNA again becomes an insulator and the base pair hydrogen bonds reform thus closing the channel. In the meantime the 5HT molecule will have been dislodged by the opening of the helix and will be taken up back into the axon terminal. The exact location of the serotonin pi cloud with respect to the pi cloud of the base pairs may be a crucial factor in this mechanism. However, a mechanism for closing the K+ pore is harder to visualize for here the membrane becomes hyperpolarized.

This basic mechanism could be used for the transport of other molecules across membranes, such as the biogenic amines themselves. (Smythies 1969, pp. 267–269)

Smythies's model is supported by evidence that 5HT and many of its analogs, including LSD-25, N,N-DMT, and harmine can bond to DNA, RNA, or both. The evidence for the binding of tryptamine and its analogs to nucleic acids is central both to an understanding of Smythies's model and also to our own hypothesis of drug action. It is quoted at length below:

Siegal and Salinas state that fluorescence studies reveal strong interaction between serotonin and nucleic acids. Yielding and Sterglanz report an interaction between LSD and native DNA, but not denatured DNA or RNA, using a reduction of native fluorescence and a change in ultraviolet absorption as criteria for binding . . .

Tryptamine and its derivates could bind to nucleic acids in one of four ways: (i) by ionic bonds between the positively charged protenated amine N and the phosphate groups; (ii) by intercalation between bases (RNA) or base pairs (DNA) and binding by pi-orbital overlap; (iii) hydrogen bonding to the spare NH and O orbitals of the base pairs in the floor of the two grooves of the helix; and (iv) single-stranded nucleic acids would offer a fourth way of binding by hydrogen bonds to the unoccupied sites on the unpaired bases.

The compounds appear to fall into three groups. If we take tryptamine itself as a standard, equilibrium is reached at approximately 9μg. tryptamine and 1,200μg. nucleic acid. The reduction fluorescence value is decreased by substitution in the 5-position by −OH or −OCH, and is increased by N,N-dialkylation with larger groups than methyl (for example, ethyl, isopropyl, butyl, benzyl). Of the latter compounds the diisopropyl and dibutyl derivatives appear to react more vigorously with RNA than with DNA. One possible explanation for these differences may derive from the fact that 5HT in solution may form a complex with itself (dimer) (by pi-cloud stocking and ion-dipole bond between the N of one molecule and the O-delta of its companion). This complex might not itself be able to bond to nucleic acid. 5HT, bufotenin, and 5-O methyl-bufotenin could form such complexes and thus less would be available to bond to nucleic acid. Tryptamine would form such a complex to a lesser extent (its N could bond directly to the pi-cloud). In the case of the higher dialkylated products the ion-dipole bond would be lessened by steric hindrance and thus more of the compound would be available to bond to nucleic acid . . .

Other substitutions on the ring induce a different reaction. Figures 5 and 6 show the results for additional compounds. This indicates that compounds with bulky ring substituents in the 5 or 6 positions (particularly, 6-chlorotryptamine) have higher reduction in fluorescence values with DNA than RNA. Thus compounds with bulky N substituents appear to bind better to RNA and some with bulky ring substituents to DNA. Figure 7 shows that there is not much difference in the reduction in fluo-

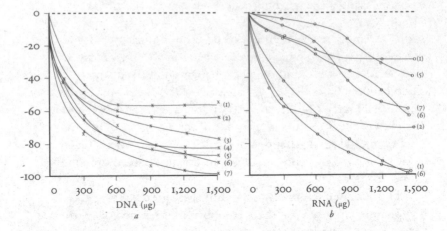

FIGURE 5

Reduction in fluorescence values for further derivatives of tryptamine on interaction with DNA (a) and RNA (b). (1) 5-benzyloxy-N, N-dimethyl tryptamine; (2) N, N-dibenzyl tryptamine; (3) 3(2-dehydroisoindolylethyl) indole; (4) 5, 6, 7 N, N pentamethyl tryptamine; (5) 6-chlorotryptamine; (6) 7-methyltryptamine; (7) 6-chloro-N, N, dimethyltryptamine.

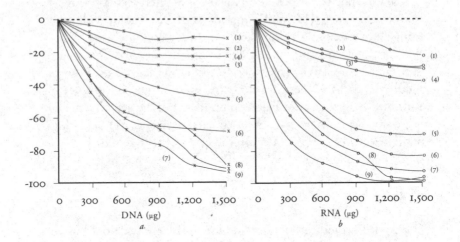

FIGURE 6

Reduction in fluorescence values for a number of tryptamines on interaction with (a) DNA, (b) RNA. (1) 5-hydroxyindoleacetic acid; (2) N, N-dimethyl serotonin (bufotenin); (3) 5-hydroxytryptamine; (4) O-methyl bufotenin; (5) dimethyltryptamine; (6) tryptamine; (7) N, N-diethyltryptamine; (8) N, N-di-isopropyl-tryptamine; (9) N, N-dibutyl-tryptamine.

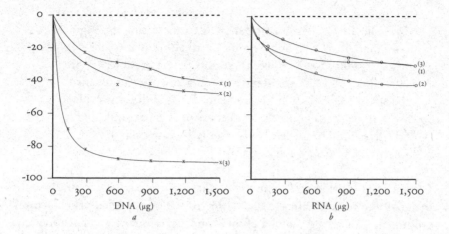

FIGURE 7

Reduction in fluorescence values for (1) 1, 2, 3, 4, tetrahydroharmine;
(2) harmaline; (3) harmine.

Figures 5, 6, and 7 from Smythies and Antun, "Binding of Tryptamines and Allied Compounds to Nucleic Acid," Nature, *223: p. 1062, Sep. 6, 1969.*

shows that there is not much difference in the reduction in fluorescence of harmaline and tetrahydroharmine in reaction with
DNA or RNA, but harmine with its bulkier ring system appears
to bind better to DNA.

These facts may be explained as follows: (i) tryptamines may
not bind to the phosphate groups of nucleic acids because the
lipophilic nature of their molecules would inhibit binding to so
hydrophilic a region; (ii) if the tryptamines bind by lipophilic
interactions with nucleic acids, that is by intercalation between
the bases of RNA and the base pairs of DNA, efficient binding
will require maximum pi-cloud overlap. In the case of RNA this
will be obtained if the tryptamine binds between two ordered
purine bases with its side-chain "out" so that maximum pi-cloud
overlap is hindered. But a large group on the side chain will not
affect binding as this will be free. In the case of helical nucleic
acid, the pi cloud is shared across the hydrogen bonds linking
the two bases. Thus the relatively small tryptamine molecule

(as compared with a typical DNA intercalator such as proflavin) could tolerate a ring substitute such as Cl increasing its length better than it would a bulky group on the N that also increases its thickness. Likewise the bulky three and four ring molecules such as harmine and LSD would have much more pi-cloud overlap capacity in DNA than in single-strand RNA. Thus this evidence would appear to support the hypothesis that tryptamine and its derivatives bind to nucleic acids mainly by intercalation. (Smythies and Antun 1969, p. 1061)

Neurotransmitters and their analogs are not the only compounds with the ability to bond to nucleic acids. One of the best-studied of such compounds is the acridine proflavin (fig. 8); note its similarity to harmine (cf. fig. 3). This compound binds by interaction between the base pairs of the double helix, resulting in a partial unwinding of the helix in the region of the intercalated molecule. Intercalated molecules are thought to be held in place by strong electronic interactions with the base pairs above and below the drug, and this results in a stabilization of the helix, as measured in the higher temperature required to denature intercalated DNA (Newton 1970).

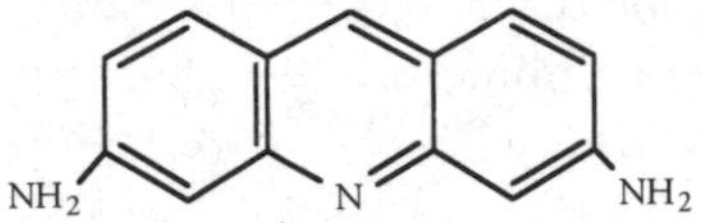

FIGURE 8   *A Proflavin Molecule*

Smythies has elsewhere theorized in even greater detail as to the nature of the 5HT bond site and possible points of comparison between 5HT and its hallucinogenic analogs:

Thus 5HT could bond to ordered single-strand RNA by intercalation (that is, pi-cloud overlap) between adjacent purine bases and two hydrogen bonds (hydroxyl to ribose ring O and ribose OH). It could bind to helical DNA by intercalation between base pairs and one hydrogen bond (either NH to deoxyribose ring O or hydroxyl H to the other deoxyribose ring), but it is not wide enough a molecule to bind to both. And it could bind to helical RNA by intercalation and no less than four hydrogen bonds . . . [see fig. 9].

The hallucinogenic derivatives of tryptamine are characterized by partial blockade of the bonding groups so that, whereas the compound can still bind to the site and prevent the subsequent attachment of 5HT, it does so without inducing the agonist effect. Blockade of the active groups is affected by the following means: (1) dialkylation of the amino group. This reduces ionic and hydrogen bonding and imposes additional steric effects. The N cannot approach so closely to the bonding atom (or), and the result will be that the indole ring will not occupy precisely the same place in the site as in the case of 5HT. The function of 5HT in this site may be concerned with charge-transfer reactions. As the pi-cloud energy in 5HT is concentrated in the 2 position the resulting slight displacement of the indole ring in the bonding of such drugs as dimethyltryptamine may disrupt this charge transfer process. A possible target in this site for the transfer of charge would be a hydrogen of the superjacent base pair (joining, e.g., the N of guanine to the O of cytosine) and thus the action of 5HT in the site might be to disrupt the H bond and thus initiate the separation of the two strands of a helical RNA. (Smythies 1969, p. 265)

In Smythies's model, the postulated ability of 5HT, or one of its analogs, to open the ionic channel by intercalating into an RNA receptor site is based on the capacity to form a charge-transfer complex with the nucleic acid. The charge-transfer mechanism will be of central significance in the presentation of our own model in the pages following. Therefore, a few general comments on charge-transfer complexes in living systems seem warranted. We encountered such comments in the observations of Albert Szent-Gyorgyi (1960):

Charge-transfer allows us to transfer an electron from one substance to another without major loss in energy, since it does not require a rearrangement in molecular structure . . .

By charge-transfer relatively inactive molecules may acquire a high reactivity. The donor, having developed a "hole" in its low-lying ground level, becomes a good acceptor, while the acceptor having acquired an electron on its high-lying excited orbital,

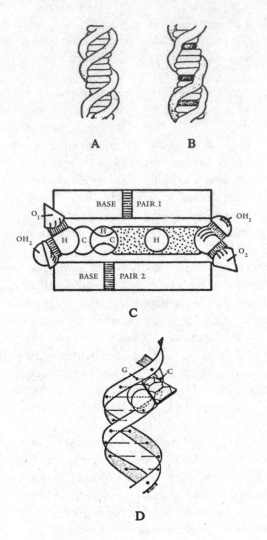

FIGURE 9   *Intercalation of Drug Molecules into DNA*

(A) A diagram to illustrate the secondary structure of normal DNA. (B) A distorted DNA structure resulting from intercalation of drug molecules. (Based on original drawings by Lermnan 1964). (C) Mode of fit of 5HT into helical RNA intercalation site. (Smythies) (D) Diagrammatic representation of the actinomycin-DNA complex based on the molecular model proposed by Hamilton et al. (1963). The cyclic peptide chains of the antibiotic are represented as circles filling the minor groove of the DNA helix for a distance of about three base pairs. B, C, and D are structural near-relatives of the harmine–nucleic acid complex.

becomes a good donor. A charge-transfer complex is something between a regular closed-shell molecule and a free radical, and the great reactivity of free radicals need not be emphasized. If the complex dissociates, as happens in extreme cases, two real free radicals are formed.

An acceptor may accept an electron also from a saturated energy band, thus creating a hole and rendering the band conductant. Conversely, a donor may donate an electron to an empty energy band, rendering this bond conductant. So charge-transfer opens the way for semiconduction into biology . . .

In valency saturated compounds electrons occupy orbitals in pairs. Electrons have their spin, and a spinning electron is a tiny magnet. Since the two electrons occupying the same orbital always spin in opposite directions, they cancel out each other's magnetic moments. However, if the two electrons become separated, as may be the case in a strong charge-transfer, they may no longer compensate one another, rendering the substance paramagnetic: as soon as the two electrons are no longer strongly coupled, and occupy different orbitals, they become relieved of the limitation of the Pauli principle according to which two electrons, forming a pair on the same orbital, must spin in opposite directions. If one of the two unoccupied electrons reverts its spin, the complex goes into the triplet state, adding a paramagnetic component . . .

There are two methods for detecting paramagnetic behavior: the magnetic balance and the electron spin resonance (ESR). The former is rather crude as compared to the latter. The signal given in ESR depends on circumstances. Free radicals given a sharp and high ESR signal extending over 10–50 gauss. If the electron is close to other unpaired electrons, it will be perturbed and may give a broad signal. Exposed to the magnetic influence of different nuclei it may split up, giving a "hyperfine" structure . . . How far a charge-transfer complex will give a signal depends on circumstances. In a weak transfer the two electrons remain strongly coupled, and so give no ESR signal, or give a signal only under strong illumination. (pp. 67–72)

Szent-Gyorgyi continues on to point out that the strength of the ESR signal given by a charge-transfer complex will be in direct proportion to the strength of the charge transfer. If strong reductants are used as donors and strong oxidants as acceptors, then the ESR signal will be correspondingly stronger.

What possible significance could the formation of charge-transfer complexes in living systems have? The following comments on its possible role in drug action are relevant here:

> We may ask, for instance, whether charge-transfer is not involved in drug action, some of the drugs acting as electron donors or acceptors. It is difficult to predict the biological effects of such a charge-transfer, for the action will not only depend on the question, whether electrons are donated or tapped off, but will also depend on the site of action. The cellular membrane, for instance, which dominates many functions of the cell, has mostly a negative charge inside and a positive one outside. So electrons donated at the inside should increase the charge and lead to hyperpolarization, and with it to inhibition, while electrons donated at the outside will decrease the potential and can be expected to cause excitation. The opposite will hold for electron acceptors. We can be prepared also to meet paradoxical results. Let us suppose that a biological substance acts by donating electrons. A drug, acting as an electron donor, may compete with a natural substance for its acceptor interfering thus with the normal course of electron transmission, this drug though itself a donor, may produce an effect which corresponds to the inhibition of electron donation. In spite of all these incertitudes we may expect one definite interrelation: If a substance exerts its biological activity by accepting or donating electrons, then it should have exceptional donor or acceptor properties. (Szent-Gyorgyi 1960, p. 1071)

Considering the preceding information relevant to charge-transfer complexes, we may ask the question: Are serotonin and its analogs likely candidates for participation in the formation of charge-transfer complexes with nucleic acids, as was suggested by Smythies? We again refer to Szent-Gyorgyi (1960) for a decidedly affirmative answer:

> Although serotonin is a somewhat stronger donor than indole, or some of its derivatives such as tryptamine, this extraordinary reactivity is characteristic for the indole formation in general and is in no way explained by the energy values of the highest filled molecular orbital . . . There seem to be other hitherto unknown molecular

indices which entail this extraordinary reactivity. There is but one general statement we can safely make about all this, and this is that if Nature developed a substance for electron transfer, then she may have given to this substance extraordinary qualities, which make it likely that Nature developed this ring naturally for services of this kind . . .

. . . It was shown that indoles are exceptionally good donors, and a great number of biologically active substances contain an indole ring (serotonin, lysergic acid, bufotenin, indole acetic acid). Attempts were made earlier by Popov, Castellani-Oisi, and M. Craft to connect pharmacological activity, like convulsant effect, with electron donation. That indoles may actually act in their biological reactions as electron donors is further suggested by the fact that the OH group, induced into the serotonin molecule at position 5 equally increases pharmacological activity and the electron-donating property. Serotonin is one of the strongest donors I ever met, though the k of the highest filled orbital is but moderately lower than that of indole (0.461). So there are still unidentified molecular parameters which greatly influence donor acceptor properties. (pp. 84–85, 108)

The possible ability of nucleic acids or nucleoprotein to function as acceptors is also touched upon by Szent-Gyorgyi (1960) in the following:

As the last item on my list of the peculiarities of the "living state" I would like to touch upon one of the most intriguing observations of the last years, that of the very broad (ESR) signal given by nucleoproteins (Blumenfeld, Kalmanson, and Shen-Pei). This signal (if really due to the protein-nucleic acid complex) indicates a density of unpaired electrons which is almost comparable to that found in metals, to which metals owe their conductivity. This finding, if corroborated, may lift a veil which now obscures the real nature and meaning of protein, nucleic acid, and nucleoprotein. (p. 134)

At this point, let us summarize briefly what has been discussed so far. We began the first section of this chapter by discussing the functions of neurotransmitters in the nervous system, and their probable chemical nature. We noted the structural similarities between many hallucinogens and the presumed neurotransmitters. The technical problems faced in any attempt to study neurotransmitters in the central nervous system were pointed out, and the indirect evidence implicating serotonin and norepinephrine as the major central transmitters was cited. We presented a diagram of synaptic events and current theories suggesting that drugs may function as false transmitters. The parallelism between regional uptake of drugs and the concentration of neurotransmitters in the brain was noted. Next, we discussed enzymatic mechanisms and the evidence that hallucinogens may arise endogenously. This led to a discussion of the possible role of the pineal, both its overall function as a regulatory mechanism of the nervous system and its possible implication in the origination of endogenous hallucinogens. In the second section of our exposition, we focused on the question of drug action at the receptor site. We cited problems inherent in this study and discussed Smythies's theory of a possible RNA or ribonucleoprotein receptor site. We noted that this could have functional consequences through alteration of the torsion of the RNA helix and the formation of charge-transfer complexes. The modes of binding of 5HT and its analogs to nucleic acids were considered in some depth. Finally, we considered the nature and significance of charge-transfer complexes in living systems and noted that indoles are excellent electron donors, while nucleic acids are equally efficient electron acceptors. Here it was also noted that strong charge-transfer complexes, such as would be expected in a nucleic acid indole complex, are characterized by a very strong ESR signal. It has been necessary to quote other authorities at such great length in the preceding pages to provide the reader with a basic grasp of many fundamental concepts and problems, which are essential to an understanding of the speculation that is to follow.

Having reached this point, we can now present our own hypothesis in broad outline. It is basically the following: What we experience as "thought" or "consciousness" has its physical basis in quantum-mechanical phenomena. We propose that the intercalation of 5HT, other neurotransmitters, and hallucinogenic neurotransmitter analogs into an RNA receptor site gives rise to three important consequences. The first of these, already proposed by Smythies, is that the intercalation forms a charge-transfer complex, which initiates the separation of the helix by polarizing the base pairs; this allows charged ions to rush through the membrane. We speculate that this intercalation may have two additional consequences. The first is that the rapid bonding and debonding of intercalators causes a rapid twisting and untwisting of the helix, and this gives rise to a vibratory oscillation of the macromolecule. This oscillation, occurring within the electrical field at the synapse, has the effect of generating an electromagnetic waveform. This signal, however, becomes absorbed at certain frequencies by low-energy electrons present in the charge-transfer complexes, which are formed by neurotransmitters intercalating into the RNA. This absorption of energy serves to modulate the signal and simultaneously saturates the energy bands in the charge-transfer complex, canceling the polarization of the base pairs, allowing the RNA strands to rejoin. Exactly this sort of absorption phenomenon is observed in electron spin resonance spectrometry, so we can refer to the proposed process as an ESR effect or an ESR signal.

Our speculation contends that the combination of modulated electromagnetic waveforms originating from the tens of millions of synapses activated at any one time is detectable to the organism by some hitherto unsuspected mechanism (possibly akin to holography) as a higher cortical experience, as thought or consciousness. Further, the signals thus generated by the nucleic acid–indole complex are reflective of the continually changing conformational topology of the nucleic acid or nucleoprotein as it exists in its superhelixed, *in vivo* state. The ESR signal generated by this mechanism might be capable of carrying information that somehow would be experienced as thought. Such information probably does not originate from the level of base pair organization, the level of the molecular code involved in genetic processes such as replication; this could not convey much in the way of "experience" to the organism. What seems more likely is that the information content of the signal is generated by the dynamic conformational changes taking place at the secondary and tertiary structural levels in the receptor. Nucleic acid in the test tube is far different from nucleic acid in its superhelixed condition in a nucleus or membrane. In its functioning, *in vivo* condition, it must be the site of furious molecular activity relating to a diversity of processes: protein synthesis, replication, charge transfer, intercalation, deintercalation, changes in torsion; all of this and more must be occurring constantly and simultaneously in living nucleic acid. Perhaps included in these regulatory functions is the production of an electromagnetic signal that is modulated by an ESR absorption effect. The modulation of this signal might be correlated to experience; it would then be a continually unfolding readout of the bioelectronic state of the neural network, experienced as the informational *gestalten* of mind and its models of the internal and external world.

To clarify the concepts associated with this speculation, it is necessary to digress into a discussion of the nature of the paramagnetic properties

associated with electron spin resonance, ESR. The theoretical foundations
of ESR are discussed by Ingram (1969):

> . . . the basic feature of ESR is its ability to detect and characterize
> the presence of unpaired electrons in a substance. The essential
> property detected by the technique is, in fact, the magnetic
> moment associated with the electron spin. Each unpaired electron
> has a spin angular momentum associated with it, which is actually
> equal to $(h/2\pi)\sqrt{-[\frac{1}{2}(\frac{1}{2} + 1)]}$, this being given by the quantum
> number $s = \frac{1}{2}$. It should possibly be explained at this point that
> the angular momentum associated with any quantum number,
> such as n, is always given by $(h/2\pi) \times n$. The reason for this is that
> the total angular momentum is precessing about a fixed axis in
> such a way that the permanent time-averaged value along this axis
> is equal to $(h/2\pi)\sqrt{-[n(n + 1)]}$, whereas the component perpendic-
> ular to this axis is averaged out by the precessional motion. This
> fact is illustrated [in fig. 11] for the particular case of the single
> unpaired electron, where the appropriate quantum number is
> $s = \frac{1}{2}$, as already mentioned. When the particular states of the
> unpaired electron are being considered, they are therefore charac-
> terized by $M_s = + \frac{1}{2}$ or $M_s = -\frac{1}{2}$, according to the orientation of
> the total angular momentum, as indicated [in fig. 10].
>
> The characterization of the different unpaired electrons in this
> way necessitates the presence of a common axis of reference, how-
> ever, and in the absence of any external applied magnetic, or
> electrical, fields, such a common axis of reference will not exist.
> Thus the unpaired electrons associated with the free radicals, or
> enzymes, present in a system standing on a laboratory bench
> would have a random orientation of their axes and would all have
> the same energy. If an external magnetic field is applied across the
> specimen, however, the electrons will now have a common axis
> of reference and will all precess so that they have a resolved com-
> ponent of either $M_s = + \frac{1}{2}$ or $M_s = -\frac{1}{2}$ in the direction of this
> applied field. General quantum conditions allow only quantum
> states in which the quantum numbers differ by unity; hence, the
> two cases of $M_s = + \frac{1}{2}$ and $M_s = -\frac{1}{2}$ are the only ones allowed for
> these single unpaired electrons.
>
> It is also evident that the application of such an external mag-
> netic field divides the unpaired electrons into two groups, those

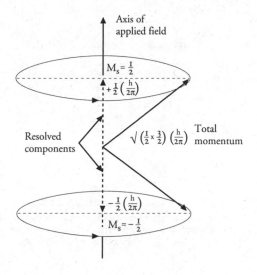

Axis of
applied field

$M_s = \frac{1}{2}$

$+\frac{1}{2}\left(\frac{h}{2\pi}\right)$

Resolved
components

$\sqrt{\left(\frac{1}{2} \times \frac{3}{2}\right)} \left(\frac{h}{2\pi}\right)$ Total
momentum

$-\frac{1}{2}\left(\frac{h}{2\pi}\right)$

$M_s = -\frac{1}{2}$

FIGURE 10

Resolved components of total spin momentum and magnetic moment along an
axis of quantization.

with their spins aligned parallel and those with their spins antiparallel to the direction of the field itself. It does, moreover, also give
different energies to the electrons in these two groups. Those
which have their magnetic moments lined up parallel to the magnetic field will have their energies reduced, whereas those lined up
antiparallel to the field will have their energies increased . . .

It has been seen that the application of the external field across
the substance containing the unpaired electrons has thus produced
an energy level splitting between them, as illustrated on the right-
hand side in [fig. 11]. The basic principle of the electron resonance
technique is now to apply electromagnetic radiation at the same
time, and arrange for the frequency, v, of this radiation to be such
that hv, the quantum of energy associated with it, is equal to the
energy difference between the two groups of electrons, that is,
$hv = g\beta H$.

The experimental technique therefore involves the application
of a strong homogeneous external magnetic field across the sam-
ple, and a simultaneous application of electromagnetic radiation

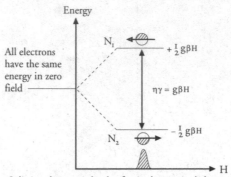

Splitting the energy levels of a single unpaired electron under
the influence of an applied magnetic field H. Resonance condition
$h\nu = g\beta H$, $\nu = 2.8 \cdot 10^6$ H c/s for a free electron.

FIGURE II

Basic electron resonance condition.

Figures 10 *and* 11 *are from Ingram,* Biological and Biochemical Applications of
Electron Spin Resonance, *pp. 3 and 4. Adam Hilger Ltd., London, 1969.*

of the correct resonance frequency. This will then supply energy to
the unpaired electrons in the lower energy level, exciting them to
the upper level and reversing their spins in the process. This
absorption of energy by the electrons as they jump to the higher
level can be detected as an actual reduction in the power of the
electromagnetic radiation passing through the system, and this
absorption can then be displayed on an oscilloscope screen, or in
any other way that is normal in absorption spectroscopy. (pp. 3–6)

Nuclear magnetic resonance (NMR) is a similar type of paramagnetic
phenomenon. Like ESR, NMR involves the generation of a signal by the
application of an external magnetic field, except that in NMR, shifts in the
orientation of the nucleus, rather than of the unpaired electrons, are measured with respect to the external field (cf. Dyer 1965). The major point for
our discussion, which would indicate that ESR rather than NMR would
function as the modulated carrier-wave, is that unpaired electrons are characteristic of charge-transfer reactions and semiconduction, and as we have
seen previously, serotonin and many of its analogs can function as power-

ful electron donors and thus may give rise to charge transfer and semiconduction in neural RNA. NMR may be involved as well as ESR in these phenomena, but the signal preceding from NMR would seem to be less specifically characteristic of the kind of quantum-mechanical interactions that we hypothesize are necessary to generate a modulated waveform.

We have seen from the observations of Szent-Gyorgyi that a strong charge-transfer complex, such as may be formed by the intercalation of an indole neurotransmitter into a nucleic acid receptor, can act to separate the electrons in the substance into two energy groups: a high-energy group with their spins aligned antiparallel to the magnetic vector of the electrical field, and a low-energy group aligned parallel to the direction of the magnetic field. Thus, the charge-transfer complex possesses all the prior conditions needed to trigger an ESR absorption effect if electromagnetic energy of appropriate frequency is passed through the system. We speculate that in the synapse this is exactly what happens: An electromagnetic wave of the correct resonance frequency is produced through a coupled electromechanical oscillation of the receptor and becomes modulated by absorption at certain frequencies. We propose that intercalation of the neurotransmitter causes this oscillation, as well as the formation of the charge-transfer complex; the rapid bonding and debonding of the intercalator causes rapid changes in torsion of the helix, giving rise to oscillation. Since this oscillation takes place in the electrical field present at the synapse, it possesses an electromagnetic component.

The interaction between the nucleic acid receptor and its intercalators could thus act as a self-contained ESR circuit: with charge transfer, on the one hand, to provide the magnetic field necessary to polarize the free electrons; and rapid oscillation in an electrical field, on the other hand, to generate the absorption effect that characterizes ESR. This absorption effect will take place only at certain frequencies, namely, those frequencies corresponding to the energy difference between the two magnetically aligned groups of electrons in the nucleic acid receptor; selective absorption at these frequencies could informationally modulate the wave.

The electromagnetic waves currently used in ESR spectrometry are radar frequencies ranging from 9,000 Mc/s to 36,000 Mc/s, which correspond to wavelengths between 3.2 cm and 8 mm. The corresponding magnetic field strengths range from 3,300 to 13,000 gauss. According to Ingram (1969), however, ESR absorption effects can be manifested using radio frequencies as low as 28 Mc/s in magnetic fields of 10 gauss. Szent-Gyorgyi (1960) has stated that free radicals show an ESR absorption effect in magnetic fields from 10 to 50 gauss. It is not clear whether macromolecular oscillation could generate the frequencies required to trigger the energy absorption that characterizes the ESR signal. An experimental approach to this model might investigate this question. To our knowledge, the possibility that macromolecular substrates oscillating in an electrical field may be capable of electromagnetic emissions at radar or shortwave-radio frequencies has not yet been investigated. It is possible that very much lower field strengths and frequencies would suffice to produce ESR effects in single macromolecules. Until experimental data is forthcoming this hypothesis must, of course, remain hypothesis.

Given, for the sake of the argument, the assumptions that (1) an electromagnetic wave of appropriate frequency is generated in the manner postulated, and that (2) this wave is modulated through absorption by charge-transfer complexes, the model still must address two questions. The first one is, through what mechanism could the organism detect the modulated carrier-wave? Second, what sort of information could be carried by the wave?

We can suggest an answer to the first question by referring to the studies, cited earlier, that show that the pineal gland is sensitive to sound, photic stimuli, temperature, and X rays. We suggest that the pineal could also function as a transducer for the detection of ESR in a feedback-type mechanism; the pineal could act as an antenna by detecting a modulated electromagnetic carrier-wave and converting it to a modulated spatiotemporal pattern of nerve impulses, much as a radio converts electromagnetic waves to sound. In this way the information carried by the signal would be reflected by modulated firing in populations of synapses; this modulated firing would in turn give rise to further modulated ESR signals (since the signal arises from processes involved in synaptic transmission), which would then trigger further modulated neural patterns. In this way this feedback mechanism could give rise to self-propagating, evolving neural processes that we experience as thought, memory, or perception. It is also conceivable that the pineal may be receptive to the ESR signals of *other* organisms as well as those of its owner. Thus, it could act as a receptor for the ESR "strum" of the biotic community and function to effectively integrate an organism into its ecology.

The question of the kind of information that the signal would carry is more difficult to answer. If the signal is generated by electromechanical oscillation of the receptor, which then becomes modulated by ESR absorption, then the signal should reflect the internal electronic state of the receptor, which in turn will reflect conformational changes taking place from instant to instant in the macromolecule. We postulate that these changes in helical torsion and tertiary topology are not merely random fluctuations but are correlated with internal and external inputs, and, thus, "model" perceptions, thoughts, and memories. Is it possible that overlapping ESRs arising from macromolecular changes occurring at many synapses could take the form of highly structured (perhaps helical) standing waveforms? Such waveforms can be viewed as spatiotemporal crystals having a vibratory "structure" (cf. Abraham 1972). Just this sort of spatiotemporal structure constitutes a holographic image, and we have noted in the previous chapter that holography seems analogous to mind in many respects.

Support for our contention that experience can somehow induce changes in macromolecules can be found in current theoretical models of learning and memory. These models are based on the concept that the storage of memory and learned behavior is mediated by changes in RNA and proteins present in the neurons. Findings showing a rise in RNA and protein synthesis following learning have furnished support for these models (Hyden 1968, p. 88). Hyden (1968) has proposed the following model for memory storage, which rests on the notion that conformational changes of macromolecules in an electrical field could be significant:

> I would like to suggest that the redundancy of the gene products
> provides a basis for the necessary richness of proteins serving as
> a mechanism for the storage of memories. Learning and experi-
> ence lead to a further differentiation of brain cells. Additional
> gene areas become active under the influence of environmental
> factors. This leads to a synthesis of a greater number of RNA
> species and proteins slightly differing from each other. The
> detailed mechanism which gives rise to these events may be the
> following. The external factors give rise to firing at modulated
> frequencies in the sensory ganglia and brain stem areas, including
> the limbic area. The modulated frequencies can split into a quad-
> rature component and a vector component. I suggest that the 90
> degree vector has a phase shift relative to the quadrature compo-
> nent. The two variables, the frequency and the phase shift, impart
> a high information content to such an electrical pattern, which
> may be decisive for the specificity of its effect. In principle, this
> effect consists in the production of a change in the ionic equilib-
> rium through field changes. In the nuclear compartment these
> field changes give rise to conformational changes: activating

enzyme proteins which in turn induce synthesis of RNA from
new areas. (p. 97)

The possibility that neurotransmitters might induce conformational
changes in macromolecules is shown by the following passage:

Elkes drew attention to an older hypothesis concerning the pur-
ported action of 5HT on the motility of glia. While the evidence
for this effect was tenuous, he felt strongly that the existence of
contractile elements in the central nervous system areas should be
seriously considered. These "contractions" might involve anything
from the folding and coiling of an ordered polymer, forming part
of a lipoprotein or mucoprotein lattice at a junctional site, to a
"visible" contraction recognizable by light microscopy. He proposed the term "micromechanical" for such phenomena and won-
dered whether the so-called neurohumoral substances could not
play a regulatory role in the specificity of such phenomena. The
well-known sensitivity of contractile tissues to agents such as 5HT
(or ACh, or NE) might be extreme examples of a deeper and more
generalized biological effect at a micellar level . . . (Smythies, in
Schmitt et al. 1971, pp. 25–26)

It must be conceded that these tentative models for learning and memory are concerned with neural functions far from those presumed to be involved with the interaction of serotonin or an analogous hallucinogen
with its receptor site. However, the fact that the hallucinogenically induced state represents a novel learning experience and at times results in
an alteration in behavior patterns indicates that the processes effected by
hallucinogens (synaptic transmission) may indeed have some influence on
learning and memory mechanisms. Just such a possibility has been suggested by Kety (1968). It seems that the question must remain unresolved
at present, since the significance of macromolecular changes occurring in
neurotransmission and memory storage is not well understood. The information we have cited, however, does seem to indicate that such changes
may function in both the processing and the storage of neural input.

One question that has not yet been considered and that unfortunately
has been discussed only very sparingly in the literature is that of whether
neural DNA, as well as RNA, could be involved in neurotransmission or
memory mechanisms, and of what possible function it might have. The
following observation with regard to DNA is suggestive:

The nerve cells share a rare characteristic with a few other cells of the organism. They do not divide. Over the life-cycle, therefore, orderliness is not maintained by means of cell division. There will be an increasing danger of errors at synthesis in the cells, which means error in function. Evidence has been presented that neurons may renew their DNA without preparing for division (Pelc 1964). Future studies will have to elucidate what happens in aging neurons, since hybridization analyses have suggested that DNA from an old animal may not be identical with DNA from a young animal (Hahn 1966).

. . . We have, therefore, as a first step, prepared brain DNA of varying degrees of purity. This DNA was injected into the ventricles of the brain of other animals of the same species. In one hour, protein synthesis was found to increase significantly. Biochemical analyses showed that the DNA had been incorporated in the recipient's brain cells in a polymerized state . . . (H. Hyden, in Koestler and Smythies 1969, p. 102)

It may be relevant to mention here the commonplace within the discipline of genetics—that only 2 to 5 percent of the genome is active at any one time, that these inactive areas can be activated by external (i.e., extracellular) factors such as hormones, and that large populations of similar nucleotide sequences exist in the DNA complements of higher organisms. It is possible to speculate on a memory mechanism, based on an interaction of intercalating amines and neural DNA, that would function on principles similar to the intercalator/RNA interaction that may be involved in neural transmission. The remainder of this chapter is concerned with a discussion of such a speculation.

For the sake of hypothesis, let us suppose that serotonin and its analogs interact with RNA at the receptor site, much in the manner postulated by Smythies, the question of the effect this could have on ESR being momentarily disregarded. We have seen from Smythies's model that serotonin intercalating into the RNA could cause a separation of the nucleotide strands and thus open an ionic "shutter" facilitating the passage of charged ions, and perhaps biogenic amines themselves, through the membrane. The preceding evidence cited indicates that injected DNA can become incorporated and polymerized in brain cells; therefore, nucleotides must be able to cross the neural membrane and also the nuclear membrane. Conventional intracellular enzymes probably facilitate the crossing of the nuclear membrane, but a mechanism facilitating outer membrane passage is more difficult to imagine. It seems possible, however, that the RNA shutter mechanism could allow the transport of small molecules, such as neurotransmitters or nucleotides, across the postsynaptic membrane. Once these molecules have penetrated the postsynaptic membrane and entered the cytoplasm of the axon, they could be transported to the vicinity of the nucleus by the mechanism of *axoplasmic flow:*

> Evidently there is some highly organized transport mechanism. It has long been known that nerve fibers are not just tubes filled with some protein jelly, but that they contain many fine structures, *neurofibrils* and *neurotubules* that run along their length. It is postulated by Ochs that after manufacture in the cell body the macromolecules are loaded onto these tubules and fibrils and travel along by some sliding mechanism, hence the uniform rate. (Eccles 1973, p. 171)

Although studies of this chemical transport mechanism have focused on the transport of macromolecules from the nucleus in the cell body to the synapse via the axon, Eccles goes on to state that reverse transport, from the axon to the cell body, does take place.

Could it be that neurotransmitters that penetrate in this manner become intercalated into the nuclear DNA of the neuron? This would seem to be at least a possibility and would appear to be a function of the ability of the amine to cross the membrane; that is, those amines would be "selected" for intercalation by (1) their ability to cross the membrane and (2) their capacity for intercalation. Thus, while certain amines present at the receptor site (e.g., serotonin) might intercalate into the RNA and open the "shutter," others might penetrate to the nucleus via the channel thus formed and intercalate into the DNA. This postulated intercalation might have two alternative effects. The intercalators might initiate separation of the nucleotide strands through charge transfer, and thus function as inductors for RNA synthesis. Alternatively, if the bound intercalators had the effect of stabilizing the helix in the manner of proflavin, rather than separating it, then it would seem that those portions of DNA involved in intercalation would be unavailable for transcription. These portions, then, would constitute the closed areas of the neural genome, which subsequent molecular events could render open to synthesis. This suggests one possible mechanism by which the base sequence of neural DNA could be "altered" without necessitating an actual change of structure; that is, given one situation in which amines are intercalated at particular sites on the

DNA, then subsequently these amines could debond from some of these sites and bond into different sites, thus "coding" a memory or learned behavior and simultaneously rendering formerly "silent" areas of the genome available for transcription and "silencing" formerly active areas. This would seem to amount to about the same effect as a restructuring of base sequences but has the advantage of not requiring an actual change in neural DNA.

On the other hand, if an ESR readout mechanism, such as that discussed previously, plays a role in making molecularly encoded information available to consciousness, an intercalation into neural DNA-inducing charge transfer would then render the intercalated portions "open" to perception via ESR. Subsequent debonding and rebonding of the amines to different sites would be reflected in a changed ESR signal. The RNA would also, of course, be expected to exhibit a change in its ESR, which would reflect the change in its structure initiated by the opening to transcription of hitherto blocked DNA sequences.

Clearly, problems are involved with experimental approaches to this model. One of the most difficult is the question of determining which amines bond at which sites. For instance, does serotonin bond into both RNA at the membrane and DNA at the nucleus, or one or the other? This amounts to asking, are certain amines "specific" intercalators for RNA, while others are specific for DNA? Or, can several species of amine bond into both sites? How might these alternatives be reflected in ESR if such a mechanism operates in the organism? At present, the only approaches to some of these questions are speculative.

We have chosen to present one such speculation. As noted in the discussion of bonding sites for indoles to nucleic acids, some compounds appear to bind better to DNA than to RNA. One such compound is harmine, and its affinity for DNA is not surprising in view of its previously mentioned similarity to proflavin. It is possible, therefore, that harmine or one of its analogs, such as 6-methoxytetrahydroharman, would exhibit a superior capability to bond to DNA if it were enabled to cross the membrane. Perhaps in the normal organism, the DNA is unintercalated by any compounds, or perhaps serotonin is the normal intercalator. When a hallucinogen such as harmine or LSD is introduced into the system, either from an endogenous source or from the external environment, it may show a greater affinity for the DNA than serotonin and bond in place of it; a stronger charge-transfer reaction may result and may produce an amplified ESR signal, facilitating greater access to stored memories and subconscious contents. Thus, a population using harmine or similar compounds in shamanic and religious practices, or an organism capable of synthesizing such highly reactive compounds internally, might well be afforded a tremendous evolutionary advantage, as it would possess an enhanced access to the informational *gestalten* of its own holographic genetic storage system.

It is also conceivable that the bonding of harmine or an analogous compound into DNA could form permanent bonds maintained by a form of superconductivity and, thus, function in the formation and maintenance of long-term memory. We have seen that compounds such as proflavin and presumably harmine have the effect of stabilizing the helix through strong pi-cloud overlap. Superconductivity could maintain such bonds indefinitely and thus ensure the longevity of long-term memory storage; it could also be involved as a mechanism for producing highly amplified ESRs from molecular substrates. The contents of long-term memories thus encoded could perhaps be selectively recalled by proper modulation of the ESR signal, by either reinforcing it or canceling it; this may be accomplished by the formation of RNA-indole complexes with ESRs in phase with the particular DNA ESR. The question of whether superconductivity may play a role in living processes deserves further investigation. Many of the ordering principles of living systems do seem to have many similarities to low-temperature systems (cf. Little 1965).

Naturally, the hypothetical model presented possesses its own peculiar problems in terms of experimental approaches, and any definitive confirmation or disconfirmation of the model would seem to depend on the development of very much more sophisticated biochemical and ESR techniques. We felt, however, that at least parts of the theory presented could be subjected to an operational test. The experimental procedures involved in this test, and the at least partially affirmative results obtained, are the subject matter of the next chapter.

Our rather freewheeling series of speculations on the molecular processes that may form the physical basis of mind is concluded at this point. We have postulated that internal and external inputs may be correlated to macromolecular changes and quantum-mechanical events that form the physical basis of mind. To say they are the physical basis of mind, however, is not to equate them to mind; this is the error of reductionism. The quantum-mechanical mechanisms we have discussed may have some properties homologous to the properties of mind as we experience it. However, mind is probably an expression of laws operating on a hierarchical level superordinate to that represented by organisms; hence, it is to be expected that it will exemplify some properties not to be found at the level of organisms alone. These are properties transcending the boundary conditions of organism and are those properties that make mind irreducible to physical or even organic structure. It is probable that the properties peculiar to mind introduce additional boundary conditions on subordinate levels, the organismic, molecular, and submolecular, so that the physical basis of mind—whatever it may be—has certain of its qualities determined by mind. If ESR forms the physical basis of mind, it probably possesses unique qualities that we would not find in the phenomenon as it is observed in the laboratory. But this relationship can never be reciprocal: Mind may determine some additional properties of ESR or whatever physical process operates at the interface of molecules and mind, but molecules and physical process, however complex, can never, by themselves, determine mind.

Chapter 6

An Experiment at La Chorrera

During the course of our investigation of the shamanic dimension, our attention was drawn to a report of *ayahuasca* usage among the Jívaro (Harner 1968); the shamans, under the influence of potent monoamine oxidase-inhibiting, harmine- and tryptamine-containing *Banisteriopsis* infusions, are said to produce a fluorescent violet substance by means of which they accomplish all their magic. Though invisible to ordinary perception, this fluid is said to be visible to anyone who has ingested the infusion. *Ayahuasca* is frequently associated with violet auras and deep blue hallucinations; this suggests that *ayahuasca* may enable one to see at ultraviolet wavelengths, and that this substance may be visible only in the ultraviolet part of the spectrum. We also had occasion to ingest synthetic tryptamines and had observed as a regular feature of the tryptamine intoxication a peculiar audile phenomenon. This is a very faint, but definitely perceivable, harmonic overtone of varying pitch and frequency that seems to emanate from inside the skull while one is under the influence of tryptamines; the exact nature of this harmonic tone eludes precise verbal description, as it varies in quality and amplitude during the course of the tryptamine experience, first manifesting itself as an extremely faint sound on the very edge of audibility, rather akin to the sound that might proceed from distant wind chimes. This sound gradually increases in volume a very few minutes after it is perceived, taking on an electric, buzzing quality that might be compared in some respects to whistling wind or running water. Understandably, one might be inclined to classify this sound as merely an audile hallucination induced by the psychoactive agent, were it not for the fact that it exhibits several specific and regularly noticeable features that would seem to set it apart from the class of hallucinated auditory phenomena, sometimes reported in literature dealing with psychedelics. One such feature is the specific association of this phenomenon with the ingestion of hallucinogens with structures close to tryptamine, that is, the psilocybin-DMT compounds and the harmine-tetrahydroharmine complex found in *Banisteriopsis caapi* and *B. rusbyana*. The reports of similar phenomena being noted for mescaline or the lysergamides are rare; while, according to Naranjo (in Efron et al. 1967, p. 389), approximately 50 percent of the subjects under the influence of *ayahuasca (B. caapi)* commonly experience an extremely loud buzzing sound, emanating from the interior of the skull,

FIGURE 12

Banisteriopsis caapi (Spruce ex Griseb.), a woody liana of the new world tropics, is a source of harmine and other harmala compounds. It is found in the equatorial areas of western South America drained by the upper Amazon's tributaries and used by the tribes of Peru, Ecuador, Colombia, and Brazil as a hallucinogenic substance. *B. caapi* belongs to the family Malpighiaceae. The same plant has various names—*caapi, ayahuasca, natema,* and *yagé*—and these names are also applied to the beverage prepared from it. Harmala compounds and their analogs (next page) are very potent monoamine oxidase inhibitors.

R=ALKYL GROUPS, e.g.,
CH₃O, OH, CH₃, etc.

ß-CARBOLINE
CORE STRUCTURE

HARMINE   TETRAHYDRO-HARMINE   HARMALINE

Principal alkaloids of *Banisteriopsis caapi* and related species.

6-METHOXY-HARMAN   6-METHOXY-HARMALAN   6-METHOXY-TETRAHYDRO-
                                             HARMAN

Alkaloids reported from Virola and related species.

TETRAHYDRO-ß-CARBOLINE   6-METHOXY-
                          TETRAHYDRO-ß-CARBOLINE

Alkaloids occurring in the brains and pineal glands of mammals.

IBOGAINE
from Tabernanthe iboga

MITRAGYNINE
from Mitragyna speciosa

Structural cogeners of ß-CARBOLINES.
They may or may not have a similar pharmacology.

97

during the course of the experience. Individual reports of the subjectively perceived phenomenon exhibit a high degree of similarity.

Our desire to pursue the investigation of this audile phenomenon at greater depth, combined with the curiosity and incredulity that Harner's report had aroused, led us to travel, in March of 1971, to the tiny mission settlement of La Chorrera, forty-three minutes south, seventy-three degrees west, on the banks of the Rio Igara-paraná in Comisaria Amazonas, Colombia. We felt that here we could carry out firsthand observations into the phenomenology of the tryptamine dimension. This region is well represented in endemic species of tryptamine-bearing psychoactive plants, among them *Virola theiodora* and other *Virola* species, *Psychotria viridis*, *Banisteriopsis caapi* (fig. 12) and *B. rusbyana*, and a lowland variety of *Stropharia cubensis* mushrooms (fig. 13) that we found to be particularly rich in phosphorylated tryptamines. Other minor psychoactive agents were also in widespread aboriginal use in this area, tobacco and coca being the most important in this respect, but these played no part in our experiments.

Ingestion of *Stropharia cubensis,* on a number of separate occasions, showed it to be of low toxicity and very nearly ideal for easy manifestation of the interior cerebral tone. We speculated that the tone is directly caused by the metabolism of the tryptamines within the cerebral matrix and might be the electron spin resonance of the metabolizing tryptamine molecules within the nervous system, somehow amplified to audible levels. We discovered that it was possible to closely imitate these tones with the voice by sounding harmonic vocal tones that quickly adjusted to the interior sounds as they moved from the audible into the ultrasonic range. Using this knowledge, it was possible to produce a vocal sound that seemed to amplify the harmonic tones perceivable inside the cranium. The vocal production of the sounds seems to rest on specific effects of the tryptamines on the motor nerves, particularly those governing the facial and vocal muscles. As with *ayahuasca,* an interior sound is commonly heard, which quite often triggers a spontaneous burst of imitative vocalizings, markedly unlike any conventional human speech or facial contortions. The tryptamines can apparently trigger a kind of rippling of facial muscles, which results in the production of a vocally modulated pressure wave.

What is more startling is that the sound, which gains in energy the longer it is sustained, can actually become visible—as if the vibrational wave patterns were shifting into the visible spectrum or inducing a vibrational excitation of the air in such a way as to affect light diffraction. These observations suggested that although the wave is produced with

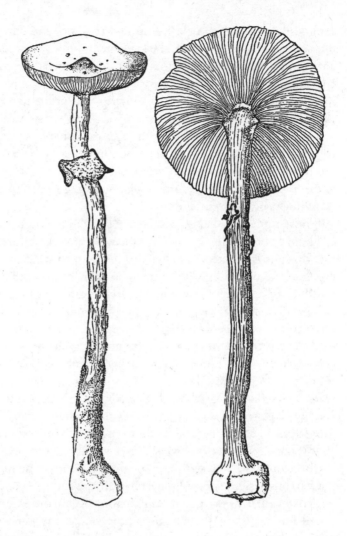

FIGURE 13

Stropharia cubensis (Earle) played a major role in the experiment at La Chorrera. These mushrooms grow gregariously on cow dung of the common species of Indian humped cattle (*Bos indicus*) and in this author's experience rarely occur in any other situation. The original type was discovered in Cuba in June of 1904. *Stropharia cubensis* has been reported from Florida, Puerto Rico, Oaxaca, British Honduras, Trinidad, Colombia, Bolivia, Argentina, and Indochina. The major psychoactive constituent has been identified by Hofmann et al. (1959) as psilocybin, that is, 4-phosphoryloxy-N, N-dimethyltryptamine. Illustration from *Les champions hallucinogènes du Mexique* by Roger Heim and R. Gordon Wasson, in Archives du Muséum National d'Histoire Naturelle, 7è série, tome 6, 1958. (Editions du Muséum National d'Histoire Naturelle, 38 rue Geoffroy-Saint-Hilaire, 75005 Paris) sound, it may possess an electromagnetic component. This peculiar wave phenomenon will continue to be generated out of the mouth and nostrils and will be visible in the surrounding air as long as the vocalizations are continued. Working from the hypothesis that this visible phenomenon might somehow proceed from the interior harmonic tones made audible through the ingestion of tryptamines, and further speculating that these tones might be caused by the electron spin resonance of the metabolizing tryptamines within the nervous system, our task became one of attempting to determine how vocally imitating molecular ESR could produce a visible standing wave and, further, of attempting to describe just what this wave might be in physical terms.

The temporal process of metabolism leads in the human brain to a special kind of phenomenon, which is thought, and the nature and texture of this thought is affected and altered in relation to what specific metabolic processes are occurring within the brain. For instance, the physicochemical state of the brain during stage IV sleep is different than when drugs are cycling in the brain, and each of these metabolic states has its special, unique form of consciousness attributed to it. It is no longer tenable to regard these processes of consciousness merely as an epiphenomenal reflection of the metabolic processes occurring simultaneously within the brain. It has been found (cf. Dicara 1970; Green et al. 1970) that this process is a two-way exchange: Metabolism gives rise to special kinds of potentiated energy states within an organism, but these energy states reflect and, in some degree, determine what kinds of metabolic processes will occur.

It is not easy to know to what degree metabolic process *is* determinable by consciousness. To assert that thought can control chemical reactions in the nervous system may seem peculiar on the surface, but it is inherently no less peculiar to say that it cannot intrude on the external world as a causal force. Clearly, thought does have causal effect; reality, as we perceive it, is largely shaped by the artifacts, both material and symbolic, of thought. Therefore, that thought can have no direct influence on the physical texture of reality is perhaps an unjustifiable assumption, for such an assumption implies that one has prior knowledge as to the boundary conditions of the interface of mind and the world. The question must remain an open one. We are reminded of Whitehead's observation that electrons blindly run either within or without the body, but within the body they blindly run according to the conditions of the body, and thought is among these conditions. The position that thought does in fact exert some influence over quantum events was included in our repertoire of operational constructs.

The brain is an extremely complex matrix of electrochemical circuitry that reacts peculiarly in the presence of certain kinds of tryptamines (but requires other tryptamines, such as serotonin, to function normally). The bizarre mental phenomena caused by tryptamines are probably related to a disturbance of normal tryptamine metabolism. It is clear that the purely chemical interaction between drug and brain occurs within the cerebral matrix. The mind, however, can be viewed as the temporal "overstructure" of the brain, which manifests, through time, in processes such as mentation, memory, and dreams. By affecting the temporal process of metabolism in the neural matrix, psychedelic drugs affect, as well, changes in its temporal overstructure, that is, mind. This suggests that psychoactive molecules may also possess a temporal aspect, which only manifests in their metabolic cycling. A static molecular diagram is essentially a misleading concept, for it can show only the physical configuration of a particular molecule. In fact, that molecule, as it functions in nature, is but one stage or structural configuration in the metabolic processes occurring within the living tissues of all organisms. We felt that this relationship was a reciprocal one, and that mind, through a conscious intervention into temporal process, could determine the outcome of certain events on the metabolic level.

This understanding of the mechanics of metabolism was combined with the notion that the sound that manifests inside the brain under the influence of tryptamines originated from the ESR created by the process of their intercalating into the neural DNA. We reasoned that it would be possible to trigger specific chemical reactions with the voice by harmonically manipulating the ESR energies and thus the charge-transfer process that causes this resonation in the molecule. The concept, as it relates to molecular electron spin resonations, can be explained more simply in terms of a vibrating string, where it was first discovered as the principle of overtonal harmonics. Suppose an open string "A" is sounded on the cello; the string sounds not only the fundamental but also a series of higher notes that are integral multiples, as defined by the speed of vibration of the fundamental one, the most important being an octave, a fifth, and a fourth apart. If the vibrating string is then touched very lightly, the fundamental note will be canceled and will sympathetically cancel the subsidiary harmonies above it, to the degree that they are harmonically close to the fundamental note.

Our reasoning regarding the ESR of tryptamines was based on a similar idea. The psilocybin complex, the methylated tryptamines, and the harmine complex are all biosynthetically derived in nature from tryptophan through a progressive cyclizing of the side-chain (cf. fig. 14). It seemed reasonable, therefore, to assume that this biosynthetic relationship is

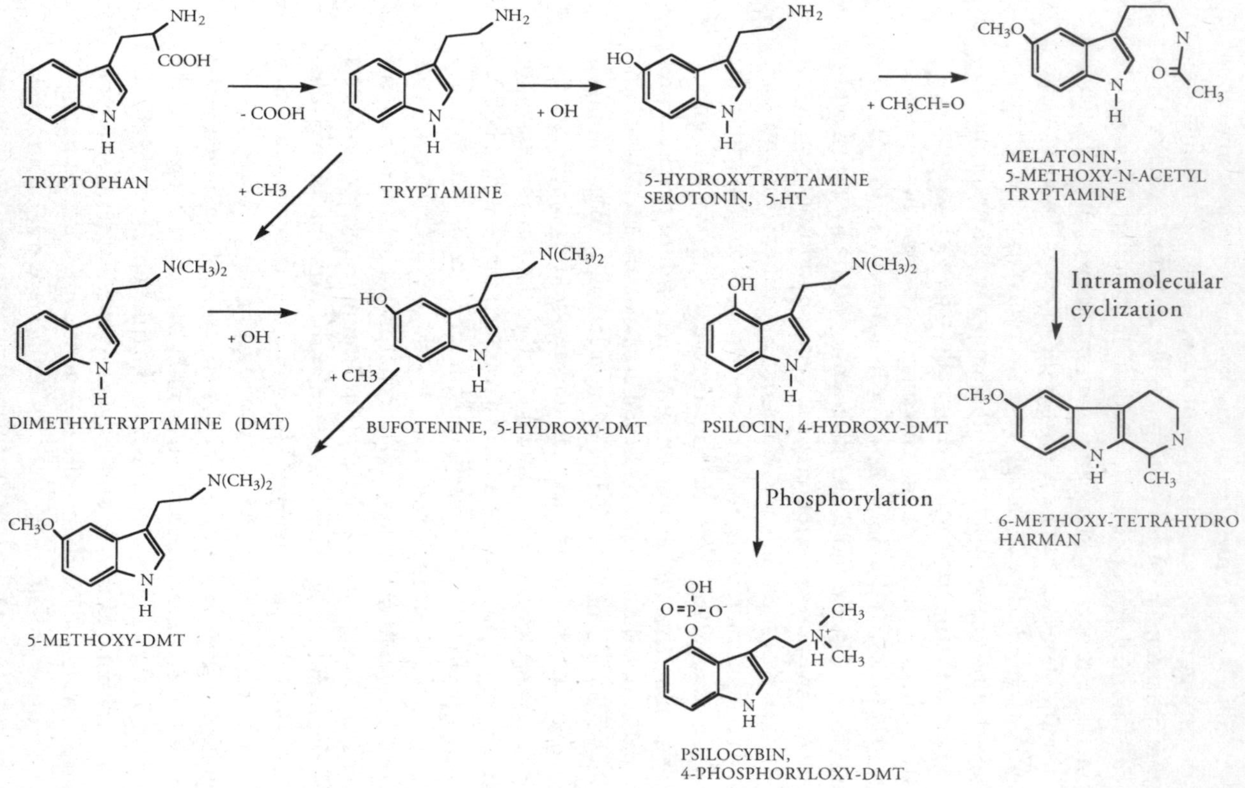

FIGURE 14 *Structures of Hallucinogens Related to Tryptophan*

Psilocin, the dephosphorylated derivative of psilocybin, is shown here in its relation to tryptamine. Note that N, N-dimethyltryptamine is closely related to psilocin. That tryptophan is a precursor of psilocybin in living organisms has been shown by Brack et al. (1961). Psilocybin and trace amounts of psilocin have been extracted from *Stropharia cubensis* by Hofmann et al.

reflected in their ESR as well, and that their absorption frequencies would be harmonic overtones of each other. If the ESR modulation of the tryptamines can be heard by ingesting the mushroom, and if this modulation can be amplified with sound, it will be absorbed at a higher frequency by the harmine complexes if these are also being metabolized within the system. This should cancel the charge transfer of the metabolizing harmine, causing it to momentarily lose its electrical resistance and behave as a superconductor. Similarly, if the modulated harmine ESR is amplified with vocal harmonics, it should be absorbed at the tryptamine frequencies and cancel the tryptamine charge transfer.

The motif and usage of *ayahuasca* in aboriginal shamanism correlates well with the premise that harmine-type compounds afford access to genetically grounded, archetypal information. The configuration of the harmine structure is ideally suited to act as a DNA intercalator. We have long speculated that the action of such compounds is due to a kind of genetic readout of molecularly coded information, which results from the harmine intercalating into the genetic material of the cerebral neurons. What has heretofore eluded explanation is the precise mechanism by which the bonding between the harmine alkaloids and the DNA-RNA matrix can take place and how, once this bond has been effected, the genetic readout can be detected by the higher cortical perceptions in the form of a psychic experience. If our theory concerning the induction of superconducting configuration within these molecules via ESR harmonics was found to be correct, this problem would be very nearly solved, for a molecule possessing zero electrical resistance would be able to sustain strong charge transfer with other superconducting molecules indefinitely. The harmine becomes superconductive only for a microsecond but then is sustained in its superconductivity through the fact of its having entered a bond state with the superconducting core of DNA. We speculate that superconductivity plays a role in the mechanism preserving the genetic message from disruption. That DNA might utilize superconductivity, or something similar, is an old idea, but it has never been demonstrated (cf. Little 1965). We suggest this may be because it is a quality of *in vivo* material, and that it is a systems property that vanishes when the genetic material is disrupted. In *What Is Life?* (1944), Schrödinger, anticipating the discovery of DNA, wrote:

> . . . to reconcile the high durability of the hereditary substance
> with its minute size, we had to evade the tendency to disorder by
> "inventing the molecule," in fact, an unusually large molecule
> which has to be a masterpiece of highly differentiated order,

safeguarded by the conjuring rod of quantum theory. The laws of chance are not invalidated by this "invention," but their outcome is modified. The physicist is familiar with the fact that the classical laws of physics are modified by quantum theory, especially at low temperature. There are many instances of this. Life seems to be one of them, a particularly striking one. Life seems to be orderly and lawful behavior of matter, not based exclusively on its tendency to go over from order to disorder, but based partly on existing order that is kept up.

To the physicist—but only to him—I could hope to make my view clearer by saying: The living organism seems to be a macroscopic system which in part of its behavior approaches to that purely mechanical (as contrasted with thermodynamical) conduct to which all systems tend, as the temperature approaches to the absolute zero and the molecular disorder is removed. (p. 69)

We speculated that information stored in the neural-genetic material might be made available to consciousness through a modulated ESR absorption phenomenon, originating in superconducting charge-transfer complexes formed by intercalation of tryptamines and beta-carbolines into the genetic material. We reasoned that both neural DNA and neural RNA were involved in this process: Serotonin or, in the case of our experiment, exogenously introduced methylated tryptamines would preferentially bind to membrane RNA, opening the ionic shutter mechanism and, simultaneously, entering into superconductive charge transfer with its resulting modulated ESR signal; beta-carbolines could then pass through the membrane via the RNA-ionic channel and intercalate into the neural DNA. The DNA-harmine complex would possess an ESR modulated at frequencies that were harmonic overtones of the ESR absorption frequencies of the RNA-tryptamine complex. The frequencies of either complex could then be harmonically amplified or canceled by modulation of the other complex.

To check our theories, we devised an experiment that was planned to trigger an intercalation of harmine into the genetic material that would sustain and stabilize its charge-transfer energy within a superconducting matrix. We reasoned that an infusion of *ayahuasca* plus tryptamine (mushroom) admixtures would allow us to do the following: (1) We would hear and vocally imitate the ESR modulation of the tryptamines as they intercalated with their RNA receptors. (2) The amplified tryptamine-RNA

ESR would be a harmonic overtone of the harmine-DNA resonation frequency, and the vocal modulation of these frequencies would cancel the two waveforms, causing both complexes to simultaneously lose their electrical resistance and assume superconducting configuration. (3) The electrically canceled harmine compound, which had been locked into superconductive bond with the DNA, would then begin to broadcast its waveform hologramatic ESR configuration through the superconducting harmine-transducing circuit. This superconductively sustained and ampli-fied resonation of the harmine-DNA macromolecule would excite the tryptamine-RNA complex into a sympathetic resonance frequency, caus-ing it to act as a radio transmitter, which would broadcast the coded infor-mation of the harmine-DNA superconducting sustainer circuit.

The modulated and superconductively sustained ESR of this macro-molecule might eventually manifest itself as a standing waveform that would, in effect, be a waveform hologram of the entire resonating macro-molecule. Such a molecule would be a superconductive holographic infor-mation storage system, containing all genetically and experientially coded information within its waveform pattern. It would respond to thought, which would be an interference pattern set up by resonating tryptamine-RNA complexes. Where the ESR set up in the cerebral tryptamine-RNA complex was in phase shift with the harmine-DNA matrix, a standing waveform would be created in three-dimensional space, which would be a hologram of an idea. Conceiving an idea would create a specific waveform pattern of tryptamine-RNA resonation; where this resonated sympathet-ically on the superconducting DNA-harmine macromolecule, that part of the molecular chain would be beheld holographically as a three-dimensional image. What is described can be considered a solid-state cybernetic circuit, macromolecular in size and sustained by superconduc-tive charge transfer. As any other solid-state circuit, the material matrix would be static, and the kinetic electrical activity would be the mobile element. The components of such a system would have a fourfold arrange-ment. The superconductive harmine-DNA complex would function as a charge-transfer power source and holographic ESR readout mechanism for informational *gestalten* stored in the *in vivo* DNA. The superconduct-ing tryptamine-RNA complex would function as a mentally triggered switch, governing the activation of the genetic readout mechanism and monitoring the input of modulated ESR frequencies from the environ-ment. The total system would be a holo-cybernetic unit of superconduc-tive genetic material in which the entirety of the DNA memory bank would be at the command of the harmine readout mechanism, activated via tryptamine harmonic interference. The tryptamine-RNA complex, besides activating the DNA-harmine readout mechanism, could function as an omnidirectional receiver for externally modulated ESR frequencies.

If we imagine the harmine-DNA complex as a radio-cybernetic matrix, then we can suppose that this matrix stores information in a regressing hierarchy of interiorized reflections of itself, in a form similar to the familiar Chinese ivory balls carved one within another, each level free to rotate independently. In response to the vibration of tryptamine-RNA charge-transfer exchanges, modulated by mind into a usable signal, information searches of any sort might be conducted through a process that we suggest might be much like the principle of retrieval of information from volume holograms. Such a process of information retrieval and image projection would never lag behind human thought. Indeed, conscious thought may be precisely this process, but occurring on a more limited scale. This limitation of scale may arise out of the way in which serotonin (5HT) reflects the ESR of the genetic material into which this neurotransmitter is continually intercalating during normal metabolism. What we are suggesting on one level is that how conscious an organism is of the world that surrounds it may be fundamentally related to the charge-transfer capacity of the endogenous DNA and RNA intercalators that the organism has evolved. Serotonin may be one of many possible resonant transmitters of the informational hologram that is stored in DNA. Harmine, we suggest, may be another, and perhaps more efficient, transmitter. Harmine may be more efficient precisely because it bonds more readily to DNA than to RNA. The rise in levels of beta-carbolines seen in pineal glands as one ascends the primate phylogeny—with the highest levels occurring in *Homo sapiens*—lends credence to the idea that the adaptation called consciousness may involve mutation of the metabolic pathways associated with serotonin, other tryptamines, and harmine. The shift of emphasis from serotonin pathways to beta-carboline and methylated tryptamine pathways is, we speculate, the molecular evolutionary event that is responsible for the intimations of transfiguration that have recently characterized mass consciousness.

It is easy to see that the actualization of a functioning system of the type described, when coupled with a controlling intellect, would be, in effect, a hyperdimensionally mobile cybernetic entity. It would be the practical equivalent of a transdimensional vehicle in that it would, in common with holographic imagery, actualize the Hermetic axiom that "What is here is everywhere, what is not here is nowhere." It would be comparable to a flying saucer that moved through time and space, not in any conventional sense but rather one that *is* all time and space, warped through a higher topology into the boundaries of conventional space-time. This is similar to Jung's understanding of the psyche and is the effect that this holo-cybernetic matrix would tend to create. If, in fact, neural DNA is the repository of information, as we postulate, then the system described would render the totality of this information available to consciousness and might include all personal memories and experiences and also all collective knowledge and experience, accumulated over the evolutionary (and possibly cultural) history of the species and reflected in its genetic makeup. Such a system would contain thousands of times the capabilities of enormous cybernetic systems in the space of a superconducting sustainer matrix only a few microns in diameter.

Success in the formation of a permanent DNA-harmine bond and the resulting permanently sustained charge-transfer process could be expected to trigger a metabolic and experiential situation with similarities to both toxic psychosis caused by abnormal tryptophan metabolism and the shamanic trance attendant upon prolonged ingestion of *ayahuasca (B. caapi)* and *ayahuasca* admixtures. In each of these situations, experimental tryptophan psychosis and shamanic trance, what is involved are alterations and inhibitions of normal amine levels in the brain. The shaman manipulates this bizarre region for culturally valid reasons and with techniques of proven efficacy. The schizophrenic is an unwilling victim, a traveler through what to him is a terrifying landscape. Using analytical premises and the operational constructs described above, we sought to carry ourselves, as modern humans, into the same numinous landscape and to offer a report of interest to empirical investigators.

Chapter 7

Psychological Reflections on La Chorrera

With chapter 6 as a basis, we approach the most difficult aspect of the La Chorrera experiment that we are called upon to discuss, the subjective psychological contents. Here is an area where we must exercise objectivity in discussing personal situations. Because we experienced what is described in this chapter, we are acutely aware of its strangeness and its incredibility. But psychology is a young science, and the neat separation of experiment and experimenter, which characterizes the physical sciences, will become an impediment to the progress of experimental psychology if taken too seriously. We would feel that we were not being completely honest and thus not as scientific as possible if we did not share with the reader the nature of the situation in which these ideas were generated. Memory will necessarily play a major part in any account of a process having temporal duration, but what a reconstructed memory fails to correctly represent is the formation of understanding as a gradual reaching out or groping that is, itself, a process proceeding through time. The experiment caused a release of unconscious imagery related to several themes of an archetypal nature. The major theme was that of transformation.

Silverman (cf. above, Part One, chapter 2) has noted two types of schizophrenia under the heading of "reactive," which he calls "essential" and "paranoid." His descriptions of the symptoms of these two types correspond well to the varieties of unusual ideation we experienced as the major confirmation of our success on the submolecular level in the two weeks following the experiment of March 5, 1971. From that date, the normal configurations of both our personalities started a sudden and immediate migration toward these two forms of reactive schizophrenia. In the early morning hours of March 5, shortly after the completion of the vocal experiment outlined in chapter 6, in the space of scarcely more than an hour, one of us entered a progressively more detached state of essential schizophrenia or classic shamanic trance.

We could feel the presence of some invisible hyperspatial entity, an ally, which seemed to be observing and sometimes exerting influence on the situation to keep us moving gently toward an experimental resolution of the ideas we were generating. Because of the alien nature of the tryptamine trance, its seeming accentuation of themes alien, insectile, and futuristic, and because of previous experiences with tryptamine in which insectile hallucinatory transformations of human beings were observed, we were led to speculate that the role of the presence was somehow like that of an anthropologist, come to give humanity the keys to galactarian citizenship. We discussed this entity in terms of a giant insect and, through the insect trill of the Amazon jungle at midday, seemed able to discern a deeper harmonic buzz that somehow signified the unseen outsider. This sense of the presence of an alien third entity was sometimes very intense, most intense in early March and from there fading off gradually.

For the next thirty-seven days, especially the next fourteen days, our shared ideation consisted of, among other themes, but as a dominant one, the idea of a shamanic journey of return from the ends of space and time to the earth, with the collected energy configuration of space-time condensed into a kind of lens or saucer, a true philosopher's stone. One of us experienced an intense transference state similar to reactive paranoid schizophrenia and accepted the paternal and curative role of shaman and psychopomp. From the sixth until the seventeenth of March, one of us did not sleep, and the other, while awake, spoke continuously, in apparent and convincing telepathic rapport with anyone he wished, in command of enormous technical erudition and a strange and rapidly evolving hyperspatial cosmogony that, following a Manichean perception, visualized the solar system as a huge light pump, wherein the light of souls is pumped from planet to planet until it finally leaves the solar system altogether and is transmitted to the galactic center.* Some of his "discoveries" were that Jupiter is the reflected image of the earth in hyperspace, is teeming with bizarre life-forms, and is somehow an essential key to unraveling the species' fate. In his interior epic, late twentieth-century history was experienced as a frantic effort to build an object, which he called "the lens," to allow life to escape to Jupiter on the heels of an impending global catastrophe.

Slowly, as the shamanic voyager neared his home, his place in space, his stitch in time, the myth making and the symptoms of election schizophrenia faded in each of us. However, the continuing process of understanding, triggered by the experiment, did not cease. Rather, it continued to stabilize and define itself with the passage of each twenty-four-hour cycle, leading out of the "crazy" poetic ideation of the early days following the experiment and into the understanding that has led us to hypothesize a new model of mind and time. Our model is, first, an effort to trace the logic of these experiences in terms relevant to the molecular levels where

* For further discussion of the archetypal theme of return to the galactic center, the interested reader is referred to *Hamlet's Mill* (de Santillana and von Dechend 1969), especially chapter 18.

the experimental superconductive intercalation of harmine may have taken place. The content of our experience has resolved itself into the logical consequences that flow from the "revealed" axiom that all phenomena are at root constellated by a waveform that is the hierarchical summation of its constituent parts, morphogenetic patterns related to those in DNA.

Although we can clearly recognize that our experience evinces the classic symptomatology associated with the two generally distinguished categories of process schizophrenia, we are unable to make the assumption that the experiment was therefore "nothing but" a simultaneous schizophrenia (cf. chapter 2). Rather, we maintain that we are, in fact, dealing with an objective phenomenon that, although of a highly peculiar nature, inexorably bound up with psychic processes, does have its basis in the molecular phenomena we were in the process of investigating. As empirical evidence for this view, we mention the following points that seem to deviate from the usual schizophrenic episode: (1) The suddenness with which the symptoms developed following our actual experiment; that is to say, within a few minutes after we completed our preplanned experimental procedures, we began to disengage from the continuum of collective perception and, at the same time, began to experience the expanded channel capacity that we had predicted would be a part of the phenomenology to be manifested if we were successful in our attempt to generate a superconducting genetic matrix harmine bond. (2) The simultaneous and dovetail aspect of our disassociation, meaning that, although both of us were exhibiting the symptoms of a type of schizophrenia, the ideas and the understanding that we were experiencing was shared. In the same way that a film running in reverse seems to present a spectacle of wild and irrational confusion, yet manages in the end to have things in their proper places, mentation and physical movement seemed to be simply the reverse of logical expectations. (3) One of us experienced eleven days without sleep and felt no strain during this same period.

More important than any of these factors (which are, after all, unique, unverified, and unrepeatable events) indicating a condition beyond simple schizophrenia are the idea models we have created out of the careful observation of the things that happened to us. It is upon this theory, and not as reporters of paranormal events, that we wish to be judged.

We argue that the theory of the hyperspatial nature of superconductive bonds, and the experiment we devised to test that theory, yielded not only spectacular subjective results but also a modular wave-hierarchy theory of the nature of time that we have been able to construe, using a particular mathematical treatment of the *I Ching*, into a general theory of systems, which illuminates the nature of time and organism and provides an idea model that explains the interconnection of physical and psychological phenomena from the submolecular to the macrocosmic level.

We cannot close these psychological reflections on our experiment without a brief discussion of the nature of the subjective experience of the hallucinogenic tryptamines that were our basic tools. To ingest *Stropharia cubensis* is to "erect a star antenna"; that is, by taking psychodynamic tryptamines into one's system, one is better able to hear and perhaps to "see" the standing wave of species' experience (as seems to be possible in some dreams). The character of the mushroom experience is almost entirely that of understanding.* We suggest that this understanding may be the amplified appearance, at the level of a higher cortical experience, of the DNA electron spin resonance. The *Stropharia* mushroom is an evidently nontoxic and easily applied tool for intensifying the phenomenon associated with gaining access to the atemporal unconscious. This case for utilization is like much else about the mushroom that partakes of the Siren's Song. In using the mushroom, one must be especially alert for transference phenomena and ego identification with the contents of the hyperactive imagination. It is not we who are doing anything; the self-revelation of the phenomenon is something that is happening to us. Alteration of monoamine oxidase (MAO) levels through the smoking of *B. caapi* bark after ingesting mushrooms is the closest approximation to smoking synthetic tryptamine (DMT) that we have found in nature. It is quite possible that in the resin of *Virola theiodora* there are even more profoundly active tryptamine and beta-carboline compounds. If some odd form of toxicity within the mushroom had a role in our experiences, it was not apparent in subsequent mushroom experiences.

It is possible that the schizophrenic episode which followed our experiment may have resulted from an irreversible inhibition of MAO. Some MAO inhibitors used therapeutically as antidepressants (notably iproniazid) can bind irreversibly to the enzyme, triggering a long-term inhibition that can only be mitigated through the production of new enzymes by protein synthesis. Studies of irreversible inhibition have shown that full recovery of normal MAO activity can require a period of ten to twenty days (Planz et al. 1972). While harmine and its analogs are known to exhibit strong MAO inhibition, this action is reversible and is on the order of three to six hours (Undenfriend et al. 1958). If, however, we succeeded in

---

* In Whitehead's phrase, this understanding is, however imperfect, "the self-evidence of pattern so far as it has been discriminated" (1968, p. 52). In the same work (p. 50), Whitehead states, "Understanding is self-evidence . . . Proofs are the tools for the extension of our imperfect self-evidence."

creating a superconducting configuration in harmine and its analogs, then we should expect that they would irreversibly bind to MAO as well as to neural DNA, and thus may have produced the symptoms that followed our experiment. MAO inhibition is reflected by a rise in 5HT levels in the brain, since synthesis continues at a normal rate, while turnover of the amine is inhibited (Planz et al. 1972). If exogenously introduced tryptamines are present in the system, these will also accumulate in the absence of MAO activity. Perhaps, in our experiment, the introduction of reversible MAO inhibitors plus tryptamines into the nervous system caused an initial accumulation of serotonin and methylated tryptamines. Subsequently, these methylated tryptamines and possibly the 5HT, having their usual conversion pathways blocked by MAO inhibition, became substrates for other enzymes such as N-methyl transferase and hydroxy-indole O-methyl transferase (HIOMT). These enzymes could further increase the levels of methylated tryptamines. Some of these amines may have been converted via the alternative enzyme pathways to psychotomimetic compounds not amenable to MAO inactivation, which might continue to accumulate in the system even after normal MAO activity had been restored. If our own theory is incorrect or incomplete, this may explain how we were able to maintain a continuous connection with the unconscious over many months.

At first we approached the psychedelic phenomenology of the *Stropharia* mushroom with perfect innocence. Now understanding has placed us forever beyond such unawareness. In comparison with synthetic psychedelics, the physical effects of *S. cubensis* compare with those of mescaline. One must be particularly sensitive to incidents that might be precursors to some sort of uncontrollable outbreak of unconscious contents. Our theory seems to indicate that, for all its concern, the ego really is not able to control the flow of events at all. If this is true and if a trance episode is a constituent part of this phenomenon, then there is nothing to be done to mitigate its inevitability. This is not, however, to be construed as a license for recklessness; on the contrary, one should act as though causality is operable and the ego in control. The mushroom is a tool that allows an insight into the state of the standing wave of mind on unconscious levels, but it is not necessary for the continuation of that phenomenon. One could forego the mushroom trance and thus eliminate a possible source of toxic reversal. Our mushroom experiences allowed us to remember and reconnect with deeper states of tryptamine ecstasy, to reconstruct and to feel the poetic-literary idea complex that was, in fact, one motivation for our program of investigation of natural tryptamines.

We refer to the dynamic yet stable, apparently self-sustaining, non-three-dimensional spatiality into which the smoking of tryptamines conveys one. We especially refer to the apparently autonomous and intelligent, chaotically mercurial and mischievous machine elves encountered in the trance state, strange teachers whose marvelous singing makes intricate toys out of the air and out of their own continually transforming body geometries. This spectacle of more than Oriental splendor is the characteristic, even unvarying, manner in which this experience presents itself. A sound, which finally can be seen as a topology, dynamically contorts itself into a form, whose voice the sound then becomes, and which it then uses to produce idea complexes presented with the specific purpose of teaching something. But this something is not easily brought back from that dimension, and this fact sets up a dynamic polarity between the ego and the content of the ecstasy. That polarity is the compass of our quest. That place or state is the area inviting exploration. In some very real sense, it is the place where ideas come from. In that other dimension, vast evolving idea complexes pass before one and are understood in an instant. And through the singing elf machines, many such object/ideas clamor (literally) for one's attention at once. In the words of H. Munn, writing of mushroom use in Oxaca, ". . . the impish mushrooms come to life, embodiments of merriment, tumbling figments of the spontaneous, performing incredible acrobatic feats" (in Harner 1973, p. 110).

The content of the experience has an emotional richness that is profoundly deep, yet so positive that one must laugh aloud. Inevitably, the subjective richness, and the apparent self-coherence of the content of the tryptamine trance, leads those who experience it to wonder after its implications for modern humans. The idea of the simultaneous coexistence of an alien dimension all around us is as strange an idea in the context of modern society as it must have been to the first shamans, whose experiments with psychoactive plants would have soon brought them to the same tryptamine doorway. What is the nature of the invisible landscape beyond that doorway? The answer to the question is linked to the question of the nature of mind. If the world beyond the doorway can be given consensual validation of the sort extended to the electron and the black hole—in other words, if the world beyond the doorway is found to be a necessary part of scientifically mature thinking about the world—then our own circumscribed historical struggle will be subject to whole new worlds of possibility.

If poetics color the science of our way, these trances are their foundations. Is this idea completely outside the realm of philosophical experience? Jonas (1966), in discussing an allegory in Philo Judaeus, which evolves from the etymology of the word Israel, "he who sees God," says:

A more perfect archetypal logos, exempt from the human duality of sign and thing, and therefore not bound by the forms of speech, would not require the mediation of hearing, but is immediately beheld by the mind as the truth of things. In other words the antithesis of seeing and hearing argued by Philo lies as a whole within the realm of "seeing"—that is to say, it is no real antithesis but a difference of degree relative to the ideal of immediate intuitive presence of the object. It is with a view to this ideal that the "hearing" here opposed to "seeing" is conceived, namely, as its deputizing, provisional mode, and not as something authentic, basically other than seeing. Accordingly, the turn from hearing to seeing here envisaged is merely a progress from a limited knowledge to an adequate knowledge of the same and within the same project of knowledge. (p. 238)

This is an excellent description of the interiorized linguistic phenomenon that proceeds and differs only in degree from the visual phenomenon, which seems, indeed, a "more perfect archetypal logos" and which, in our experience, defines the tryptamine trance experience. If the physical brain is analogous to a holographic plate, can sounds in certain ranges penetrate the skull in such a way as to make audile holograms (visual images) appear in 3D space or in the mind-brain of another organism? This matter stands completely unresearched, although audilely induced wave interference patterns have been illuminated with lasers to produce hologramatic images (cf. chapter 4).

We are not alone in suggesting that the tryptamine compounds are somehow vitally involved with the mysteries of language and language formation:

The Mazatecs say that the mushrooms speak. If you ask a shaman where his imagery comes from, he is likely to reply: "I didn't say it, the mushrooms did." No mushroom speaks, that is a primitive anthropomorphization of the natural, only man speaks, but he

who eats these mushrooms, if he is a man of language, becomes
endowed with an inspired capacity to speak. The shamans who eat
them, their function is to speak, they are the speakers who chant
and sing the truth, they are the oral poets of their people, the doctors of the word, they who tell what is wrong and how to remedy
it, the seers and oracles, the ones possessed by the voice. "It is not
I who speak," said Heraclitus, "it is the logos." Language is an
ecstatic activity of signification. Intoxicated by the mushrooms,
the fluency, the ease, the aptness of expression one becomes capable of are such that one is astounded by the words that issue forth
from the contact of the intention of articulation with the matter
of experience. At times it is as if one were being told what to say,
for the words leap to mind, one after another, of themselves without having to be searched for: a phenomenon similar to the automatic dictation of the surrealists except that here the flow of
consciousness, rather than being disconnected, tends to be coherent: a rational enunciation of meanings. Message fields of communication with the world, others and one's self are disclosed by the
mushrooms. The spontaneity they liberate is not only perceptual,
but linguistic, the spontaneity of speech, of fervent, lucid discourse, of the logos in activity. For the shaman, it is as if existence
were uttering itself through him . . . words are materializations of
consciousness; language is a privileged vehicle of our relation to
reality. (Munn, in Harner 1973, pp. 88–89)

Summation of our Amazon experience is not easy. In the wake of our
experiment there have been, besides enormous disruptions of statistical
norms in the form of accumulations of meaningful coincidences, instances of physical phenomena absolutely beyond current understanding.
Telepathic phenomena, especially, in our subjective judgment, were manifest several times during this period. These experiences go an enormous
distance toward convincing us that we are indeed involved with a paranormal phenomenon that may violate the usual laws of conventional physics.
These experiences have been the continuing motivation for our attempt
to empirically demonstrate the existence of this phenomenon. The violations have to date been inexplicable by any theory save the organismic
general theory of systems we have elaborated. It is this continuing self-
explication on the part of the phenomenon and the resolution of the

explication into a general theory of systems or process that sets our experience apart from the general gnosis of shamanism or schizophrenia. Because this theory makes assertions about reality, it invites careful empirical investigation. It is for this reason that, while cultivating a suspended judgment, we endeavor to allow the phenomenon every opportunity to reveal and refine itself.

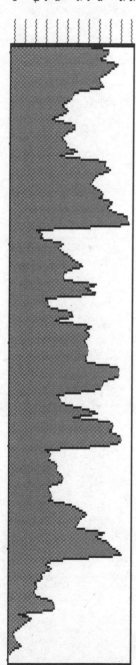

1.0273335
0.9345933
0.8418565
0.7491108
0.6563666
0.5636233
0.4708801
0.3781368
0.2853936
0.1926504
0.0999011
0.0071569

Part Two

Time,

Change,

and

Becoming

Introduction

In Part Two we will be concerned with some of the speculations arising out of the apparent functioning of the audilely induced intercalation of harmine into the genetic matrix. These speculations have arisen in the months, and now years, that have followed upon our original experiment. These extrapersonal thought processes arose in a temporal sequence of steady self-amplification and explication; internal contradictions have been few.

The chapters that follow require what may appear at first as a sharp shift of focus. The discussion now moves from the methodological and philosophical bases of our experiment to a rather formal exposition of the calendrical potentials offered by the structure of the sequence of the hexagrams used in the classic Chinese divinatory system, the *I Ching*. This concern may appear to be far removed from the molecular basis of Amazonian shamanic trance, but in fact divination is the especial prerogative of the shaman, whatever the cultural context. It is one of the major signs of a shaman's command of a superhuman condition. The three-thousand-year-old King Wen sequence of the sixty-four hexagrams of the *I Ching* is among the oldest structured abstractions extant, yet the nature of the ordering principles preserved in that sequence remains unelucidated. The *I Ching* is a mathematical divinatory tool of great age whose probable origin is the mountainous heart of Asia—the home of classical shamanism and Taoist magic—it is a centrally important part of humanity's shamanic heritage that is rich in implications. Chapter 8 traces some of the implications the *I Ching* may have had for neolithic China and its intuitions concerning time. We chose to examine the *I Ching* and its relation to temporality and organism because, in the months following our experiment, their specific similarities seemed to force themselves upon us. It is our supposition that the unconscious contents which our experiment made accessible were constellated around the *I Ching* because it is particularly concerned with the dynamic relationships and transformations that archetypes undergo; it is deeply involved with the nature of time as the necessary condition for the manifestation of archetypes as categories of experience. The *I Ching*, through its concern with detailing the dynamics of change and process, may hold the key to modeling the temporal dimension that metabolism creates for organisms, the temporal dimension without which mind could not manifest.

Our *tentative* assumption is that the intense involvement we experienced with this problem arose out of the functioning of the harmine-DNA complex and the intensified broadcast of the structurally modulated ESR of that unusual molecular configuration. Chapter 9 examines the hypothesized resonance calendar of the previous chapter from a point of view that seeks to isolate the irreducible elements in such a hierarchical view of time and then to treat them as the system by which organisms order their world-describing cognitive categories. The later chapters of Part Two will elevate the temporal variables contained in the *I Ching* calendar to the level of a possible general law of nature descriptive of temporal variables in macrophysical as well as quantum-mechanical systems. In chapter 10 we discuss the nature of the order of the King Wen sequence and then present techniques for graphically mapping the proposed temporal continuum. Chapter 10 carries the mapping process to a new level of refinement by presenting techniques for a comparative numerical quantification of every point in the hierarchy relative to a zero state. The cosmology such a general law of nature would make necessary is examined in chapter 11, which deals with the part of astrophysics relevant to the cosmic view of the atemporal shaman. Chapter 12 discusses the teleology a temporal hierarchy implies. In chapter 13 we discuss quantification of the hierarchy and the opportunities it offers for attempts to experimentally test its empirical existence. A systems approach to charting the parameters of the historical future is also outlined. Chapter 14 discusses evolution and freedom in the light of the above.

Chapter 8

The *I Ching* as Lunar Calendar and Astronomical Calculator

The *I Ching* is an oracle system of great age in wide use in China since around 1000 B.C. It consists of sixty-four hexagrams, or six-line figures. Lines in a hexagram may be solid (—) or broken (- -), and a hexagram is read from bottom to top. The resulting sixty-four permutations upon these simple rules (figs. 15 and 16) were believed by the Chinese to reflect universal categories, or archetypes, that could shed light on one's fate if one properly consulted the oracle. The method of consulting the oracle has changed over the centuries. Originally bones were used; later forty-nine stalks of yarrow; still later coins were tossed. None of this will concern us here. Neither will we be concerned with the voluminous commentaries, doctrines, and interpretations of the *I Ching* that began in the early Han dynasty and continue today. These matters are discussed thoroughly in Wilhelm (1964) and Needham (1954, 1965).

Our concern will be with facts that predate history, and with which no commentary can claim to be contemporary. We will be concerned with the primary unit of the *I Ching,* the hexagram. We will examine in detail its three-leveled hierarchical structure. The King Wen sequence, the oldest preserved human abstract sequence, will occupy us in later chapters as we seek for its ordering principles, make assumptions, and advance hypotheses. In this chapter, we will lay the groundwork for these more theoretical discussions by detailing what we believe neolithic China was doing with the *I Ching,* and hence why it was structured as it is.

Though the origins of the *I Ching* are uncertain, Joseph Needham (1954) adopts the position of Li Ching-Chhih that ". . . the canonical text originated from omen compilations which might be as old as the 7th or 8th century [B.C.], though it did not reach its present form before the end of the Chou Dynasty" (p. 307). Needham goes on to say: "The first extension of the system of the *kua* (hexagrams) seems to have taken place during the early Han period, when they were brought into systematic association with sidereal movements and hence with the passage of time" (1954, p. 329). In a footnote to the above we find: "Alternatively W. Eberhard suggests . . . that the *I Ching* hexagrams were connected with some pre-Chhin calendar system" (Needham 1954, p. 329n).

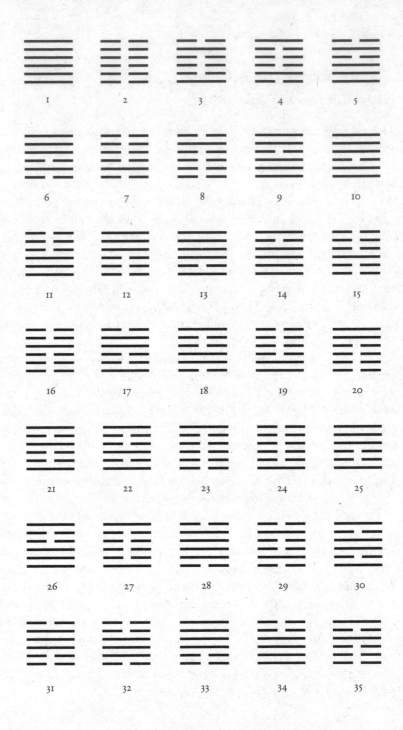

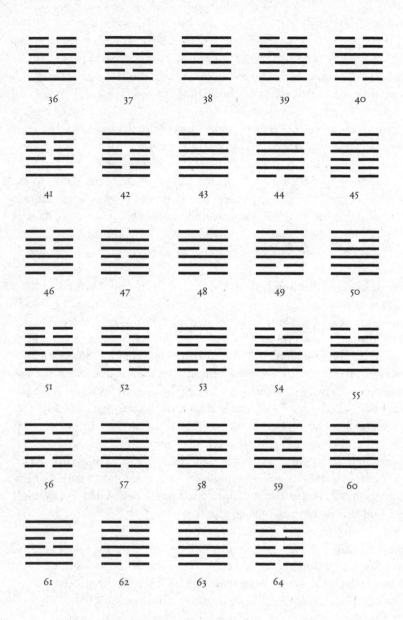

FIGURE 15

The King Wen arrangement of the sixty-four *I Ching* hexagrams.

This chapter will suggest in a speculative way a possible form that this lost calendar may have had. Since we are not sinologists, the case will be made around a single objective fact. We will extrapolate this fact through the use of only two assumptions concerning ancient Chinese culture and psychology. These assumptions are widely enough held among commentators on Oriental culture that they may be regarded as secure statements of a broad consensus. Of central interest is the coincidence of the duration of thirteen lunations and the number 384. The true value for the duration of a lunation is 29.530588 days. Examination of oracle bones dated to the thirteenth century B.C. has, according to Needham, led to the conclusion that at that time the length of the lunation was known to be 29.53 days.

29.53 days × 13 = 383.89 days

The nearness of this number to 384 is made significant when one realizes that 384 is the number that arises when sixty-four is multiplied by six, six being the number of *yao* or lines in a single hexagram. This last sentence introduces one of the assumptions by which we will advance the argument. It is the assumption of hierarchical or resonance thinking in Chinese intellectual constructs. In this case, it is the notion that what is done with the *yao,* the most basic element of a hexagram (multiplication by six to form a hexagram), might also be done with the entire set of *yao,* the complete sequence of sixty-four hexagrams. This idea that operations carried out on one level are elegant and efficacious if carried out in a similar way on other levels is intimately related to our second premise. This is the idea of cyclical recurrence of events and situations on many different scales of duration. The importance of these ideas in ancient China has been widely noted. An example of each will suffice. First, resonance thinking:

> Much has already been said about the importance in the Chinese worldview of action at a distance, in which the different kinds of things in the universe resonate with one another. In the 5th century A.D. Shih Shuo Hsin Yu we find the following:
> "Mr. Yin, a native of Chinchow, once asked a (Taoist) monk, Chang Yeh-Yuan, 'What is really the fundamental idea *(thi)* of the Book of Changes *(I Ching)?*'
> "The latter answered, 'The fundamental idea of the *I Ching* can be expressed in one single word, Resonance *(Kan).*'
> "Mr. Yin then said, 'We are told that when the Copper Mountain (Thung Shan) collapsed in the west, the bell Ling Chung

responded (ying), by resonance, in the east. Would this be according to the principles of the *I Ching?*"

"Chang Yeh-Yuan laughed and gave no answer to this question." (Needham 1954, p. 304)

On cycles:

... Nothing could be more striking than the appreciation of cyclical change, the cycle-mindedness, of the Taoists. "Returning is the characteristic movement of the Tao (the Order of Nature)" says the *Tao Tê Ching.* "Time's typical virtue," wrote Granet, "is to proceed by revolution." Indeed time *(shih)* is itself generated, some thought, by this uncreated and spontaneous *(tzu-jan)* never-ceasing circulation *(yün)*. (Needham 1965, p. 6)

It is established, therefore, that striking correlations exist between a count of 6 × 64 days and lunar motion. The 384-day year is a lunar year of thirteen lunar months. Such a lunar year has been determined to be 383.9 days or .1 day less than 384 days. Therefore, the cycle loses 2.4 hours (.1 day) each 384 days. If one were to adopt 384-day-long years as a calendar and insert one intercalary day every ten of such years, making every tenth year 385 days long, this calendar would lose one day every 454.5 of its years. Thus, the calendar would be accurate to .0022 day loss per 384-day year. This is accurate indeed as calendars go.

That neolithic calendars in China were lunar is generally regarded as established. The two most likely year counts would necessarily be 384 days (13 lunations) or 354 days (12 lunations). Three hundred eighty-four, if used as a day count, seems to have resonances with the durations of other astronomical cycles of longer duration. To demonstrate these resonances, it is necessary to continue to apply the same principles of hierarchical extrapolation that link the sixty-four hexagrams to a duration of 384; that is, multiplication of subunits into larger modules via numbers inherent in the structure of the *I Ching:* Six or sixty-four. We suggest that the 384-day lunar year discussed above was viewed by the calendar makers of early China as a hexagram. This idea would have arisen as a natural consequence of observing the relationships between the six *yao* of a hexagram and the six small cycles of sixty-four days, each of which together formed the 384-day year. At this point in the process, it is reasonable to suppose that the Chinese love of cycles, hierarchies, and resonances would have led them, having cognized the 384-day year as a hexagram, to assume that 64

TABLE I   *Permutations of I Ching Hexagrams*

Base		Multiplier	Multiplicand	Astronomical Unit
64 days (# of hexagrams in *I Ching*)	×	6 (# of *yao* in a hexagram)	384 days	13 lunations
384 days	×	64 (# of hexagrams in a sequence)	67 solar years, 104.25 days	6 minor sunspot cycles (11.2 years)
67 solar years, 104.25 days	×	64 (# of hexagrams in a sequence)	4306+ solar years	2 Zodiacal Ages (1 per trigram), 4400 years approx.
4306+ solar years	×	6 (# of *yao* in a hexagram)	25,836 solar years	1 complete procession of the equinoxes, 26,000 years

----

FIGURE 16

Calendrical properties operating in the *I Ching* bear a relation to a lunar year of thirteen lunations and to the equinoctial precession, as well as to sunspot cycles.

× 384 days was a natural division of time. Once begun, the process need know no end. And indeed, 384 × 64 × 64 also shows interesting resonance periods. In fact, several phenomena that have been found to be cyclical appear to have relationships of correspondence to the calendrical hierarchy on one of its levels. As an example, we may point out that the 67.35-year cycle (384 days × 64) is composed of six *yao* cycles of 11.225 years; this is in astonishing agreement with the average sunspot cycle, whose duration is given as 11.2 years. What is perhaps even more startling is that the cycle of sunspot frequency discloses a 33.33-year period along with its 11.2-year period. The 33.67-year duration of the trigrammatic cycle is within one-third year of this duration. It is an established fact that sunspot cycles produce a periodicity in plant growth:

The growth of trees is accelerated during sunspot maxima; thus the eleven-year sunspot cycle is reflected in the increasing and decreasing width of the annual rings of trees. This effect is so reliable that archaeologists use it to date the establishment of ancient settlements. (Knoll, in Campbell 1967, p. 291)

Periodically, in mental hospital wards, aggressive patients show intense surges of activity . . . Such outbursts occur only sporadically but are striking enough to have invited study. At Douglas Hospital in Montreal, continuous, round-the-clock observation studies of patients over periods of several months did, indeed, show a picture of such periodic outbursts. Correlations between increased aggression and staff on duty, changes in menu, medication, or visiting days were too weak to explain the group behavior . . . When no explanation could be found, Dr. Heinz Lehmann compared his hospital data against data from the U.S. Space Disturbance Forecast Center in Boulder, Colorado. There appeared to be a correlation between solar flare activity (sun spots), geomagnetic disturbances, and excitement on the ward . . . Since sun flares are bursts of gaseous material, high energy particles that influence the ionosphere, causing changes in magnetic fields on earth, a relationship is not impossible. Sun storms sometimes cause a noticeable deflection in a compass needle. Perhaps, since the brain is at least as sensitive as a fine compass, it also responds to large magnetic disturbances. (Luce 1971, p. 14)

And sunspots were familiar to ancient Chinese:

As Ionides and Ionides have said, Chinese astrological conclusions were for once perhaps right in maintaining a connection between celestial and terrestrial phenomena. Though not at present generally admitted, it is not impossible that the sun-spot period may be connected, through meteorological effects, with events of social importance, such as good and bad harvests. Such a correlation is indeed maintained for Japanese rice crop famines since A.D. 1750 by Arakawa. Conceivably the basis of the association made in the *Chi Ni Tzu* book . . . between the 12-year Jupiter cycle and an agricultural production cycle, may really have been, as Chatley suggests, the 11-year sun-spot period. Correlations between the periodicity of sun-spot maxima and other phenomena such as aurorea, using in part Chinese data, have been attempted by several workers. (Needham 1954, vol. 2, p. 436)

One reason advanced for the use of a sexagenary cycle in the historical Chinese calendar is that it is perhaps five repetitions of the approximately twelve-year cycle of Jupiter (cf. above). Might it not be that five Jupiter cycles equaling one sixty-year cycle and the solar year calendar of 360 days were a clumsy replacement for an early sixty-four-year cycle of 384-day years (67+ solar years) that also very accurately kept the sunspot cycle of 11.2 solar years.

The earliest Chinese dynasty whose calendar is known is the Chou. According to W. Eberhard, a 384-day year did exist in late Chou times, although it was regarded as an intercalary year with the usual year of twelve months being 354 days. Seven such intercalary years were inserted in every nineteen years, that is, into the Lunar Metonic cycle (W. Eberhard, personal communication, 1974). This "mixed calendar" may represent a transition form from an earlier time when years of 384 days were used exclusively.

In addition to the correlations to lunations and sunspot cycles cited, there is yet another cycle of celestial movement that appears to be "built into" the hierarchical *I Ching* calendar. This cycle is the zodiacal world year generated by the slow precession of the equinoxes.

> . . . the equinoctial "points"—and therefore, the solstitial ones,
> too—do not remain forever where they should in order to make
> celestial goings-on easier to understand, namely, at the same spot
> with respect to the sphere of the fixed stars. Instead, they stub-
> bornly move along the ecliptic in the opposite direction to the
> yearly course of the sun, that is, against the "right" sequence of
> the zodiacal signs . . . This phenomenon is called the Precession
> of the Equinoxes, and it was conceived as causing the rise and the
> cataclysmic fall of ages of the world. Its cause is a bad habit of
> the axis of our globe, which turns around in the manner of a
> spinning top, its tip being in the center of our small earth-ball,
> whence our earth axis, prolonged to the celestial North Pole,
> describes a circle around the North Pole of the ecliptic, the true
> "center" of the planetary system, the radius of this circle being of
> the same magnitude as the obliquity of the ecliptic with respect to

the equator: 23 ½°. The time which this prolonged axis needs to circumscribe the ecliptical North Pole is roughly 26,000 years, during which period it points to one star after another: around 3000 B.C. the Pole star was alpha Draconis; at the time of the Greeks it was beta Ursea Minoris; for the time being it is alpha Ursea Minoris; in A.D. 14,000 it will be Vega. The equinoxes, the points of intersection of ecliptic and equator, swinging from the spinning axis of the earth, move along with the same speed of 26,000 years along the ecliptic. (de Santillana and von Dechend 1969, pp. 58–59)

Various mathematical treatments of the phenomenon of nutation (a small periodic motion of the celestial pole with respect to the pole of the ecliptic) introduce uncertainty into the duration of this year; de Santillana gives it as 25,920 years, while Flamerion shows it as 25,780. Both these figures are in disagreement with the value contained in standard astronomical tables, 25,725 years. We have already shown that 64 × 384 days gives a duration (67+ years), sixths and halves of which have relation to sunspots. When the 67+ year cycle is similarly treated (multiplied by 64), a duration of 4,302+ years is obtained. One-sixth of this number seems to have no significance astronomically; however, one-half of this number equals 2,153 years. This number is very close to the 2,200-year length of a "zodiacal year"—the number that results when the duration of the precession (25,700 years) is divided by the twelve zodiacal signs, giving zodiacal "ages" approximately 2,200 years in duration. The correlation is too close to be accidental. It can only enhance our respect for the prehistoric astronomy of the Chinese, since it has long been assumed that no one could have detected the equinoctial precession before it was allegedly discovered by Hipparchus in 127 B.C. It was natural that the Han astronomers should wish to incorporate into their astronomy the sidereal periods of planetary revolution. Their thought was that at the beginning of a world cycle there had been a general conjunction of the planets and that at the end of the world this would happen again. This notion of a general conjunction occurs in Hellenistic literature and may derive from Berossus and the Babylonians.

Discovery of calendrical properties operating in the *I Ching* that appear to bear a relation to a lunar year of thirteen cycles and to the zodiacal world year, as well as to sunspot cycles, suggests a possible historical speculation. The Chinese year has an average duration of 360 days. It is in essential agreement with the lunar Metonic year developed in fifth-century Athens. The thirteen-month lunar *I Ching* calendar is composed of 13 ×

29.53 days; $12 \times 29.53 = 354.4$ days, while a solar year is 365.25 days. The average of these numbers is 359.85, or within .15 of an average Chinese year. Richard Wilhelm (1964), in discussing the age of the *I Ching* and its attribution to the legendary figure Fu Hsi, says: "The fact that he (Fu Hsi) is designated as the inventor of the linear signs of the Book of Changes means that they have been held to be of such antiquity that they antedate historical memory" (p. xxxviii). Other scholars agree:

> Eberhard believes that it is possible to trace several local calendars in very ancient times and that it was this which gave rise to the idea that there had been official calendars of the Hsia, Shang and Chou "dynasties." Jao Tsung-I has described an interesting calendrical diagram, with text, inscribed on silk and of Chhu State provenance, dating from about the 4th century. Han calendars have been studied by Shinjō and by Eberhard & Henseling . . . (Needham 1954, vol. 2, p. 391)

It is possible to suggest that in neolithic China the sequence of 64 hexagrams $\times$ 6 was actually known and used as a calendar. This calendar was very early displaced by the more seasonally oriented, yet less astronomically functional 360-day solar year calendar.

One can only speculate how and why this may have happened. Perhaps the astronomical rationale behind the 384-day calendar had degenerated into a secret knowledge, confined to a ruling or priestly class that came into conflict with a popular, rationalistic, antiesoteric faction that sought the elimination of the thirteenth lunar cycle in order to reform the calendar to more nearly conform with the solar year. W. Eberhard (personal communication, 1974) has pointed out that traditionally in China the number thirteen has not been highly regarded; it is a prime number and as such is not reducible to two (female) or three (male) or four or nine. For the traditional Chinese, twelve preserves harmony and thirteen disturbs it. This Chinese attitude may be a clue to the non-Chinese origin of the *I Ching* and the thirteen-month lunar cycle calendar possibly associated with it. In Han times, the *I Ching* was called the *Chou I* and was assumed to have originated with that dynasty in the far northwest of China. A calendar and astronomy being introduced from outside of China would naturally encounter resistance.

If this controversy became overt and violent, we can imagine the occurrence of events similar to the book burning of 213 B.C., which may have resulted in all but complete destruction of the thirteen-month lunar calendar and knowledge of its relation to the hexagram sequence. The superstition that each new dynasty or reign period must make all things new is very old in China and has often resulted in changes in the calendar after times of social crisis. It would be some time after the adoption of a reformed solar calendar before the loss of astronomical utility through abandonment of the lunar 384-day calendar would be realized. After such a time, from the middle Chou onward, the knowledge of how to construct the lunar calendar may have existed only in scattered fragments and cryptic sayings such as represent the earliest extant commentary material on the *I Ching*. Wilhelm (1964) reproduces this material as the *Shuo Kua*—Discussion of the Trigrams. Some of the ambiguities in this material seem to be dissipated by the assumption that a hierarchical hexagram sequence calendar is being referred to.

The relative clumsiness of the traditional Chinese calendar seems to lend support to this idea that it conceals an older, reformed lunar calendar. The traditional Chinese calendar had an average length of 360 days, into which two intercalary months were inserted every five years. This means that a lunar year of twelve months would have 354.4 days per year, which is 5.6 days short of the average duration of 360 days. The solar year, on the other hand, is 5.25 days longer than the 360-day year. When 10.85, the sum of 5.25 + 5.6, is taken times 5 (the five years into which the two intercalary months are inserted), the result is 54.26 days, which is approximately five days less than exactly two lunar months. These calculations show that, in spite of the insertion of the two extra lunar months every five years, this calendar—if we assume lunar months of 29.53 days were used—would still gain 4.8 days every five years; compare this to the loss of one day every 454.5 lunar years for a thirteen-month lunar year of 384 days, with only one intercalary day every ten years. This latter represents a level of accuracy improved by a factor of many thousands. Even in comparison with the Gregorian calendar in use in the modern West, this calendar is more accurate by a factor well over one hundred. The Gregorian calendar adds one day every four years; the *I Ching* calendar adds one day every 454.5 of its 384-day years, with the insertion of one intercalary day every ten years. Even without this latter insertion, the proposed *I Ching* lunar calendar is more than twice as accurate as the Gregorian.

Insight into the Chinese view of calendars and their makers is afforded by examination of hexagram 49, Revolution. Hexagram 49 specifically connects great revolutions with calendrical reforms, and the Confucian commentary on the Image goes further and specifically connects the role of the shaman with that of a calendar maker: "The Image: Fire in the Lake, the Image of Revolution. Thus the Superior Man sets the calendar in order and makes the seasons clear" (Wilhelm 1964, p. 201). The Commentary interprets in part as follows: "Arrangement of the calendar is suggested by Tui which means a magician, a calendar maker" (Wilhelm 1964, p. 202). The Judgment adds:

> Times change, and with them their demands. Thus the seasons
> change . . . In the world cycle also there are Spring and Autumn
> in the life of peoples and nations, and all these call for social trans-
> formations . . . In the course of the year a combat takes place
> between the forces of light . . . and . . . of darkness, eventuating
> in the revolution of the seasons. Man masters these changes in
> nature by noting their regularity and marking off the passage
> of time accordingly. In this way order and clarity appear in the
> apparently chaotic changes of the seasons, and man is able to
> adjust himself in advance to the demands of the different times.
> (Wilhelm 1964, p. 202)

In the above, we suggest that the "changes of the seasons" may be a poor translation; since the progress of the seasons is not "apparently chaotic," a cycle of epochs or psychological "seasons" may be indicated. This entire passage appears to obliquely refer to the kinds of temporal cycles "hidden" in the *I Ching* and to hint at its esoteric function as a calendar and astronomical calculator.

Chapter 9

Order in the *I Ching* and Order in the World

L. L. Whyte pinpointed the problem at the center of the crisis in biology in his *Internal Factors in Evolution* (1965). Whyte says this:

> The fundamental spatial and temporal laws of the developing organization of local processes are still obscure.
>
> What is missing? Possibly knowledge of certain crucial facts, but certainly a sufficiently clear formulation of the problem. We cannot expect to understand organization until we know what we are looking for *in terms of mathematics* [italics mine]. The use of mathematical standards alone can clarify the aim of a theory of organization . . . The mathematical task, as I see it, is to identify the *Coordinative Conditions* (C.C.), i.e., the general algebraic conditions expressing the biological spatio-temporal coordination, the rules of ordering which must be satisfied (to within a threshold) by the internal parts and processes of any cellular organism capable of developing and surviving in some environment. The C.C. are the expression of geometrical, 3D, or perhaps kinematic rules determining the necessary 3D or spatio-temporal network of the relations of the atoms, ions, molecules, organelles, etc., in a viable organism. They are necessary in the individual, not merely statistical over assemblies. The C.C. must cover all the fundamental aspects of the unity of organisms . . .
>
> The C.C. are not merely *morphological,* expressing relative spatial positions and orientations within the ordered system (not in an arbitrary external frame), but *morphogenetic,* representing a one-way tendency towards the development of stationary forms. In other words the C.C. not only define an *invariant characteristic configuration* which tends to persist through all the normal transformations of the system (i.e., through growth, functioning, reproduction, etc.) but also a "dynamic" *tendency towards ordered equilibrium,* i.e., a self-ordered and self-stabilizing process. Thus the C.C. are the mathematical conditions which cover not only the *homeostatic* (feed-back control, etc.) properties of the organism, but also its *one-way* development. Indeed from a logical and mathematical point of view the stationary properties must be secondary consequences, arising under limiting conditions, of a

one-way developmental principle. Ontogenetic development is
theoretically primary to homeostasis and cyclic function.

    The C.C. may be a single set of conditions applying at all
levels of structure, from the nucleus of the germ cells to the organism as a whole, or they may be a hierarchy of conditions. They are
certainly *strong*, in the sense that they impose a high degree of
order, but they are *not maximal*, for they leave many parameters
free to vary (fluid regions, flexibility, mobility, learning, successful
mutations, etc.). (pp. 33–36)

Whyte discusses the schema of Coordinative Conditions as they might
be applied to living systems. Our own thought, in accordance with the
formative first principle of organismic philosophy as developed by Whitehead (cf. chapter 3), has been to extend the idea of organism to all processes and systems in the universe and therefore to seek a general systems
theory or set of C.C. quite as applicable to events on the macrogalactic or
inner-atomic levels as to the specifically biological realm. As Albert Wilson points out:

It is interesting to note that the gravitational potential of the universe is near the Schwartzchild Limit, the theoretical maximal
value for potential. These *quantitative* equivalences indicate that
there probably exist basic causal *qualitative* relations between the
structure of the universe and the properties of the atom and its
nucleus (the question of the direction of causality being open).
(A. Wilson, in Whyte et al. 1969, p. 120)

Whyte (1965), amplifies the character of the system theory being sought:

It will be recalled that the C.C. are the algebraic expression of the
3D geometrical and kinetic conditions determining the spatial and
temporal relations of parts and process in all viable organisms.
Our assumption here is that the conception of the C.C. and their
actual form will one day be as commonplace to structural biolo-
gists as Maxwell's equations are now to physicists. The C.C. are
out there in nature, just as much as Maxwell's equations. What
can be said of them today?

    They are certainly set in 3D space, not in some higher abstract
manifold. They are time-scaled, i.e., contain natural units of

length and time (or the equivalent), though in many circumstances organic structures and processes vary greatly in spatial and temporal scale. Moreover, the C.C. probably employ collective parameters, i.e., global variables associated with organic systems as a whole and their internal relations, and not with ultimate parts. The C.C. must be capable of representing both relatively stable structures and the formative processes which generate them . . .

. . . What is missing? Individual structural facts covering *stationary* aspects are being collected at an unprecedented rate, but the basic theoretical principles of a structural and *dynamic* synthesis are lacking. What character must these principles possess? What must be their aim?

The answer is surely beyond doubt. What is lacking is a *mathematical conception of the character of the unity of organism, and of organic subunits . . .* (pp. 103ff.)

Whyte goes on to pose seven questions inviting further research, three of which have special import for our own work:

4. In view of the unique theoretical scope of chiral (skew or screw) forms which are capable of determining both polar-electrical and axial-magnetic correlations, and of the prevalence of helical arrangements and left-handed amino acids in organisms, are the C.C. related to helical pulsations, i.e., to change in helical angles?

5. Do all vital processes involve pulsating structures undergoing simultaneous cycles of geometrical deformation and electro-magnetic polarization? If so do mutated genotypes have to be capable of conforming to such pulsations?

6. Are the C.C. the expression of an ordering tendency, related to the movement towards minimum potential energy of complex low temperature systems, which can account both for the genesis of life and for its maintenance? (1965, pp. 110–111)

With all of the preceding in mind, we now advance to our own version of the Coordinative Conditions and their interrelationships. Our operational premise has been that cognitive categories, memories, mentation, and even archetypal deep structures are phenomena whose genesis is to be sought in conformational changes at the molecular level; specifically, that such mental phenomena reflect dynamic processes and structural modifications mediated by DNA during the performance of its function of homeostatically regulating the organism and its storing of information as reflexes and memories. This premise, that cognitive categories reflect organizing principles at work in the physical structure of the human organism, allows us to examine abstract and symbolic systems of thought from a new point of view, from a point of view that asks, "What do the structures of rituals, divinatory processes, and other appealing and persistent, yet nonrational idea systems reflect concerning the physical organization schema that lie at the foundation of brain and mind?" This method was anticipated by Jung, who examined myth and religion to reveal the structure and dynamics of the psyche.

There can be little doubt that Jung regarded the *I Ching* as a repository of archetypes, just as the *I Ching* says of itself that it "contains the categories of all that is." "Stilling of the heart" techniques, physical techniques that retard normal autonomic processes and allow deep and sustained periods of inspection of the organization of the psyche are at the heart of Taoist yoga and Chinese alchemical thinking. It seems conceivable that, if one grants that the organization of the psyche reflects the organization of its physical foundations, shamanic and yogic techniques that allow deep insight into the organization of consciousness and its categories might also allow their practitioners to gain an intuitional sense of the nature of physical organization. In the West, the Pythagoreans exemplify an early philosophical school in possession of ecstatic techniques and concerned with the organization of matter. It is reasonable to suggest that these concerns were congruent in ancient China as well. Our intuition has been that consciousness could not fail to reflect the shifting modalities of the energy continuum of metabolism that is its ground. We believe time to be not a homogeneous medium, but a flux of variables or a field of nonstochastic perturbations of the flow of probability. We feel that the quantum theory was the announcement of the discovery of these laws in microphysical systems, and that elucidation of the nature of organism will somehow involve the extension of the idea of temporal variables into a hierarchical theory that recognizes quantized flux phenomena at every level of space-time organization.

The King Wen sequence of the *I Ching* represents for us, as well as for the ancient Chinese, a neolithic intuition concerning the structure of psychic time, arrived at through the slow growth of folk traditions concerning the nature and order of the internal categories. As mind arises out of organism and organism out of inorganic matter, is it possible that the *I Ching* sequence holds a reflection not only of psychic organization but also of the nature and order of the temporal variables that are its stated concern to describe? Such variables may be the formative boundary conditions with which evolving life had to cope, and which it came to reflect. In judging this hypothesis, we should not lose sight of the fact that all science is done in just this way; flashes of creative insight, which are nothing more than revelation of the organization of the psyche, are found to map onto a part of reality and thus are validated as true. Experiment always plays a part in such a process; we cannot know if experiments, as we would conceive them, were ever undertaken with regard to these theories. We know nothing of the methods of pre-Han science. The *I Ching* appears occult to the West, since we have an automatic assumption concerning the nature of time and causality. But this assumption hides from us the nature of time and organism. Perhaps the ancient Chinese were not so unfortunate. The dependency of Western physical science on physical instrumentality is so great that we cannot imagine achieving insight into the organization of matter without such instruments. Actually, an advanced psychology might achieve insight into the C.C. through entirely internalized techniques of manipulating and observing the organism. Since long before history, such techniques have been the special province of the shaman.

Before turning to the King Wen sequence of the sixty-four hexagrams of the *I Ching* and what that sequence may reveal of the order of the temporal variables, we should first examine some of the special properties that are possessed by the number sixty-four apart from any other considerations.

It is well known that sixty-four codons, of three nucleotide units, are used by DNA and RNA to specify amino acids used in protein synthesis. What is not so well known is the rule proposed by the anthropologist Anthony F. C. Wallace that limits the maximum number of entities that can be contained in a folk taxonomy to sixty-four. Since a taxonomy is a "map" of conceptual categories, his idea has importance for our own theory of conscious organization:

> . . . The hypothesis, which we shall call the "2^6 Rule," is, then, that *irrespective of race, culture, or evolutionary level, culturally institutionalized folk taxonomies will not contain more than 2^6 entities* and consequently will not require more than six orthogonally related binary dimensions for the definitions of all of the terms [italics his].
>
> . . . In the area of cultural semantics, we are suggesting that a somewhat similar principle applies . . . *the evolution of cultural*

complexity is limited, in so far as folk taxonomies are concerned, by
the two-to-the-sixth-power rule [italics his] . . . What is limited is
the complexity of the taxonomies which are components of the
various cultural sub-systems. (Wallace 1961, p. 462)

The *I Ching* is just such a taxonomy, "a group of symbols . . . which denote mutually exclusive but jointly exhaustive subsets of referents within a
set denoted by a cover symbol and which (unlike names) are defined by
unique combinations of values on two or more conceptual dimensions"
(Wallace 1961, p. 462).

Wallace's work supports our contention that there is a definite relation
between the categories of experiential archetypes and the numerical foundations of the *I Ching*. With that fact as a beginning, we turn our attention to the King Wen sequence of the sixty-four hexagrams to seek the
nature of the order of that sequence for what it might reveal about time
and metabolism.

The earliest arrangement of the hexagrams of the *I Ching* is the King
Wen sequence. It was this sequence that was chosen to be studied as a possible basis for a new model of the relationship of time to the ingression
and conservation of novelty. In studying the kinds of order in the King
Wen sequence of the *I Ching* a number of remarkable discoveries were
made. It is well known that hexagrams in the King Wen sequence occur in
pairs. The second member of each pair is obtained by inverting the first.
In any sequence of the sixty-four hexagrams there are eight hexagrams
that remain unchanged when inverted. In the King Wen sequence, these
eight hexagrams are paired with hexagrams in which each line of the first
hexagram has become its opposite (yang changed to yin and vice versa).

The question remains as to what rule or principle governs the arrangement of the thirty-two pairs of hexagrams comprising the King Wen sequence. Here we find ourselves in an intellectual terra incognita; no
known basis exists for determining why pairs are arranged as they are or
why one member of a pair precedes another. Our intuition in seeking a solution to these problems was to look at the first order of difference. First
order of difference refers to how many lines change as one moves through
the King Wen sequence from one hexagram to the next. The first order of
difference will always be an integer between one and six. When the first
order of difference within pairs is examined it is always found to be an
even number. Thus all instances of odd values for the first order of difference occur at transitions from one pair of hexagrams to the next pair.

When the complete set of first order of difference integers generated by the King Wen sequence is examined, they are found to fall into a perfect ratio of three to one; three even integers to each odd integer. The ratio of three to one is not a formal property of any or most sequences but was a carefully constructed artifact achieved by arranging hexagram transitions between pairs to generate fourteen instances of three and two instances of one. Fives were deliberately excluded. This exclusion of fives is also not a necessary property of the system. We may be sure that the King Wen sequence has been consciously constructed to discriminate against a change of five lines as one moves from one hexagram to another through the sequence. The case of hexagrams 38 and 39 is particularly instructive in this regard.

Previously we noted that, as a natural consequence of the system, there would be eight instances where inverting a hexagram would have no effect, and so all lines must be changed to their opposites. When we examine Table II (fig. 17), however, we find that there are in fact nine such cases. One, the synthetic case, is the transition from 38 to 39. If the arrangement of the thirty-two pairs was random, we could expect other instances where the second term in one pair and the first term in the following pair happened to be opposites with an order of difference of six. But, in fact, this situation occurs in the sequence only in this one case. If there was a conscious effort to include only the eight necessary pairs with the differences of six, why was the additional occurrence of the value allowed? The answer appears to be directly related to the absence of first order of difference values of five noted above. If the order of the natural pair 39 and 40 were to be reversed, the value of the change between 39 and 41, which would then follow 39, would be five. The fourteen threes and two ones constitute sixteen instances of an odd integer occurring out of a possible sixty-four. This is a three to one ratio exactly. As it is a property of the system that the transition values within pairs will give even values, we can conclude that of the transition values that could be consciously manipulated in a final arrangement, those were chosen in which the odd and even transitions were equally and exactly apportioned.

Our conclusion is that the King Wen sequence was ordered, aside from the already stated rules that generate the hexagram pairs, on the following rules:

1. Order among the thirty-two pairs was determined by a wish to absolutely exclude transition situations with a value of five.

TABLE II   *Change in the King Wen Sequence*
(First Order of Difference between Sequential Hexagrams)

HEXAGRAM 1 = 6	HEXAGRAM 17 = 6	HEXAGRAM 33 = 4	HEXAGRAM 49 = 4
2 = 2	18 3	34 = 4	50 = 4
3 = 4	19 4	35 = 4	51 = 4
4 = 4	20 3	36 = 2	52 = 1
5 = 4	21 2	37 = 4	53 = 6
6 = 3	22 2	38 = 6	54 = 2
7 = 2	23 2	39 = 4	55 = 2
8 = 4	24 3	40 = 3	56 = 3
9 = 2	25 4	41 = 2	57 = 4
10 = 4	26 2	42 = 4	58 = 3
11 = 6	27 6	43 = 2	59 = 2
12 = 2	28 2	44 = 3	60 = 1
13 = 2	29 6	45 = 4	61 = 6
14 = 4	30 3	46 = 3	62 = 3
15 = 2	31 2	47 = 2	63 = 6
16 = 2	32 3	48 = 3	64 = 3

Value	Times occurring	% of 64	Rank
1	2	3	2, 4, 3, 6, 1
2	20	31	5 does not occur
3	14	22	
4	19	30	
5	0	0	
6	9	14	
	———	———	
	64	100	

FIGURE 17

We viewed the King Wen sequence as a continuum and intuited that the ordering principle related to a quality that connected the unrelated pairs of hexagrams.
We were led to compare the first order of difference, or degree of change, as one
moves through the King Wen sequence.

2. Order among the thirty-two pairs was secondarily determined by a
similar wish to absolutely exclude transition situations with a value of one,
except in cases where this would interfere with rule (1). (Note: Only two

instances of transitions with a value of one occur, and both cases occur in situations where reversing the members of the pairs involved [pairs 53–54 and 61–62] would cause transition values of five.)

3. A three to one ratio of even to odd transitions was maintained.

As if these synthetic symmetries were not enough, in addition we find that when the first order of difference of the King Wen sequence is graphed it appears random or unpredictable (fig. 18A). However, when an image of the graph is rotated 180 degrees within the plane and superimposed upon itself, it is found to achieve closure at four adjacent points (fig. 18B).

While this closure might logically be expected anywhere in the sequence, it in fact occurs at the conventional beginning and end of the sequence.

More than 1.2 million hexagram sequences were randomly generated by computer (all sequences having the property possessed by the King Wen sequence that every second hexagram is either the inverse or the complement of its predecessor). Of these 1.2 million Wen-like sequences, 805 were found to have the properties of a three to one ratio of even to odd transitions, no transitions of value five, and the type of closure described previously. Such sequences were found to be very rare, occurring in only .07 cases or approximately one in every 1,769 of the Wen-like sequences.

For these reasons we were led to view the King Wen sequence as a profoundly artificial arrangement of the sixty-four hexagrams. Look carefully at figure 18B. Review in your mind the steps from the King Wen sequence that led to it. Notice that it is a complete set of the sixty-four possible hexagrams, running sequentially both forward and backward. Since it is composed of sixty-four hexagrams of six lines each, it is composed of 6 × 64 lines or 384 lines or *yao*. One might make an analogy and say that figure 18B is to the King Wen sequence as a cube is to a square. Figure 18B is composed of the same elements as the King Wen sequence but it has more dimensions.

The point that we wish to make in this discussion is that the first order of difference among the hexagrams, as they are read in a linear sequence, was consciously and deliberately ordered in very ancient times. Why this was done we cannot yet say, but the fact that it *was* done validates our contention the these mathematical qualities of the *I Ching* were factors of which the neolithic Chinese were well aware. Whether they graphed the first order of difference, as we have done in figures 18A and B, is moot. Graphing is not necessary; simple numerical quantification of the orders of difference gives the idea of the continuum of the sequence. Nevertheless, establishing the values of the first order of difference among the hexagrams

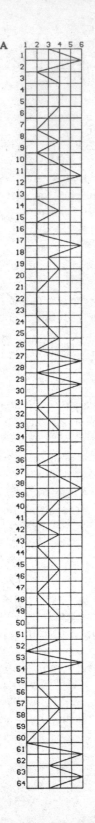

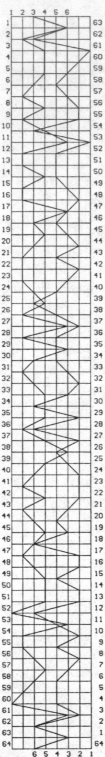

FIGURE 18

Graphing the first order of difference of the King Wen sequence displays a singularity: The first and last three positions have similar values. Thus closure occurs at both ends of the graph when it is rotated in two dimensions and placed next to itself (fig. 18B).

as a conscious part of the pre-Han traditions causes us to believe that it is valid to examine the graph to see why such care was taken with the order of its first order of difference values.

Although the graph appears relatively unstructured, it is evident that it contains a singularity: The first and last three positions of the graph are congruent mirror images of each other. Thus, congruence occurs at both ends of the graph when it is rotated in two dimensions and placed next to itself (cf. fig. 18B). While an arrangement with closure might have placed any two hexagrams opposite each other, what we in fact find is that the hexagrams opposite each other are such that the numbers of their positions in the King Wen sequence when summed are always equal to sixty-four.

The graph that this whole process generates (fig. 18B), or at least the two columns of value differences that are its numerical equivalent, seems to us to have been at the basis of the King Wen sequence. Our case has been thus far, we hope, a logical extension of qualities clearly important to those who organized the *I Ching* into the King Wen sequence.

Now we will turn to the question, why was this particular sequence of first orders of difference so important? What did it mean to its makers; what were they seeking to model with it? In chapter 8 we attempted to reason toward the structure of a multileveled hierarchical calendar that we believe was used in pre-Han China, a calendar based on the *I Ching* and simple mathematical extrapolations of it. In the present chapter we have argued that the King Wen sequence was ordered so as to give special attention to the first order of difference among the hexagrams, when they are taken in linear order. The nature of the first and last three of these first-order-of-difference values suggests that each was designed to be paired with its opposite number in a reversed sequence to form a backward- and forward-running continuum of the first order of difference. This continuum may be numerically displayed or actually graphed as in figure 18B.

To answer the question, "Why was this done?" we must recall the principles used to construct the calendrical hierarchy that emerged from chapter 8. We believe those principles should be applied to the graphic portrayal of the continuum of the backward- and forward-running sequence that the wave of figure 18B represents. Figure 18B is a graphic picture of the entire sequence of the *I Ching*, yet we propose that it was treated as the smallest unit in a series of hierarchical macro-hexagrams. In other words, we believe that the oracle-constructing Chinese viewed the complete set of forward- and backward-running valuations of the first order of difference of the King Wen sequence as equivalent to a line, a *yao*, and, therefore, open to the same manipulation as lines are subject to in the *I Ching* and the *I Ching* calendar; that is, multiplication by six and sixty-four.

Above, we stated the opinion that these operations were undertaken with a desire to portray what was known to the Chinese concerning time—observations made on the basis of a sophisticated and interiorized psychological view of the world. We believe that the quantum-mechanical parameters of mind eventually may have become accessible to observation and description through such an approach. A perfected organismic psychology might have evolved into a science of process in organism at every level of organization far more easily than the static Western physical sciences. The world as dynamic process, an idea basic to Vedic and Taoist viewpoints, makes the wave mechanics of postquantum physics seem quite natural, although in the Western scientific tradition it marks an extreme reorganization of thought that involves nothing less than the abandonment of determinism and materialism.

To extend our hypothesis, we will consider the space-time continuum as a modular wave-hierarchy. This hierarchy is composed of waves that have, on the most simple level, the configuration that is generated by figure 18B. The energy map of changes plotted backward upon itself forms pairs that, when added together, always equal sixty-four. The graph was seemingly constructed to be superimposed backward upon itself, suggesting to us that time was understood to function with the same holographic properties that have long been an accepted part of the phenomenon of the perception of three-dimensional space. This also suggests that interference patterns are characteristic of process. Living beings especially illustrate this: They are an instance of the superimposition of many different chemical waves, waves of gene expression and of gene inhibition, waves of energy release and energy consumption, forming the standing wave interference patterns characteristic of life.

We hypothesize that the wave description generated by this combining of the two graph lines is the simple form of a more complex wave that utilizes the simple wave of figure 18B as the primary unit in a system of such units, combined in the same way as lines are combined into trigrams and then hexagrams in the *I Ching* (cf. fig. 19). We will argue that this more complex wave (fig. 19) is a kind of temporal map of the changing boundary conditions that exist in space and time, including future time. Time, like light, may best be described as a union of opposites. Time may be both wave and, ultimately, particle, each in some sense a reflection of the other. We have called the quantized wave-particle, whatever its level of occurrence within the hierarchy or its duration, eschaton (fig. 19):

. . . Koestler addresses the question of what to call entities that belong to hierarchical systems. They have two aspects, ". . . the functional units on every level of the hierarchy are double-faced as it were; they act as wholes when facing downwards, as parts when facing upwards." (Koestler 1967.) He elects to designate these "Janus-faced" entities by the term *holon* (from the Greek *holos* = whole plus the suffix *on* as in proton or neutron suggesting a particle or part). We note that Gerard uses the term *org* to designate the same concept . . . (D. Wilson, in Whyte et al. 1969, p. 288)

This construct may best be understood as a reflection in the temporal dimension of the patterns that impart structural order to organisms and their view of the world. Space-time within this idea model is entirely composed of these hierarchically nested waves. Each such wave is exactly like all the others, their differences arising out of their relational positions in the hierarchy. Each wave, by itself, contains the entire modular hierarchy through its being a reflection of organization on higher and lower levels in an extensive continuum (cf. fig. 19). These wave systems, in duplicating themselves on various levels, lose none of their original properties. We hoped to map temporal variables using a wave-mechanical and holographic theory which holds that the ingression of novelty into the temporal continuum might conform to the wave described in figures 18B and 19.

The claim that any spatiotemporal span can be described by wave mechanics may sound deterministic, but such is not the case. The nature of time is conditioned by space and vice versa, so that the individual, by utilizing energy in proper ways, can go to the places and think the thoughts that will hold him (within the vicissitudes of the wave-hierarchy as it constellates his historical position) as close to an ideal as possible. An organism is confronted with possibilities just as a particle is confronted with probabilities:

The initial state will be represented, complete with the uncertainties which it involves, by a certain initial form of the associated wave. The later changes of the wave can be predicted exactly by the equations of Wave Mechanics: but this does not mean an absolute Determinism for the corpuscle, since knowledge of the wave at every instant only enables us to assign certain probabilities to the various hypotheses tenable as to the position and momentum of the corpuscle. In a word, then, while the older Mechanics claimed to apply exact and inexorable laws to every phenomenon,

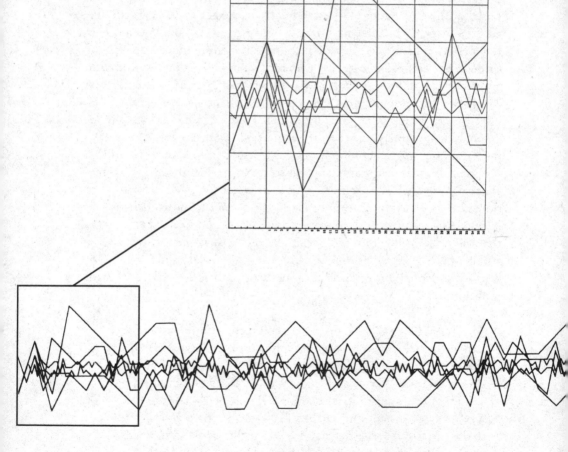

FIGURE 19

The Eschaton is a universal and fractal morphogenetic field, which was hypothesized to model the unfolding predispositions of space and time. This structure was decoded from the King Wen Sequence of the *I Ching* and was the central idea that evolved in the wake of the events of La Chorrera. The complex three-leveled form utilizes figure 18B as its primary unit. Six such structures in a linear arrangement compose the smallest level of the eschaton, two make up the middle level, and a single large version of 18B is superimposed over these and becomes a third level unifying the other two. This arrangement is similar to the structure of a hexagram: six lines form two trigrams, which in turn compose a hexagram.

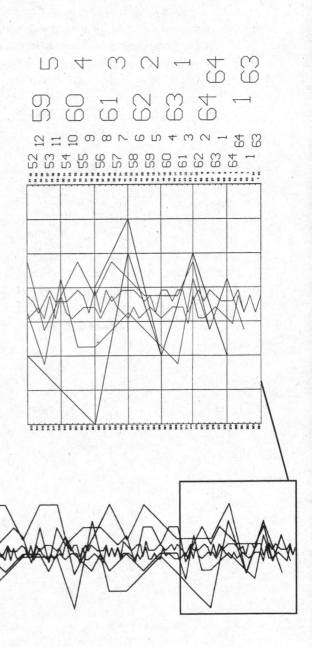

the new Physics only gives us laws of probability, and though these can be expressed in exact formulae, they still remain laws of probability. Thus in every physical phenomenon there remains a margin of uncertainty; and it is possible to ascertain that this margin of uncertainty is measured, in a way, by the constant, h. Figuratively, it has been said that there was a crack in the wall of physical Determinism, whose size was measured by Planck's constant, h; and thus the latter receives a somewhat unexpected interpretation: it is supposed to be the limiting barrier of Determinism. (De Broglie 1970, p. 246)

These ideas have implications for the physicist, philosopher, and psychologist. Simply put, we are saying that the wave-hierarchy of energy that regulates the ingression of novelty into time thus constellates the world of our experience in its entirety and therefore also in all of its possible subsets, so that in any span of time or space, if one can determine where to begin the generation of the wave description, space-time under examination will be quantified relative to an ideal zero state to as great a depth as one wishes to resolve the levels in the wave-hierarchy. This explication is quantitative, and yet may also utilize the linguistic framework that the *I Ching* commentaries provide.

Chapter 10

The King Wen Sequence as a
Quantified Modular Hierarchy

Chapter 9 introduced the simple wave we have construed out of the King Wen sequence through a particular graphing technique. In chapter 9, use of the simple wave as the primary unit in a modular hierarchy was alluded to and exhibits were offered to demonstrate the ordering principles of the King Wen sequence. This simple wave of the backward- and forward-running transitions in a single complete King Wen sequence of the *I Ching* (fig. 18B) can easily serve to model the physical structure of a single helical strand of DNA and its transformations: replication, duplication, and RNA transcription. These are *in vitro* functions of DNA and do not shed light on the dynamic and harmonic relations that exist in the *in vivo* world of the cell nucleus. The single-strand functions of DNA are well understood, but systems properties that appear in a living cell have not even begun to be clarified.

If the constant intercalation of 5HT into bond sites between codons, now a recognized part of 5HT metabolism (cf. fig. 9), does significantly alter ESR patterns in DNA, then it seemed likely to us that interference patterns that such a shifting of ESR signatures would generate might provide the mechanism for the hologramatic standing wave that the living system has developed to model within itself the world it encounters beyond itself. Only 10 percent of DNA is involved in protein synthesis. The functions of the other 90 percent are uncertain, but we suggest that an organism's entire internal horizon of experience is created and maintained in the energy continuum, which neural DNA regulates and maintains. Thought and reflection may be holographic functions that take place against the background of the energy flow of metabolism that DNA controls. It is this flow of energy that is experienced by organisms as the phenomenon of time itself. Organisms evolved in and became patterned in response to this flow.

We hoped to apply the idea of a modular hierarchy to the simple wave, using the kinds of resonance cycles our calendrical studies implied, and thus to generate maps of the continuum of temporal variables. If our speculation is sound, such maps should function as graphs of the continuum of metabolic energy, which we call time, and should thus have relevance to the individual and to his or her life—the ontogenetic expression of

DNA—as well as to history or species' time, which is DNA's phylogenetic expression. To do this, we have chosen to treat the simple wave (fig. 18B), which is itself a composite expression of the entire *I Ching*, as a primary unit in a hierarchy in which every level is structured on the same principles as are the levels above and below it. This is termed a *modular hierarchy:*

> The central idea in a modular hierarchy is the *module* which is a structure or a system that may be regarded both as a *whole*, decomposible into submodules identified with a lower level, and as a *part* combinable into super-modules identified with a higher level.
> . . . The term "module" being used here in this general sense need not be precisely defined, however, we may ascribe two fundamental properties to modules. First, a module possesses some sort of closure or partial closure (Wilson 1969). This closure may be topological, temporal, or defined by some operational rule as in group theory. Second, modules possess a degree of semi-autonomy with respect to other modules and to their context. These two properties appear to be common in all modular hierarchies. (A. Wilson, in Whyte et al. 1969, p. 115)

Recall from chapter 8 that the primary unit in the *I Ching* is the line, or *yao.* A full sequence of sixty-four hexagrams contains 384 *yao.* Hierarchically situated above the *yao* is the hexagram, composed of six *yao,* which traditionally has been divided into two subunits of three lines each. Such subunits are called trigrams, and two trigrams form one hexagram. Following the same principles of construction, we have arranged six simple graphs in sequential order. These are analogous to the six lines of a hexagram. Over these we have superimposed, in sequential order, two more simple waves, each three times the size of the six small waves. These two larger waves are equivalent to the two trigrams in any hexagram. Superimposed over the sequence of six and two is a final simple wave, standing for the entire hexagram, a single wave six times larger than the six waves on the primary level and twice as large as the two waves on the intermediate level (cf. fig. 19). The three-leveled structure thus generated is a more detailed version of the simple graph (fig. 18B) and is analogous to a hexagram. When this modular hierarchy is extended to further levels, this complex wave preserves the relation of a single hexagram to the entire *I Ching* sequence, becoming part of a still larger hierarchy of which it is only $1/64$ of the whole. Each tri-leveled module exists as $1/64$ of a still larger module. Such a complex wave has at its primary level 384 parts in sixty-four primary subunits, just as the complete *I Ching* sequence of sixty-four hexagrams has 384 *yao*. We know that a duration of 384 days is nearly exactly thirteen lunar cycles. Given this and the idea that organic macromolecules may have arisen in response to periodicities in astrophysical forces, especially gravity, we suggest that lunar cycles may have had a formative influence on the structural organization of the DNA. We also speculate that a cycle of lunar influences of 384 days' duration may be a kind of natural calendar important to all life that has evolved on earth. Such a 384-day lunar cycle would be a primary cycle of biological importance and might be a subset in a hierarchy sixty-four times larger than itself. We have called such a 384-day cycle a lunar year and believe such a year to be but one level in a hierarchy of many levels, each described by the wave of figure 19.

Such a hierarchy would require twenty-six levels to describe the totality of temporal existence. Our assumption was that figure 19 is descriptive of all, and any one, of these levels. When figure 19 is used as a 384-day lunar calendar, each day is entirely under the hexagramatic influence of three pairs of hexagrams, one part on each of the three levels. It is the influence of smaller cycles on each level (cf. Table III, fig. 20) that adds the "color," tone, and feel to the experience of being, and it is these lesser scales and the interphases between them that are responsible for those "minute particulars" that give life its depth and ambiguity and render a deterministic prediction concerning a spatiotemporal moment impossible. General predictions based on larger time scales form the empirical basis of our investigation of this sort of *I Ching* hierarchy and its relation to time.

A lunar year is a temporal process that forms a hexagram, a total energy *gestalt*, in space-time. This form requires 6×64 days to complete, because it is composed of six parts (lines or *yao*), each of which requires sixty-four days to complete itself. Not only is a lunar year $\frac{1}{64}$ of a larger cycle, which is $\frac{1}{64}$ of a still larger cycle (cf. Table I, fig. 16), but the lunar year is itself composed of sixty-four parts, each described by the same complex wave that models it. These "hexagrams" are of six days' duration. Such six-day cycles are themselves wholes composed of sixty-four parts, each a replica of the whole and so on down through shorter and shorter cycles until cycles are reached whose duration is on the order of Planck's constant. Further division of time cycles has no meaning for physics, and so it is here that divisions cease. It is at this level that the modular hierarchy has its ground and origin. Our view is that various temporal levels are overtonal harmonics of a quantum-mechanical flux of cyclical and irreducible temporal variables. If one entertains the idea that our universe may possess such a time scheme, one is led to contemplate the problem of the nature and necessity

TABLE III   *The Levels and Durations of the Temporal Hierarchy**

1	2.280×10^{18} sec	(72.25 billion [10^9] years)	divided by 64 =
2	3.562×10^{16} sec	(1.129 million [10^9] years)	" " " "
3	5.566×10^{14} sec	(17, 638,000 years)	" " " "
4	8.697×10^{12} sec	(275,600 years)	" " " "
5	1.359×10^{11} sec	(4,306 years, 97.5 days)	" " " "
6	2.123×10^{9} sec	(67 years, 104.25 days)	" " " "
7	3.318×10^{7} sec	(384 days – 13 lunations)	" " " "
8	5.184×10^{5} sec	(6 days)	" " " "
9	8.100×10^{3} sec	(135 minutess)	" " " "
10	1.266×10^{2} sec	(127 seconds)	" " " "
11	1.978 sec	(1.98 seconds)	" " " "
12	3.090×10^{-2} sec	(.03 seconds)	" " " "
13	4.828×10^{-4} sec	(range of low-frequency sound) "	" " "
14	7.544×10^{-6} sec	(range of low-frequency radio) "	" " "
15	1.179×10^{-7} sec	(range of high-frequency radio) "	" " "
16	1.842×10^{-9} sec	(range of ultra-high- frequency radio)	" " " "
17	2.877×10^{-11} sec	(range of extremely high- frequency radio)	" " " "
18	4.496×10^{-13} sec	(range of infrared)	" " " "
19	7.026×10^{-15} sec	(range of visible spectrum)	" " " "
20	1.098×10^{-16} sec	(range of x-ray radiation)	" " " "
21	1.715×10^{-18} sec	(range of gamma radiation)	" " " "
22	2.680×10^{-20} sec	(range of gamma radiation)	" " " "
23	4.188×10^{-22} sec	(range of gamma radiation)	" " " "
24	6.543×10^{-24} sec	(range of gamma radiation)	" " " "
25	1.022×10^{-25} sec	(range of gamma radiation)	" " " "
26	1.597×10^{-27} sec	(range of Planck's constant)	

* All second values were calculated to twelve significant integers and then rounded off to four.

FIGURE 20

Table III displays a modular hierarchy of temporal intervals requiring twenty-six levels to describe the totality of temporal existence. Our notion was that Figures 19, 25, and 26 are descriptive of all and any one of these levels.

scheme, one is led to contemplate the problem of the nature and necessity of the final time such a theory requires.

The eventual result of a self-enfolding of the temporal continuum at levels of the hierarchy of long duration might be likened to a visible condensation of the hologram of mind expressed as a radiant image, a standing waveform. Organisms are involved in a process of endlessly refining their cognition of the world. No final projection of the nature of this phenomenon can be made, and, in fact, even though every statement is a part of the truth, it is also very much defined by the boundary conditions under which it was formulated. During the second century, the Alexandrian thinkers, specifically Clement, focused their attention, when dealing with the Apocalypse, on the nature of the resurrection body; the question of the time of the appearance of the Son of Man was deemed a matter of lesser interest:

> In that Great Day men will be reunited to their bodies. This is the undoubted assurance of the Scripture. But it constituted one of the great difficulties of the time. Christians were perplexed by it; heathen controversialists poured upon it unmixed ridicule and scorn. Origen, like Clement, found a solution of all his doubts in the teaching of St. Paul; but he refined upon this in a way peculiar to himself. The resurrection body will be the same that we now inhabit, and yet not the same. Not the same because spiritual and glorious, because again its material substance will be entirely different. Yet the same, as our body of today is the same with our body of twenty years ago; every particle is changed, yet the body as a whole is not changed. The soul has a vital assimilative "spark" or "principle," which lays hold of fitting matter, and shapes it into a habitation suited to its needs. The same process by which it repairs the daily waste of our organisms now will enable it then to construct a wholly new tenament for itself. The Origenist monks are said to have believed that the Resurrection Body would be spherical, and this opinion is charged upon Origen by Justinian.
> (Bigg 1913, pp. 271–272)

The theory of shared genetic memory and DNA bioelectronic reflection of its environment may yet yield sufficient data for a relatively clear understanding of humanity's (and the shaman's) persistent intuition of an afterlife and the collective transformation, which we suspect is imminent and is creating the present shock of chaos at the end of history. The question of the moment of this true rupture of plane is difficult; it seems most millenarian speculations decode as giving critical importance to the age in which they were composed.

In a modular hierarchy of space-time such as we propose, the total energy resident in the continuum can be supposed to be totally resident in each resonant subset. This idea follows necessarily from the assumption of organismic thought that the entire hierarchical continuum is resident in its modular parts. The fold of temporal limitation and particularity that defines a nexus of space-time is the place where modes of connection typical of a higher spatial dimension ingress into the world of normal space-time. That place is, in a sense, everywhere; that is, it is potentially anywhere. The modules are members of a quantized, or discretely expressed, hierarchical structure that on each level manifests the same form met in the primary level. The problem of the moment of the involution of such a temporal hierarchy into its short epochs is interesting. As moderns and necessarily skeptics, we have assumed that although the hypothesis points toward an eventual involution of the temporal manifold, a concrescence, there is little likelihood of such an event occurring in the immediate present.

We believe space-time to be a flux of novelty whose variables are predictable. Using this supposition, we shall attempt to quantify the ebb and flow of temporal parameters and, thus, to chart the future course of novel ingressions into space-time (cf. Appendix). This is not, in principle, a difficult task. What is required is a logically coherent technique for assigning a quantified value to every point in the modular hierarchy. Empirical investigation of a hypothesis of a flux of temporal parameters cannot go forward until this is done. Quantification of every point in the hierarchy, with the ideal and terminal state quantified as zero, would give a relative scale of values. We used these relative values to map the intensity of novelty's ingression into the history of space-time. We did this to research the contention that this schema does map novelty's ingression into the real world. Only through quantification can a consensus concerning the meaning of the wave be achieved; otherwise, the wave and its interpretation are no better than a mystical doctrine. We have achieved a quantification of the wave through a set of operations that are at once logically rigorous and at the same time preserve our intuitions concerning what the graph is. Our attack on this problem began with an examination of the simple wave of figure 18B.

Thirteen discrete line types comprise any simple version of the graph. These thirteen lengths are displayed in figure 21. As these lengths are

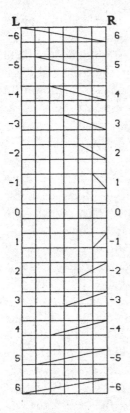

FIGURE 21

Thirteen discrete line types comprise the simple
version of the wave in figure 18B. To quantify
the degree and direction of skew of individual
lines, one direction of skew is designated positive, the other negative. L values are used for the
left side of the simple wave and R values are used
for the right side.

always discrete units, we can assign to them values that are ascending integers. The values in figure 21 allow a quantification of line length. To quantify the degree and direction of skew of individual lines, one direction of
skew is designated as positive, giving lines skewed in that direction positive values. Lines skewed in the opposite direction are given negative values. This gives values adequately preserving and quantifying line length
and direction of skew. The values labeled L in figure 21 are used for the
left side of a simple wave while the values labeled R, which are the same
values but with their sign reversed, are applied to the right side of any simple wave. Since the sign is important only in combining values across
scales but is ignored in the final graphing of combined values, either set of
values may be applied to either the right or left side. However, whichever
schema is chosen must then be followed throughout. Figure 22 represents
the version of the values of the simple graph that we have used.

It is important to note that the valuations in figure 22 are valuations of
the simple wave on the smallest scale of a single complex wave. The relative proportions of the three levels in the complex wave are preserved and

quantified by multiplying the valuations of the linear scale in the appropriate way. To assign a value to a position on the trigramatic scale, the valuation of that position on the linear scale (fig. 22) is multiplied by three because the trigramatic scale is three times larger than the linear scale. In a similar manner, the hexagramatic positions are assigned a valuation by multiplying their linear-level valuations by six, again because the hexagramatic scale is six times larger than the linear. Figure 22 uses the value scheme in figure 21 and is the version of value assignments we have used in all our calculations.

Note that in figure 22 all parallel lines, regardless of the distances separating them, reduce to zero. Thus, while the operations discussed so far have allowed quantification of skew direction, proportional ratios of the wave's parts, and the degree of departure from the parallel state, they have not provided a quantified account of the fluctuating distances between the two parameters of the wave. The procedure for obtaining these values is similar to, but distinct from, the procedures outlined above.

Figure 23 shows the seven types of divergence, congruence, and overlap that points in the simple wave may display. The two possible assignments of positive and negative numbers are shown to the right and left sides in figure 23. We have chosen to use the right-hand schema to preserve the intuition that overlap tends to carry a situation toward the zero state rather than away from it. Figure 24 shows the values this series of point assignments generates when applied to the simple wave. In figure 25 the valuation for skew, parallelism, and relative proportion have been combined in the manner discussed above. The 384 positions and their corresponding values are the quantification of the trileveled wave of figure 19. These same values are graphed as a single line graph in figure 26. Figure 25, which is the data base of figure 26, is the primary valuation scheme for any complex wave, and the process of quantifying a given time in the modular hierarchy of complex waves will necessarily begin with reference to the values of figure 25.

Figure 26 graphs composite values for a single complex wave. These values are displayed in figure 25. Figure 26 reduces the complex, trileveled, bidirectionally flowing complex wave of figure 19 to a single line moving in only one direction. Figure 26 preserves certain qualities of the complex wave (fig. 19): its divergence from the zero state where lines are parallel, the direction and degree of skew of pairs of lines, the relative proportions of the three levels, and the distances between the fluctuating parameters of the various component waves. Figure 26 does not reflect the shift of values that would occur if the single-line complex wave were nested into a partic-

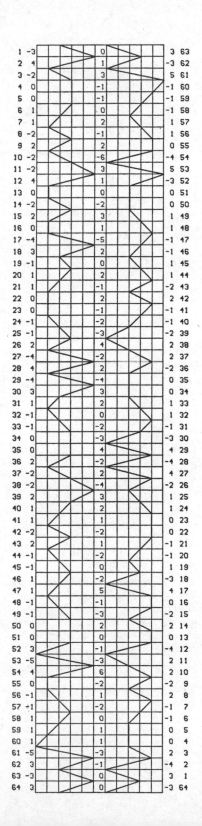

1	-3	0	3	63
2	4	1	-3	62
3	-2	3	5	61
4	0	-1	-1	60
5	0	-1	-1	59
6	1	0	-1	58
7	1	2	1	57
8	-2	-1	1	56
9	2	2	0	55
10	-2	-6	-4	54
11	-2	3	5	53
12	4	1	-3	52
13	0	0	0	51
14	-2	-2	0	50
15	2	3	1	49
16	0	1	1	48
17	-4	-5	-1	47
18	3	2	-1	46
19	-1	0	1	45
20	1	2	1	44
21	1	-1	-2	43
22	0	2	2	42
23	0	-1	-1	41
24	-1	-2	-1	40
25	-1	-3	-2	39
26	2	4	2	38
27	-4	-2	2	37
28	4	2	-2	36
29	-4	-4	0	35
30	3	3	0	34
31	1	2	1	33
32	-1	0	1	32
33	-1	-2	-1	31
34	0	-3	-3	30
35	0	4	4	29
36	2	-2	-4	28
37	-2	2	4	27
38	-2	-4	-2	26
39	2	3	1	25
40	1	2	1	24
41	1	1	0	23
42	-2	-2	0	22
43	2	1	-1	21
44	-1	-2	-1	20
45	-1	0	1	19
46	1	-2	-3	18
47	1	5	4	17
48	-1	-1	0	16
49	-1	-3	-2	15
50	0	2	2	14
51	0	0	0	13
52	3	-1	-4	12
53	-5	-3	2	11
54	4	6	2	10
55	0	-2	-2	9
56	-1	1	2	8
57	-1	-2	-1	7
58	1	0	-1	6
59	1	1	0	5
60	1	1	0	4
61	-5	-3	2	3
62	3	-1	-4	2
63	-3	0	3	1
64	3	0	-3	64

FIGURE 22

The values of figure 21 are used to quantify the degree and direction of skew of the simple wave of figure 18B. The exterior columns of numbers are hexagram numbers, the interior columns of numbers are the quantified values.

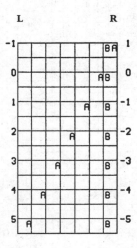

FIGURE 23

The seven types of divergence, congruence, and overlap that end points of line segments of the simple wave of figure 18B may display.

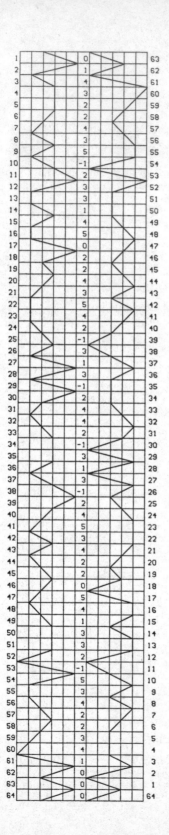

FIGURE 24

The values generated when the right-hand series of point valuations of figure 23 are applied to the simple wave of figure 18B. The exterior columns of numbers are hexagrams and the interior columns are the quantified values.

ular position in a modular hierarchy of complex waves, each level of which was sixty-four times larger than its predecessor. In such a case, figure 26 would serve as a schema of values to be combined through superimposition with the values associated with whichever one of the sixty-four segments of the next largest level it is to be nested in. These latter values have first been multiplied by sixty-four, indicating their membership in the next larger level in the hierarchy. Thus, sixty-four variants of figure 26 would be generated, and it is these variant waves that we have treated as the temporal maps of a given historical span. The mathematical details of the nesting of one level of the hierarchy in another have been implemented in the Timewave Zero software. Peter Meyer has contributed a mathematical formulation of the theory in the Appendix, pp. 211–220. The components of the valuation of each of the 384 positions in figure 19 are shown in figure 25. The values displayed in figure 25 are the basis of the quantified maps of temporal flux upon which rests this notion of a fractal and hierarchical structure of time. Note that the order of the values in figure 25 are the reverse of the order of the values as plotted in figure 26.

The last three of the 384 segments of the wave on any level possess singularities that quantify as zero (fig. 26, lower right corner). When the wave on a given level enters those segments of itself that are zero states, it ceases to contribute boundary constraints to its subsets on lower levels. The cessation of boundary constraints imposed by higher levels in the hierarchy causes a quantized drop toward the zero state each time that a cycle enters its terminal phase on any level in the hierarchy. Such quantized transitions from one modality to another are called "changes of epochs" by Whitehead. The appearance of life in an inorganic world, of consciousness in an unconscious world, or of language in a world without language are all examples of such epochal transitions. Our lives are filled with such transitions, but they are terminations of relatively short cycles in the quantified hierarchy. Terminations of cycles or epochs of really long duration cause extreme accelerations toward the zero state. This idea is similar to Whitehead's conception of concrescence and the Vedic conception of world ages that grow shorter as they tighten around an axis point. The spiral image of the Christian Apocalypse is another example of this intuition that time is a series of tightening cycles around a quantized transformation (cf. Cohn 1970).

A perfect, self-consistent proof that figure 26 does adequately conserve four qualities—divergence from the zero state where lines are parallel, the direction and the degree of skew of pairs of lines, distances between the parameters of the component waves, and the proportions of these three

Quantification Values

Pos	Value	Pos	Value	Pos	Value	Pos	Value	Pos	Value	Pos	Value
1	10	33	38	65	31	97	32	129	43	161	44
2	13	34	28	66	34	98	22	130	40	162	34
3	12	35	38	67	41	99	32	131	47	163	55
4	20	36	32	68	40	100	4	132	46	164	57
5	20	37	44	69	38	101	4	133	38	165	53
6	22	38	47	70	33	102	7	134	36	166	50
7	36	39	49	71	38	103	27	135	41	167	52
8	38	40	33	72	34	104	30	136	52	168	53
9	32	41	37	73	26	105	34	137	62	169	25
10	32	42	32	74	17	106	25	138	47	170	20
11	33	43	51	75	18	107	23	139	43	171	24
12	33	44	47	76	48	108	23	140	45	172	17
13	41	45	49	77	50	109	49	141	47	173	19
14	34	46	41	78	43	110	40	142	31	174	10
15	39	47	40	79	38	111	51	143	36	175	36
16	40	48	37	80	33	112	19	144	43	176	37
17	32	49	63	81	35	113	11	145	23	177	29
18	32	50	63	82	23	114	15	146	19	178	48
19	39	51	62	83	25	115	44	147	21	179	49
20	44	52	71	84	24	116	41	148	30	180	50
21	40	53	77	85	41	117	47	149	32	181	29
22	33	54	75	86	40	118	48	150	31	182	37
23	33	55	26	87	38	119	49	151	42	183	32
24	32	56	30	88	41	120	47	152	41	184	30
25	40	57	26	89	45	121	53	153	31	185	26
26	50	58	22	90	43	122	52	154	32	186	27
27	44	59	23	91	71	123	53	155	26	187	38
28	17	60	28	92	79	124	43	156	34	188	43
29	20	61	35	93	68	125	38	157	5	189	38
30	22	62	33	94	66	126	36	158	9	190	36
31	37	63	33	95	70	127	42	159	13	191	36
32	39	64	30	96	68	128	42	160	45	192	36

FIGURE 25

Displays the values associated with each of the 384 positions in the complex wave of figure 19. All calculations involving valuations of any point in the *I Ching* hierarchy will begin with reference to these values.

Pos	Value	Pos	Value	Pos	Value	Pos	Value	Pos	Value	Pos	Value
193	34	225	14	257	49	289	14	321	61	353	38
194	37	226	24	258	52	290	18	322	52	354	36
195	36	227	22	259	35	291	16	323	51	355	53
196	44	228	24	260	34	292	30	324	50	356	47
197	44	229	38	261	32	293	26	325	26	357	55
198	46	230	41	262	27	294	29	326	28	358	56
199	38	231	43	263	32	295	33	327	29	359	60
200	34	232	23	264	28	296	36	328	40	360	63
201	44	233	21	265	32	297	40	329	50	361	25
202	26	234	22	266	35	298	31	330	35	362	20
203	31	235	41	267	36	299	29	331	57	363	24
204	33	236	41	268	30	300	29	332	57	364	17
205	37	237	39	269	28	301	49	333	55	365	19
206	40	238	65	270	31	302	40	334	61	366	14
207	41	239	64	271	30	303	51	335	62	367	16
208	42	240	61	272	37	304	19	336	57	368	13
209	44	241	47	273	25	305	21	337	19	369	15
210	44	242	51	274	53	306	21	338	23	370	24
211	33	243	52	275	51	307	34	339	21	371	25
212	38	244	53	276	56	308	35	340	26	372	26
213	34	245	41	277	47	309	23	341	26	373	5
214	27	246	55	278	46	310	46	342	27	374	13
215	27	247	28	279	44	311	41	343	30	375	8
216	26	248	30	280	47	312	45	344	29	376	6
217	42	249	26	281	51	313	41	345	21	377	2
218	40	250	42	282	49	314	42	346	22	378	3
219	42	251	43	283	57	315	43	347	24	379	4
220	47	252	40	284	53	316	43	348	22	380	7
221	50	253	53	285	56	317	42	349	35	381	2
222	52	254	51	286	64	318	42	350	39	382	0
223	19	255	51	287	64	319	60	351	43	383	0
224	17	256	48	288	66	320	60	352	39	384	0

FIGURE 26

The Eschaton Mathematically Formalized

Here the complex three-leveled structure of figure 18 is seen at the bottom, and the waveform that is the result of its quantification appears as the single line graph in the middle. This wave is the formal equivalent of the more complex structure in figure 18 from which it derives. A blowup of the end point of the wave displays details of its fractal nature. According to the notion of temporal dynamics put forth here, this terminal section of the wave is where novelty is predicted to aggregate. The quantification achieved here moved this speculation from the merely hypothetical into a realm where empirical investigation of the descriptive and predictive potential of the waveform vis-à-vis history and biological evolution could proceed along ordinary scientific lines.

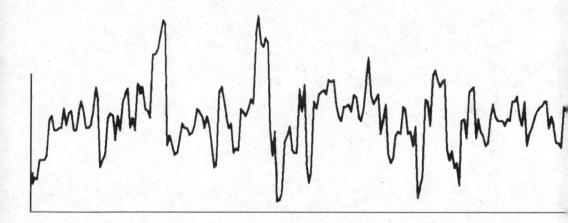

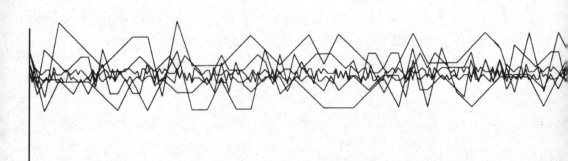

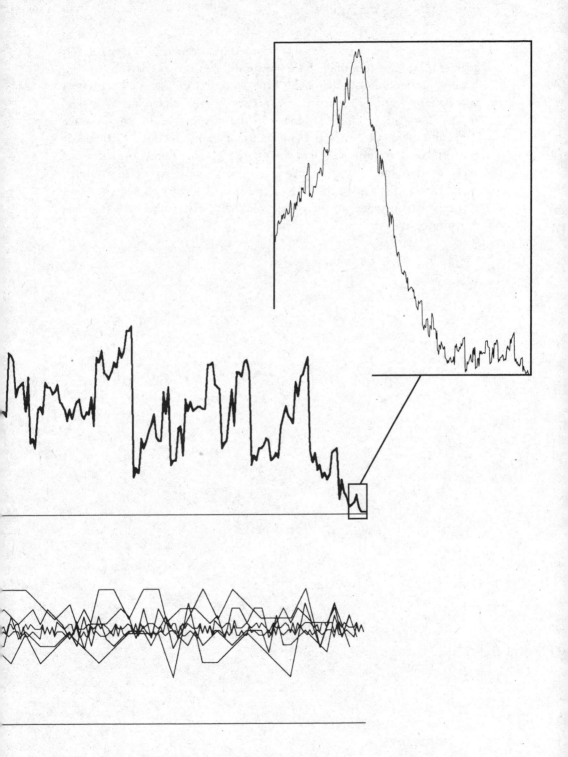

qualities relative to other levels—is afforded by comparing any two graph segments assigned to a single time but on different scales relative to an arbitrary termination date that is the same for both. Any two such segments will be found to be similar in form yet preserving their relative proportions. This demonstrable fact confirms the idea that the complex wave (fig. 19) is adequately reflected and its useful values retained throughout the series of operations that generate figure 26. What figure 26 achieves is a clarity and simplicity of expression lacking in the trileveled complex wave. Figure 26 is a quantification of operational constructs, which makes this modular hierarchy of temporal variables a valid subject for rigorous scientific investigation.

Chapter 11

The Temporal Hierarchy and Cosmology

Concrescence is Whitehead's term for the process that *is* any given actual entity:

> Concrescence is the *growing together* of the many into the unity
> of a one . . . The initial phase of a concrescence is composed of
> the separate feelings of the disjunctively diverse entities that make
> up the actual world of the actual entity in question. Subsequent
> phases effect the *growing together*, the *concrescence*, of these many
> separate feelings into one unity of feeling, which is termed the *sat-*
> *isfaction* of that actual entity. "'Concrescence' is the name for the
> process in which the universe of many things acquires an individ-
> ual unity in a determinate relegation of each item of the 'many' to
> its subordination in the constitution of the novel 'one'" (PR 321).
> With the attaining of its satisfaction an actual entity is completed
> and *perishes*—i.e., it becomes a datum for fresh instances of con-
> crescence. (Sherburne 1966, pp. 212–213)

The modular wave-hierarchy is described by an energy map of changes
running forward and backward upon themselves, much like an alternating
current (cf. fig. 19). Fung Yu-Lan (1947) has made clear the traditional
place this idea has long occupied in Chinese thought:

> The content of the course of transformation in the universe is
> a process of construction-plus-destruction in things. And this
> process of construction-plus-destruction in things is the opening
> and shutting referred to in the explanations of the *Ch'ien* and
> the *K'un*. The constructive part of the process is equivalent to
> the "coming forward," the destructive part is equivalent to the
> "going away." A whole act of coming forward, plus a whole act
> of going away, that is transformation. This going and coming has
> no end to it, and just because this is so, therefore the universe is
> without limit of time. Therefore it is said, "the unceasing moving
> one way and the other is designated as effective evolving." The
> process is without limit, because what comes must go and what
> goes must come back again: The advancing thing also retires and
> the retiring thing comes back again. (p. 98)

We are attempting to make mathematically explicit a description of the Tao that is no different from that proposed by the third-century Chinese thinker Wang Pi:

> What he [Wang Pi] was trying to describe was perhaps a series of fields of force (as we might call them), contained in, but subsidiary to, the main field of force of the Tao, and each manifesting itself at different points in space and time. He believed that to each of these there corresponded one of the hexagrams of the *I Ching*, its sufficient characterization being given in the *thuan* or "explanation" attached to it in the Book of Changes. In this way man could know the most important "dominant factors" or "root causes" of things, and feel able to affirm with unshakable faith that though there was manifold complexity in the universe, there was no confusion. (Needham 1954, vol. 1, p. 322)

In the West, the idea of the universe as arising from the ceaseless ebb and flow of an underlying medium may be traced to Pythagoras and Heraclitus. Whitehead's organismic philosophy makes the same assumption: ". . . we shall conceive each primordial element as a vibratory ebb and flow of an underlying energy, or activity" (1967, p. 35). Whitehead has nicely anticipated our turning to science for a judgment on the truth of this view:

> We must first ask whether there is any evidence to associate the quantum theory with vibration. This question is immediately answered in the affirmative. The whole theory centres round the radiant energy from an atom, and is intimately associated with the periods of the radiant wave-systems. It seems, therefore, that the full hypothesis of essential vibratory existence is the most hopeful way of explaining the paradox of the discontinuous orbit. (1967, p. 36)

Like an electron or an organism, a spiral galaxy suggests itself as an expression on one level of the partially achieved state of concrescence. The concrescence that our own small planet, a subunit in the hierarchy from electron to galaxy, is now experiencing is of enormous importance to us as a species, yet there is no certain fate to which we can entrust ourselves. The self-evidence of the fact of freedom and its logical necessity for meaningful thought means that no phenomenon functions with absolute mechanical certainty. This is the fact, at once sobering and exhilarating, that quantum physics has secured. It may be that the fate of evolution on earth, with its escape, or no, from catastrophe, is of no concern to the larger universe, much in the way that the death of millions of cells occurs in higher organisms as a normal part of metabolism. This supremely rational idea finds strong support in the existential "myth," which Hans Jonas elaborates in his essay on immortality. Our hypothesis is as rigorous and mathematical as we can make it, yet all science springs from some myth; and Jonas (1966) speaks eloquently of a myth that our own notion shares:

> In the beginning, for unknowable reasons, the ground of being,
> or the Divine, chose to give itself over to the chance and risk and
> endless variety of becoming. And wholly so; entering into the
> adventure of space and time, the deity held back nothing of itself;
> no uncommitted or unimpaired part remained to direct, correct,
> and ultimately guarantee the devious working-out of its destiny in
> creation. On this unconditional immanence the modern temper
> insists. It is its courage or despair, in any case its bitter honesty, to
> take our being-in-the-world seriously: to view the world as left
> to itself, its laws as brooking no interference, and the rigor of our
> belonging to it as not softened by extramundane providence. The
> same our myth postulates for God's being in the world. Not, however, in the sense of pantheistic immanence; if the world and God
> are simply the same, the world at each moment and in each state
> represents his fullness, and God can neither lose nor gain. Rather,
> in order that the world might be, and be for itself, God renounced
> his own being, divesting himself of his deity—to receive it back
> from the Odyssey of time weighted with the chance harvest of
> unforeseeable temporal experience; transfigured or possibly even
> disfigured by it. In such self-forfeiture of divine integrity for the
> sake of unprejudiced becoming, no other foreknowledge can
> be admitted than that of *possibilities* which cosmic being offers in
> its own terms: to these, God committed his cause in effacing himself for the world.
>
> And for aeons his cause is safe in the slow hands of cosmic
> chance and probability—while all the time we may surmise a
> patient memory of the gyrations of matter to accumulate into an
> ever more expectant accompaniment of eternity to the labors
> of time—a hesitant emergence of transcendence from the opaqueness of immanence.

. . . And then he trembles as the thrust of evolution, carried by its own momentum, passes the threshold where innocence ceases and an entirely new criterion of success and failure takes hold of the divine stake. The advent of man means the advent of knowledge and freedom, and with this supremely double-edged gift the innocence of the mere subject of self-fulfilling life has given way to the charge of responsibility under the disjunction of good and evil. To the promise and risk of this agency the divine cause, revealed at last, henceforth finds itself committed; and its issue trembles in the balance. The image of God, haltingly begun by the universe, for so long worked upon—and left undecided— in the wide and then narrowing spirals of pre-human time, passes with this last twist, and with a dramatic quickening of the movement, into man's precarious trust, to be completed, saved, or spoiled by what he will do to himself and the world. And in this awesome impact of his deeds on God's destiny, on the very complexion of eternal being, lies the immortality of man.

With the appearance of man, transcendence awakened to itself and henceforth accompanies his doings with the bated breath of suspense, hoping and beckoning, rejoicing and grieving, approving and frowning—and, I daresay, making itself felt to him even while not intervening in the dynamics of his worldly scene: for can it not be that by the reflection of its own state as it wavers with the record of man, the transcendent casts light and shadow over the human landscape? (pp. 275–277)

If the wave model is a valid general theory of time, it should be possible to show why certain periods or places have been particularly rich in events that accelerate the creative advance into novelty, and also to show where and when in the future such events might be expected to recur.

To carry out this operation, a personal computer has proven indispensable. A group of programs implementing these ideas has been written by our colleague Peter Meyer. We call this program Timewave Zero.* This software takes these theories and discoveries concerning the *I Ching* and creates time maps based upon them. These time maps or novelty maps show the ebb and flow of connectedness or novelty in any span of time from a few days to tens of millennia. The theory is not deterministic; it

---

* Timewave Zero is available in the Mac or MS/DOS environment from Dolphin Software, 48 Shattuck Square #147, Berkeley, California 94704.

does not say what will happen in the future, only the levels of novelty that *whatever* happens will have to fulfill. As such it operates as a map, or simplified picture, of the future (and past) behavior of whatever system is being studied. At this point perhaps a picture is worth more than words, so let us look therefore at figure 27 on page 172.

This is a novelty map of the eight thousand years that immediately precede the end of the Mayan Calendar on December 22, A.D. 2012. First let me explain that we chose the end of the Mayan Calendar as the "end date" for this graph because we found good agreement between the events that comprise the historical record and the wave itself when this end date was chosen. The end date is the point of maximized novelty in the wave and is the only point in the entire wave that has a quantified value of zero. We arrived at this particular end date without knowledge of the Mayan Calendar, and it was only after we noticed that the historical data seemed to fit best with the wave if this end date was chosen that we were informed that the end date that we had deduced was in fact the end of the Mayan Calendar.

In figure 27, and indeed in all the novelty maps, when the graph line moves downward, novelty is assumed to be increasing. When there is movement away from the base line, novelty is assumed to be decreasing in favor of habitual forms of activity. Time is seen as the ebb and flow of two opposed qualities: novelty versus habit, or density of connectedness versus disorder. In figure 27 we see clearly that one trend toward greater novelty reached its culmination around 2700 B.C., precisely at the height of the Old Kingdom pyramid-building phase; then a countermovement toward predictable forms of behavior asserted itself and increased in importance until around 900 B.C. At that time, around the time of the consolidation of Mycenaean sea power, the tendency toward habituation was overcome and replaced by a long cascade into greater and greater novelty that reaches its culmination early in the twenty-first century.

The career of novelty is revealed to be a process that is punctuated by subprocesses. These mitigate, modify, and influence an overall general tendency toward greater and greater novelty. Notice that the last fifteen hundred years of figure 27 are highly novel times that have played themselves out at levels of novelty very close to the horizontal axis, the maximized "zero state." Let us look at those last fifteen hundred years more closely.

Figure 28 is a graph full of precise predictions that to my mind demonstrate the force of Timewave Zero. The thing to notice is the very precise way in which episodes of historical advance or novelty are precisely indicated by steep descents in the wave. Such agreement between the historical

Time Wave Zero

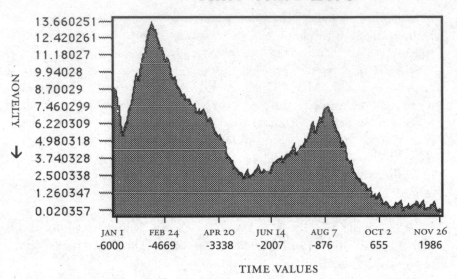

FIGURE 27

8012 years, from 6000 B.C. to A.D. 2012. In figures 27 through 30 the values on
the left of each graph are a numerical quantification of novelty. The maximum
novel situation has a value of zero; hence, values tend toward zero as the end
date is approached. In these graphs the end date is assumed to be December 21,
A.D. 2012.

record and the ebb and flow of the wave argues strongly that the Timewave
is in fact able to accurately portray the evolution of historical patterns of
change.

The theory of time that is implied by the Timewave is a theory of time
as a fractal, or self-similar, wave. Fractals have recently come into vogue in
many branches of the natural sciences, and the reader wishing a thorough
exposition of this new area of mathematics should consult Benoit Mandelbrot's *The Fractal Geometry of Nature*. A fractal wave comes quite naturally equipped with an extensive set of internal resonances that show a
formal, but acausal, linkage between events and periods of time that may
be widely separated from each other in space and time. So, for example,
when we look at events of the one hundred years leading up to the Mayan
calendrical termination, we see that the graph is topologically similar to
the graph that we said applied to the past several thousand years. My interpretation of this is that it means that shorter duration subsets of the

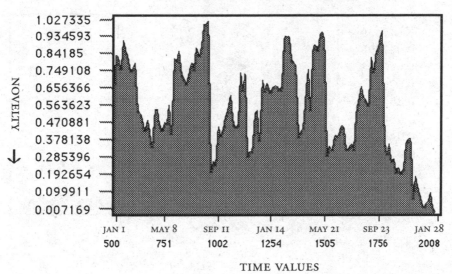

Time Wave Zero

NOVELTY ↓

Y-axis values
1.027335
0.934593
0.84185
0.749108
0.656366
0.563623
0.470881
0.378138
0.285396
0.192654
0.099911
0.007169

JAN 1	MAY 8	SEP 11	JAN 14	MAY 21	SEP 23	JAN 28
500	751	1002	1254	1505	1756	2008

TIME VALUES

FIGURE 28

1512 years, from A.D. 500 to A.D. 2012. The oscillatory character of historical novelty from the Fall of Rome until the European Enlightenment is clearly visible.

fractal curve of time are microversions of the larger pattern in which they are embedded. Such an idea lays the basis for understanding such phenomena as fads, fashion, and the occasional wave of historical obsession that characterize society; for example, see figure 29.

Notice that with figure 29 we leave the realm of modeling of past historical events and move into the area of prophecy proper, for a portion of figure 29 actually refers to a portion of time that has yet to undergo the formality of actually occurring. Let us zero in on the point in which the wave passes out of the past and into the future (fig. 30).

Here we see twenty years, with December 19, 1989, in the middle. Ultimately it is in the mind of the reader to decide, based on his or her own knowledge and feeling, whether the wave descriptions of the portions of the twentieth century that we are all living through are correctly mapped by Timewave Zero.

Timewave Zero is an exploratory idea system and a software package that runs on personal computers. It is the broadcast output of the naturally superconducting experimental deoxyribonucleic matrix transceiver

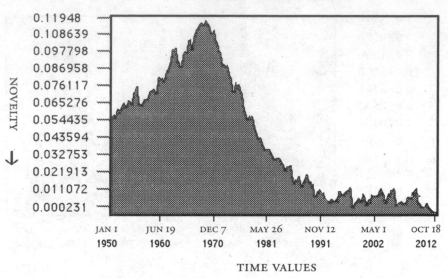

FIGURE 29

63 years, from January 1950 to December A.D. 2012.

operating in hyperspace. We believe that by using such ideas as a compass for the collectivity, we may find our way back to a new model in time to reverse the progressive worldwide alienation that is fast turning into an eco-cidal planetary crisis. A model of time must give hope and overcome entropy in its formal composition. In other words, it must mathematically secure the *reasonableness* of hope. This theory, and indeed the mathematical theory of dynamic systems generally, does this by securing in a formal manner the process by which transformation can naturally arise and persist out of a background of flux.

It becomes increasingly clear that we are now experiencing a similar period marked with extreme density of novel ingressions, a time when the rational and acausal tendencies inherent in time may again reverse their positions of dominance.

The stupendous idea of an end of time is an attempt to negate the eternal stasis, to break the circle. All peoples who have awakened to the suffering and hope of the *condition humaine* have arrived at this idea. The magnificent image of the Norse *ragnarok* . . . is perhaps

Time Wave Zero

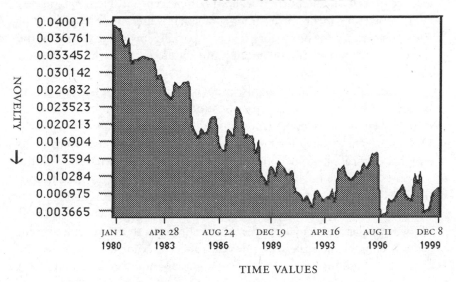

FIGURE 30

20 years, from January 1980 to January A.D. 2000.

its most radical form. But, each in its own way, the other peoples who have created a world for themselves have also appointed an end to it; Indians, Persians, Greeks, Arabs, and Jews . . . Thus the prophet Zacharias can say that it will be light at eventide. This final time revolutionizes the course of the world.

The irruption of a time that is impossible, of an event that falls out of the cycle—we are familiar with this notion, from the fishes that remain hanging on the limbs of the trees in the Deucalion, to the mountain that is transplanted into the sea in the sermon of Jesus. (Van Der Leeuw, in Campbell 1967, pp. 338, 340)

Gnostic intuitions of the first and second century suggested that energy is the "divine light" that is trapped in matter and that energy, in order to free itself, must evolve itself through progressively subtler stages until it generates self-reflecting consciousness, which can then evolve techniques for freeing all energy from matter. Like this myth, all ideas of salvation, en-lightenment, or utopia may be taken to be expressions in consciousness of the drive of energy to free itself from the limitations of three-dimensional space and "return to the Father," that is, return to the uncontaminated essence of itself in an epoch of realized concrescent satisfaction. Concrescent satisfaction includes the notion of energy unbounded by space or time. This means for our theory that at especially low-value regions of the modular wave-hierarchy a quantum jump should occur in the concrescent process.

What this advance of novelty is, and what the process of becoming may be seen to be in essence, is the revelation of the interspecies' mind. In human beings, it is approached through the nonmetabolizing neural DNA scattered through the body, and for humans it becomes apparent as a higher cortical phenomenon, an experience, as a confrontation with the Jungian "collective unconscious." This revelation and its integration into the field of shared experience is a process of transformation of the previously limited ego. The many magnitudes of duration in which the levels of the modular hierarchy of waves can be supposed to be operable exceed, at both ends of the scale, any physical processes known to occur in the universe. These magnitudes or "cosmic epochs" are shown in figure 20, Table III. For example, the time during which ½ of the hydrogen is consumed in the thermonuclear reaction $H^2 + H^2 \rightarrow He + n$ is approximately .00003 second, that is, of the same magnitude as the .000048 figure for the thirteenth cycle projected in the wave model. Similarly, the age of matter in the universe is now tentatively placed at 1.5×10^{10} years; our final figure on the macroscale is nearly five times larger than this, but we suggest that the first nearly 3×10^{10} (30 billion) years were simply passed with diffuse primal hydrogen (and perhaps antihydrogen) entering the space-time continuum very gradually. In any case, some 15 billion years ago, matter began to gather in sufficiently dense aggregates to give rise to the temperatures, pressures, and magnetic fields necessary for star formation. In the light of these time scales and events, the cosmogonic myth argued for becomes the following.

Nearly 36 billion years ago, almost twice as long as the age that modern astrophysics supposes to be the age of the universe, the set of mutually reflective relations that constitute the paired universe of matter and antimatter began to enter and, thereby, define three-dimensional space. Following a major shift of epochs, hydrogen began to appear spontaneously near the center of the spatial topology. Denser atomic materials followed in due course; first helium, via the Critchfield formula for H-H fusion, which can proceed in pure hydrogen. All of these material entities spring at their point of origin from the same source as the topological manifold of space, that is, from a higher spatial dimension. Why a higher spatial dimension is ingressing at an ever-accelerating rate into space-time we shall perhaps not understand until we achieve, through a concrescence of time, a return to the higher topological dimension. "We" in this case means the interspecies' network of DNA shared by all life. As in Jonas's myth, deity thus achieves a redefining and clarifying of the nature of itself through the efficacy of its works. Whatever the reasons energy entered space-time, each expression of itself in time has taken the form of a further sophistication of organization. The path of return sought by evolution on all levels is through antientropic organization. The original particles, which began entering the space-time continuum some 36 billion years ago, had, by 12 billion years ago, given rise to the epoch of the primal aggregate of the Big Bang theory, although the great majority of stars are less than 5 billion years old. This wave-hierarchy theory of time manages to avoid some of the dualisms inherent in the Steady State of Big Bang schools of cosmological theory, since it offers a mechanism by which an entire universe can spring into existence and yet not violate any physical laws while doing so. In its general outlines, the cosmology that our theory has built into it is in accord with recent ideas put forth by Edward Tryon. Both his model and ours predict a universe that is homogeneous, isotropic, and closed and consists equally of matter and antimatter. All of these contentions are consistent with, and supported by, the present state of astrophysics. We have proposed that quantum-mechanical phenomena organize matter at every level; Tryon (1973) suggests that the universe itself is a very large instance of a quantum-mechanical phenomenon that is a commonplace when of brief duration. Tryon points out that universes can spring from nothing without violations of physical law so long as they have specific properties. Chief among these is the requirement that such a universe must have a zero net value for all conserved quantities. The quantities that physics considers conserved fall into two categories, continuous and discrete. It is the discrete quantities that characterize the elementary particles: spin, strangeness, electric charge, and so on. These quantities have equal magnitude, but opposed signs, in the case of particles and antiparticles. All that the laws of discrete conservation imply, therefore, is that if a universe appears from nowhere, it must consist equally of matter and antimatter. It is very possible that we live in a universe that possesses zero net values for all of its conserved quantities. Such a universe could well have sprung from nothing:

> To indicate how such a creation might have come about, I refer
> to quantum field theory, in which every phenomenon that could
> happen in principle actually does happen occasionally in
> practice, on a statistically random basis. For example, quantum

electrodynamics reveals that an electron, positron and photon occasionally emerge spontaneously from a perfect vacuum. When this happens, the three particles exist for a brief time, and then annihilate each other, leaving no trace behind. (Energy conservation is violated, but only for the brief particle lifetime δt permitted by the uncertainty relation $\delta E \delta t \sim h$, where δE is the net energy of the particles and δh is Planck's constant.) The spontaneous, temporary emergence of particles from a vacuum is called a vacuum fluctuation and is utterly commonplace in quantum field theory.

If it is true that our Universe has a zero net value for all conserved quantities, then it may simply be a fluctuation of the vacuum, the vacuum of some larger space in which our Universe is imbedded. In answer to the question of why it happened, I offer the modest proposal that our Universe is simply one of those things which happen from time to time.

One might wonder how a vacuum fluctuation could occur on such a grand scale. My answer is in two parts. The first is that the laws of physics place no limit on the scale of vacuum fluctuations. The duration is of course subject to the restriction $\delta E \delta t \sim h$, but this merely implies that our Universe has zero energy, which has already been made plausible.

The second part of my answer lies in the principle of biological selection, which states that any Universe in which sentient beings find themselves is necessarily hospitable to sentient beings. I do not claim that universes like ours occur frequently, merely that the expected frequency is non-zero. Vacuum fluctuations on the scale of our Universe are probably quite rare. The logic of the situation dictates, however, that observers always find themselves in universes capable of generating life, and such universes are impressively large. (We could not have seen this universe if its expansion-contraction time had been less than the 10^{10} yr required for *Homo sapiens* to evolve.) (Tryon 1973, pp. 396–397)

The universe is subject to cycles of temporal variables, occurring on many levels and generating appropriate forms of novelty on each such level. Life's epoch began one to two billion years ago—1.3 billion years on our scale. Eighteen million years ago brings one to the closure of the next smallest level. This occurred at the height of the age of mammals. One sixty-fourth of this 18-million-year cycle is a cycle whose inception was

275,000 years ago, a time that corresponds well with the emergence of *Homo sapiens.* One sixty-fourth of this cycle brings us to the cycle that epitomizes what might properly be called historical time, that cycle which began 4,300-plus years ago, around 2300 B.C. The duration of the cycle next encountered is 67-plus years, and we have assumed the most recent such epoch to have begun in 1945. The end of World War II and the development of atomic weapons and their use in war are forms of novelty whose appearance attended the shift of epochs that created the postmodern world. If our understanding is correct, then this same 67-plus–year cycle at, or near, the end of a 4,300-year cycle will terminate around the year 2012 (cf. fig. 27).

Language and its appearance is a recent instance of concrescence. It is a recent form of novelty, having been in existence not more than a million years. As a concrescence occurring in our species, it may provide a clue to the path that evolving human novelty will take in the future. In the case of language elaboration, we have an excellent example of the way in which what must first have been a freakish mutational ability became overnight a species-transforming novelty, emerging from the foundation of mammalian organization. We suggest that the unique mode of being that language represents may have become manifest as follows.

Human beings must have discovered the use of fire shortly after acquiring prehensile thumbs. Certainly evidence argues that humans possessed fire long before the first tools were made. Once the discovery of fire was made, the element necessary for humanity's correct intervention in energy's struggle to free itself was present. With the introduction of fire into the *Homo sapiens* community, the stage was set for the invocation of the logos. Around their fires, humans dragged the carcasses of the hunt and the plants that the group deemed useful as food or fuel. It is reasonable to suggest that in this coincidence of plants, bone tubes emptied of their marrow, fire, and the restless prehensile hands of early humans, eventually the peculiar psychological states attendant upon the smoking of tryptamines, or the MAO inhibitors occurring in the same biosynthetic chain, would be discovered. In describing *Australopithecus,* a human ancestor, Lord Ritchie-Calder (1961) says, "They lived in limestone caves and there is evidence they may have used fire . . . they appear to have been carnivorous, because in the caves there are animal bones . . . and antelope limb bones. These antelope bones are interesting because they have been smashed to extract the marrow" (p. 43). Recent excavations at Non Nok Tha in Thailand indicate that one of the most technologically advanced cultures in the world of 13,000 B.C. existed there. The graves at Non Nok Tha yielded the bones of *Bos indicus,* the Indian zebu. The manure of this species of cattle is the preferred environment of Colombian varieties of *Stropharia cubensis* mushrooms.

Once any hallucinogenic effect were discovered, it would, as it represents contact with a tremendum, be surrounded with ritual. This usually means dancing and, especially important for our argument, singing and chanting. Once ritual use of a tryptamine-containing plant is exercised in the presence of vocal sound, the chemical basis for spontaneous seizures of unconsciously modulated sound and its signification of a tremendum would be present. The beginning of language may be such glossalialike phenomena. Shortly after such practice found even slight usage, one could expect that the correct union of signed sound and cognitive category would occur, and language, as the prototype of a "more perfect archetypal logos," would be discovered—discovered within the confines of ritual, a kind of preconscious understanding of the requirements of energy for its transformation and liberation. Following the acquisition of language, the advance into novelty, now in part self-reflecting, continued on a higher level. The most recent of these major new levels of coordinated organization may be embodied in the epoch of electronic communications and the furiously evolving postrelativistic consciousness of the twentieth century.

Language is the embodiment of meaning. Meaning signifies organization, and there is no organization without purpose. What is the purpose of organization? Is it perhaps to retard entropy? In such a case, the meaning of meaning for that which apprehends meaning is the necessity to purposefully create and maintain order. Note "retard", not "reverse"; according to the Second Law of Thermodynamics, entropy cannot be reversed; in localized areas, however, it may cease temporarily. In organisms this situation occurs, and it also occurs in low-temperature systems that mutate to states of higher order instead of "going over" into disorder. Transference of the properties of microevents occurring in quantum-mechanical systems to macrosystems, a phenomenon exhibited by superfluids, might, if found to have a wider occurrence in nature, offer some explanation for the emergence of natural levels of order. Research has already shown that in some biological processes microphysical events are decisive (cf. Prigogine et al. 1972).

Chapter 12

Toward a Physics of Concrescence

The story of the evolution of physics in the twentieth century is the story of the elaboration and acceptance of a wave-mechanical conception of the primary nature of matter. No model of matter can fail to take into account that contemporary physics has recaptured a Pythagorean intuition too long forgotten by the followers of the commonsense physics of Newton. Common sense is gone from physics; Planck banished it when he discovered the discrete nature of radiation, and Heisenberg's Principle of Uncertainty made a return to the notion of simple location forever impossible. Our own theory is thoroughly kymatic, or wavelike.

The parallels between the classic behavior of waves and the graphs we have elaborated is interesting because they seem to argue strongly that there is no inconsistency involved in discussing the modular hierarchy we propose in wave-mechanical terms. One model of wave activity that has found acceptance in quantum mechanics is that of French physicist Prince Louis de Broglie. The accepted understanding of de Broglie's wave is that "the highest intensity of these waves at any point of the space to which they are confined gives us the probability of finding the electron at that particular point if we carry out a special experiment designed for that purpose. They are so to speak 'waves of probability'" (Gamow 1964, p. 57). It is interesting that the modular hierarchy of the *I Ching* also is a "wave of probability," and that if the electron is conceived of as a concrescence, then, naturally, at the point of maximum symmetry (the zero state) of the wave, one might expect its appearance. Such a theory would have clear application to atomic physics if the various quantum states met within the atom could be shown to be determined by zero, or near zero, states (maximum symmetries) within the short epochs of the *I Ching* hierarchy. The *I Ching* wave and the postquantum atom may not really possess distinct particularity. The property of the *I Ching* wave-hierarchy, determination of morphology through ingression of temporal variables, may simply represent a description of a set of laws operating within the atom but previously ignored. Modern physics is haunted by a plentitude of particles; an elegant theory should reduce such particles to a coherent substratum.

In *The Ambidextrous Universe*, Gardner (1964) observes:

> The positron was the first anti-particle to be discovered. Every elementary particle is now known to have a corresponding

anti-particle. The two particles are alike in all respects except that they are opposite in the sign of any quantity (represented by a plus or minus quantum number) that is conserved . . . In other words all conserved quantities must be of opposite sign so that when the particle and anti-particle come together, these quantities will cancel each other, leaving nothing but pure energy (photons). In the case of the photon and the neutral pi-meson, particle and anti-particle are one and the same. (p. 211)

He speaks of ". . . entertaining examples of mutual annihilation by a left-right encounter. In most cases the two structures involved are helices of opposite handedness" (Gardner 1964, p. 250). In this vein we refer to C. H. Hinton's (1887) speculation:

If we consider a twist and its image, they are but the simplest and most rudimentary type of organism. What holds good of a twist and its image twist would hold good of a more complicated arrangement also. If a bit of structure apparently very unlike a twist, and with manifold parts and differences in it—if such a structure were to meet its image structure, each of them would instantly unwind the other, and what was before a complex and compound whole, opposite to an image of itself, would at once be resolved into a string of formless particles. A flash, a blaze, and all would be over. (p. 172)

We have speculated that the vacuum fluctuation of space-time is a holographic modular hierarchy whose individual levels possess properties in common with the King Wen sequence of the *I Ching* and the morphology of DNA. We have suggested that within this hierarchy time could, though hologramatically homogenized, be said to be moving in two opposed directions. Hinton and others, in trying to imagine a hypothetical meeting between human and antihuman, or galaxy and antigalaxy, always conceive the meeting as occurring in normal, three-dimensional space, and thus necessarily entailing a point of first contact and an approach or closure of linear distance in three dimensions. This sort of meeting of matter and antimatter can only result in a violent, complete, and spatially localized energy conversion, which is not particularly interesting. We can suppose that in such a case the Leidenfrost phenomenon would act to inhibit the reaction. This phenomenon is named after the German physician who studied it during the nineteenth century. As a drop on a hot surface evaporates, a layer of steam forms between the drop and the surface; this insulates the drop and appreciably slows its evaporation. The analogy between this phenomenon and events likely to follow upon a meeting of matter and antimatter has already been suggested by Hans Alfven (1966):

> The first contact between koinomatter and antimatter will result in annihilation, but the attendant generation of energy will create a force that separates the two. In the Leidenfrost phenomenon . . . a layer of steam is formed between the drop and the plate. In our more ambitious experiment, a layer is similarly formed to separate the koinomatter and antimatter. Reasoning by analogy, we may expect this to bring about an annihilation that is relatively slow and small in scale. It need not be more intensive than to ensure the formation and maintenance of an adequate insulating layer. (p. 52)

If, however, instead of a three-dimensional approach of an object and its antimatter reflection, we imagine that these two universes were never spatially distinct, but rather were somehow coextensive in space-time (one occupying a higher spatial dimension than the other), each the antimatter image of the other, and each existing in holographic matrices that confer spatiotemporal ubiquity to all of the contents of each, then it is possible to imagine a meeting between universe and antiuniverse, which would have a much more profound effect than simple annihilation. Such a meeting could only occur across the complete topology of the entire space-time continuum (or across the topology of an astronomical macrostructure, like a galaxy, if the topology of space-time is discontinuous over extragalactic, or extraclustral, distances). The meeting of a material matrix possessing hologramatic properties and its antimatter reflection would result, it is true, in mutual annihilation of both matrices, but not in the sort of localized explosion that would ensue from their meeting in three dimensions. Rather, the annihilation through mutual cancellation would occur at every point in both matrices *simultaneously,* something impossible in a three-dimensional collision, where Leidenfrost's effect would impede the reaction. The meeting of antimatter and its reflection in normal space seems unlikely, since both kinds of matter, the particles to build such matter at any rate, have already been detected "right here" on earth. Were a collision in normal space to occur between two universes, one of matter and one of antimatter, the reaction (since it would represent a total energy conversion) would possess, as the surface of its expanding spherical shock wave, fusion processes that would accomplish the initial plasmization of matter caught in the expanding reaction; the partial energy release, represented by the fusion processes, would itself be converted in the matter/antimatter reaction moving behind it. The matter/antimatter interphase would occur in a plasmic atmosphere of free ions; matter in modes of organization that occur outside the fission process would not be generated by the expanding total energy conversion reaction.

A very different situation would occur were the collision of the two continua to occur in the hologramatic kind of spatiotemporal organization we are suggesting may exist. In such a situation, the mutual annihilation of both continua would occur simultaneously at all points in both matrices. Only photons would be left, and they would presumably retain the structure they had possessed as matter, and its stereoisomeric reflection in antimatter. This idea of an event occurring simultaneously throughout the four-dimensional space-time continuum is at variance with the assumptions of relativity. Nevertheless, Whitehead (1967) preserves this concept in his philosophy, and following him, we have preserved it in our methodology:

> It only remains to add that Einstein would probably reject the theory of multiple space-time systems which I have been expounding to you. He would interpret his formula in terms of contortions in space-time which alter the invariance theory for measure properties, and of the proper times of each historical route. His mode of statement has the greater mathematical simplicity, and only allows of one law of gravitation, excluding the alternative. But, for myself, I cannot reconcile it with the given facts of our experience as to simultaneity, and spatial arrangement. There are also other difficulties of a more abstract character.
> (p. 122)

It is possible to suggest that relativistic effects are operating within each wave-particle conceived as a four-dimensional space-time continuum, but that the equations of relativity should be inserted within those equations, descriptive of the properties of holographic matrices: convolutional integrals and Fourier transformations.

In trying to imagine this meeting of universes, we should abandon the idea of a localized explosion and imagine, instead, a universe whose physical laws suddenly cease to operate—as matter and antimatter achieve simultaneous, ubiquitous cancellation—leaving, in the wake of the closure of the vacuum fluctuation, the photonic forms existing and able for the first time to obey laws relevant to themselves as photonic holograms (forms), rather than as photonic holograms expressed through matter or antimatter, as objects or antiobjects. Such a process, though farfetched, would utilize a set of naturally occurring phenomena (vacuum fluctuations and higher dimensional matrices) to create the sort of basic ontological mutation in the nature of matter such as, we suggest, may characterize some future shift of epochs. The photonic shell, left in the wake of fourth-dimensional merging of holograms of matter, and of antimatter, may be the key to a clearer understanding of the archetype of a paradisiacal existence at time's end. The spiral implosion of time may entail the universe, and every entity in it, meeting and canceling its antimatter double to create, through this union of opposites, an ontological mutation from matter to photonic form, which represents tremendous freedom.

Myth anticipates these ideas in the Mandaean conception of the soul as a light double, which exists in a higher dimension, and which one meets after death (cf. Drower 1962). If such a meeting between our universe and its reflection could be imagined to be possible in some not-so-distant future, relative to the age of the universe, then the existence of life and self-reflecting consciousness could be seen as emergent properties that are a natural consequence of the temporal flow of a universe that has entered the short epochs that precede a final concrescence. We see the experiment at La Chorrera as part of a tapping in on a growing sense of the imminence of a major shift of epochs on some level that must be stirring in many species and individuals. In our experiment, an intuition of such a possible change was achieved through techniques bioelectronic and shamanic, whose revelation, through a transpersonal *zeitgeist*-like phenomenon, marks a form of election. If the theory of the bonding of harmine into nucleic acids (briefly, while metabolizing, or permanently, through audilely induced bonds) is correct, and if the resulting signal or shift in metabolic mode were to be found to effect and restructure higher cortical processes, we would be on the way to validating intimations that an epoch-terminating event, long in the making and critical to the creative continuation of human evolution, is at last coming to fruition. The investigations at La Chorrera then emerge as fortuitous events made possible by a correct use of free will in the light of the constraints inherent in the present epoch.

Certainly, if a partial concrescence is achieved in a three-dimensional focus, then the temporal continuum of normal space-time will be unaffected and continue. Any partial concrescence would leave intact a continuum of successive events, and as investigators of this phenomenon, it is up

to us to anticipate these successive events. Although each time is an overtonal harmonic of other moments, there is a thread of creative advance
running through time along the helix of closure represented by life's approach to new epochs. The quantified hierarchy (cf. figs. 27 through 30 in
chap. 11 and fig. 32 in the Epilogue) appears to describe the vicissitudes of
past history with some accuracy, but the same description gives such a piv-
otal role to the twentieth century that reason dictates skepticism. The critical role of our own era is a fact only if the assumption of the cyclical,
ever-condensing nature of time is correct. If time is an eternal process, then
it may be open-ended or cyclical, but not the latter in such a way as to ever
yield the actual concrescence this idea calls for. That could happen only if
the temporal cycles were to constantly shorten themselves around a temporal axis. The idea of an "axis time" is common to Continental theology:

> We write: "Anno Domini 1951." This means that we measure time
> from a centre. This centre determines the time that follows it, and
> the time which preceded it strove toward this centre. Our histori-
> cal numbering of the years tacitly presupposes a caesura between
> the era before the birth of Christ and the era which came after it.
> Our history is oriented toward a centre. (Quispel, in Campbell
> 1967, p. 85)

Such a leading of energy toward a center can only end in transformation. What the temporal axis is like, as an experience, has been the continuing puzzle of our experiment and of much of human history:

> Of final time itself we see nothing. There is only God . . . Here
> all dimensions are effaced, including the fourth dimension, of
> time. But the biblical concept of eternity is no abstract timeless-
> ness, no *aeternitas,* but a *me olam ad olam.* Final time begins in the
> midst of historical time. In the New Testament as elsewhere it is
> announced to the peoples by omens—adunata and wonders. But
> it also sets its stamp upon time. In the ancient world, including
> Egypt, there was an eschatological schema, according to which
> a time of decline and despair heralded the advent of final time.
> The historical events were read into this schema, as conversely
> the event that seceded from time was read into history. (Van Der
> Leeuw, in Campbell 1967, pp. 348–349)

The moment of concrescence may occupy the same position with respect to time that a magnetic pole of the earth occupies relative to the geomagnetic field of the planet. Like the poles, which are physically characterized by climatological extreme, the temporal pole would mark a temporal extreme, the most extreme moment of density of the ingression of novelty, but like the poles, it would not be apparently different from its space-time environment. Such an understanding of time would mean no definitive concrescence could take place.

Our theory is one of a progressive spiral involution of time toward a concrescence, rather than a theory of a static hierarchy of waves, eternally expressed on many levels. This is because the terminal positions in the King Wen wave naturally quantify as zero states. The natural consequence of this is that the terminal sections of an epoch do not contribute to the valuation assigned to lower levels of that particular section of the hierarchy. This results in a progressive drop of valuations toward the zero state as any epoch enters its terminal phase. Only in the situation of final concrescence does the valuation on all levels actually become zero. In fact, the quantified definition of absolute concrescence is that it is the zero point in the quantified wave-hierarchy.

The paradox of the concrescence is that as one approaches it, one becomes more free, but through recognition of the boundary conditions of that modality into which one is becoming absorbed. Once concrescence is achieved, ego and Tao are perceived as one, or rather, only Tao is perceived, but as though it were ego.

> The final phase in the process of concrescence, constituting an actual entity, is one complex, fully determinate feeling. This final phase is termed "satisfaction." It is fully determinate (a) as to its genesis, (b) as to its objective character for the transcendent creativity, and (c) as to its prehension—positive or negative— of every item in its universe. (Whitehead 1969, pp. 30-31)

A persistently recurring idea concerning a sudden apparent suspension of natural laws is the assumption, which the *I Ching* also makes, that natural laws are not eternal absolutes, but rather flux phenomena that operate over long periods of time. Though it is commonly assumed that human time is cosmically insignificant in terms of duration, actually this does not appear to be the case. Whitehead (1968) notes that ". . . span of existence is merely relative to our habits of human life. For inframolecular occurrence, a second is a vast period of time" (p. 157). When a span of human time is compared not only to the varieties of duration persisting in the macrocosm but to those in the physical microcosm as well, where magnitudes like $.655 \times 10^{-27}$ erg seconds are met with (cf. fig. 20, Table III, in chap. 10), the position of humanly cognizable time among the classes of time necessary for the functioning of the physical universe is more correctly seen to rest in the middle; so that from the standpoint of a temporally deconditioned and impartial observer, the appearance of life in the last few seconds of a cosmic hour of creation is equally as unlikely as, given the self-evident existence of life, the appearance of consciousness in the closing seconds of yet another cosmic hour devoted to the career of life. Each of these acts, with *deus ex machina* endings, must be seen objectively as being no less improbable than that in the closing seconds of an Act III, the curtain might be rung down by a concrescent transformation that would fulfill the equation life is to nonlife as consciousness is to life as X is to consciousness. One point more: These three propositions are not really equally improbable. Given the first, the second is more likely; given the first and second, the third grows almost necessary.

Achievement of the zero state can be imagined to arrive in one of two forms. One is the dissolution of the cosmos in an actual cessation and unraveling of natural laws, a literal apocalypse. The other possibility takes less for granted from the mythologems associated with the collective transformation and entry into concrescence and hews more closely to the idea that concrescence, however miraculous it is, is still the culmination of a human process, a process of toolmaking, which comes to completion in the perfect artifact: the monadic self, exteriorized, condensed, and visible in three dimensions; in alchemical terms, the dream of a union of spirit and matter. Presumably, were such a hyperspatial tool/process discovered, in a very short time it would entirely restructure life's experience of itself, of time, space, and of otherness, and then it would be these effects which would follow rather than precede the concrescence, and which, through their atemporal influence on the content of visionary experience, would be seen to have given rise to the "apocalyptic scenario" in the expectation of so many ontologies. The appearance in normal space-time of a hyperdimensional body, obedient to a simultaneously transformed and resurrected human will, and able to plumb the obligations and opportunities inherent in this unique juncture in energy's long struggle for self-liberation, may be apocalypse enough.

What we now require is an empirically verifiable experimental confirmation of the idea of a modular wave-hierarchy in time, or of the importance of nucleic acid ESR for consciousness. The quest for such experiments may prove elusive for the following reason: The dependence of scientific methodology upon inductive thought has caused it to construct its rules of admissible evidence against the admission of phenomena that cannot be repeatedly triggered by experimental means. Against this point of view, which assumes the absolute homogeneity of time, our own theory assumes at its very heart that time itself is a medium of variables in flux, and that as such, every moment is different from every other moment. This is actually a more consistently conservative position than science's logically unfounded use of induction. Nevertheless, this position holds out the possibility that, unless we are able to exactly determine and predict the temporal boundary conditions operating in a given moment, we may not be able to devise an experimental procedure that would effectively prove or disprove this theory. Elimination of inductive assumptions, and formulation of clear and quantified definitions of the boundary conditions inherent in the waveform, is only part of the problem. We must also understand that, even if the wave theory of time is correct, we would find it difficult, if not impossible, to prove, unless we had chosen a temporal moment of major concrescence from which to generate the wave. Only in such rare cases would the wave conform to observed experience on every temporal level of the hierarchy.

Even in the case of a major or final concrescence, confirmation would not occur in a 72-billion-year cycle that had these condensing subcycles operable until the last four days, or, more probably, until the last several hours of the cycle. Figure 20, Table III, makes clear why this is so. We suggest that each cycle has within itself "revelatory intervals" where, in garbled, or distorted, form, intuitions of the species' history-culminating entry into concrescence emerges into the conscious collective life of the psyche to fertilize idea systems in formation there. Such intervals are quantifiable as low-value approaches to an ideal zero state. Figure 32, in the Epilogue, displays the values of Frame 384. Frame 384 is the terminal frame in the hierarchy of sixty-four-nested cycles, each with 384 variables. As such, it represents the last epoch on any level; it maps the epoch immediately preceding concrescence on any level. Does it describe the ingression of novelty into history since 2300 B.C.? We submit not only that it does but that Frame 384 also graphs the ingression of novelty into our own epoch, from 1945 to 2012.

It is difficult to imagine a universally pleasing method of comparing two distinct historical events against each other and against a quantified scale of their respective degrees of advancement into novelty. This being so, comparison between the 4,306-year scale and the current 67-plus–year cycle, with resulting judgments concerning the degree to which the two may complement, and reflect, each other, must rest purely and finally in the mind of the beholder. If the relation between the 4,306-year cycle and the 67-plus–year cycle were established, so too would be an idea implicit in this, that the terminal 67-plus–year cycle contains, condensed and intensified, all the themes and changes of the 4,306-year cycle. When we turn to the next smaller cycle, the 384-day lunar year, the problem is made more complicated by the obvious loss of objectivity. Logical extension of this idea would indicate that the terminal 6-day cycle should be as much a condensation of the themes of the last 384-day cycle as that cycle is of the last 67-plus–year cycle, or as that is to the last 4,306-year cycle. Although more than 72 billion years are necessary for the first six quantized transitions of level, those remaining, though continuing the same mathematical progression, require only 384 days to complete themselves. In other words, half of the becoming of the 72-plus-billion-year-old universe, half of the unfoldment of the hierarchically structured totality of its laws, will occur, given the correctness of these time cycles, during the last .3 seconds of its existence. The rise of life, the appearance of civilization, the discovery of atomic energy, each represents the revelatory interval associated with crossing one of the quantized barriers to condensation into the next smaller cycle; yet in the last 135 minutes, eighteen such barriers will be crossed, thirteen of them in the last 75×10^{-4} seconds. Trying to imagine what passage through these barriers might be like pushes one's imagination to the limit of hyperbole. The shorter twenty of the progressively lengthening twenty-four cycles that comprise the entire temporal hierarchy occur within the last 384-day cycle.

The concept of a revelatory interval clarifies the idea that apparent miracles, that is, extremely improbable occurrences, are actually instances when the operating laws of one cycle achieve a sort of harmonic cancellation with another cycle whose operating laws are more restrictive of molecular activity. This understanding of the nature of miracles is that they are instances when phenomenological modes common to different temporal modalities than the one being experienced break in upon natural laws mistakenly assumed to be eternal constants, disrupting and distorting them. This explanation applies equally to miracles of the sort ascribed to Christ or Simon Magnus, or to such "miracles" as the existence of life in a largely inorganic cosmos or the existence of consciousness in a cosmos where such a complex level of organization is apparently rare. Natural laws are not constants, but descriptions of statistical norms that are valid only when applied within the limits of the specific epoch in which they are encountered. This idea aids one trying to visualize the various levels of condensation through which this phenomenon will pass and present itself as it moves, ever more rapidly, through the shortening epochs.

Chapter 13

The Wave of Time

The idea model is complete in its outlines from particle to cosmos, but nevertheless, what remains significantly outside understanding is the process by which the nature of the present-at-hand will transform itself at the onset of a major shift of epochs. Certain themes that we associate with nonordinary reality or concrescent precursors have yet to be connected with the events since March 1971. The speech-become-visible phenomenon has played no real part in experiences since that time; yet it was just that feature, the outstanding peculiarity of tryptamine ecstasy, that led us to the Amazon originally (cf. p. 96). Triggering a flood of shared mental imagery might be accomplished via vocally modulated audial phenomena that would illuminate hologramatic images of the imagination-modulated vibration from ionic tryptamines, especially serotonin, metabolizing *in vivo,* perhaps in the pineal gland. We suggest that charge transfer involving such tryptamine ions may be the chemical analogs or the reflection in physical matter of ongoing processes of thought and idea formation. A major shift of epochs might allow these audio-holograms to become telepathically shared or to condense and appear as light or even matter.

> Up to now we have often opposed light and matter, the latter being associated with mass and often with electricity, while the former always appears free from inertia and charge. But if these two fundamental entities of the physical world appear to oppose one another, they are none the less related because they are both special forms of energy. In principle, therefore, there is nothing against the view that energy, while always conserving itself, can pass from the material to the luminous form and vice versa. We know today that it is actually so; this fact breaks down the barrier which seemed to separate light and matter and, to complete the enumeration of the fundamental properties which assure light a privileged place amongst the physical entities, we can now add that *light is, in short, the most refined form of matter* [italics his]. (de Broglie 1955, pp. 67–68)

The notion of concrescence signifies an abyss of ambiguity, for once the monadic hierarchy enters the short epochs preceding concrescence, the normal limitations of three dimensions will be obviated. In the last $2\frac{1}{4}$ hours of the duration of space-time, all of the cycles must, *in some sense,* be repeated several times. What the last epochs of time will be like, as all things are gathered and focused toward concrescence, remains mysterious.

We do not yet know whether the cycle of time we are studying is time caused by the submolecular energy exchanges in living macromolecules, and thus a biological phenomenon. We speculate that quantum-mechanical constraints have configured life and imposed boundary conditions on it, and that DNA is configured as it is because it reflects some quantum-mechanical or astrophysical organizing principle that makes no discrimination between the organic and the inorganic but is as responsible for the nature of nonorganic processes as it is for the manner in which the cell or the mind is organized. If this is not the case, and the waveform applies exclusively to DNA-based organisms, then this would return the problem of the origin of the inanimate universe to the cosmologists, and thus fail in its attempt to serve as a general theory of systems. The correlation of the mechanics of the wave to solar processes, lunar movements, and equinoctial precession argues that to suppose this a systems theory of biological processes exclusively is to make an unnecessarily limiting distinction.

Since the wave maps variables reflected in the organization of the psyche, it naturally has heuristic potential as a mnemonic engine. Surveying and intensifying one's understanding concerning these retrogressing time cycles is like a preliminary course in atemporal navigation. The standing wave-hierarchy contains everything now in the state called active imagination; presumably, it will exist some time in the future as the state called objective, or shared, reality. Comprehension of this unity in a particular or dynamic manner, rather than the quiescent and static total comprehension of the entire information field represented as some kind of enstasis, is a way of seeing, a shamanic path, and is accomplished through application of "right method" to the unitary information field. Anyone using the quantified frames of the hierarchy, especially when applying them to history or to the lunar year, should note that numbers rest on lines that designate "days"; yet there are "dawn lines," and the day lying between two position numbers is a day that runs from dawn to dawn. The idea that days begin and end at dawn is third century and Gnostic, according to Jonas; later, it was carried over by Manichaeans. We adhere to this idea because during the experiment in March 1971, it was clear that, as far as daily energy cycles in the environment are concerned, dawn and, secondarily, dusk are the moments of the opening of the "crack between the worlds." In fact, after March 4, 1971, and until we left La Chorrera, the time of the onset of maximum self-revelation of ingressing novelty was quite literally concurrent with the sunrise, beginning at the "crack of dawn" each morning. This moment on our scale is the end of one day and the beginning of another.

We believe that the importance of the dawn moment is rooted in the relationship between light and living organisms. That such circadian or daily cycles of light-induced metabolic fluctuations exist is well documented. Research has shown that 5HT (serotonin) in the pineal gland is light synchronized. 5HT is the very metabolite that may allow us the experience of self-reflecting consciousness. This idea clarifies at the neuro-humoral level the intuitive connection felt by all peoples between the rising of the sun and the differentiation of the self out of unstructured chaos; indeed, the connection may be one of cause and effect.

> Pineal serotonin fluctuates, rising and falling in a daily rhythm. Its persistence after blinding suggested that this rhythm is endogenous but synchronized by light and dark. Like melatonin, its levels in the pineal seemed to respond to light entering through the eyes, transmitted as nerve messages along the inferior accessory optic tract. But unlike melatonin, its increases and decreases were not explained by enzyme activity. The story was evidently more complex and interesting than anyone had forecast, for pineal serotonin seemed to follow an endogenous, circadian rhythm that was entrained by light and darkness in a manner not thoroughly understood. (Luce 1971, p. 126)

Thus, our understanding is that a maximum density of novel connection occurs at dawn in any cycle large enough to encompass at least one dawn moment. This assertion might be investigated using the methods of evaluation that J. B. Rhine developed to evaluate "psychic" phenomena. A group tested only at the propitious moment each day might be easily compared with a different group examined daily at a different time or with a group whose testing had taken no account of the time the test was administered.

The nearness of a major concrescence to our own time seems a self-evident fact, implicit in the excesses of all sorts that characterize the history of the twentieth century. Two methods for computing possible dates of a future concrescence have been found suggestive. The first is simple and involves simply propagating 67-plus–year cycles and their subsets forward in time, with various shifts in the alignment of the scales. The software implementation of the wave, Timewave Zero, allows any date to be studied, and appropriate computer programs could be written to search among many dates for a "best fit" of quantified historical data to the quantified wave-hierarchy. The problem with this, and all approaches of this sort, lies in finding a method of quantifying historical data.

The second approach to a search of possible dates for future concrescence is more subtle and takes account of the precession of the equinoxes (cf. p. 130). Because of the precession, the solstice and equinoctial nodes precess or move backward against the background of the fixed stars that comprise the zodiac. In a 26,000-year zodiacal great year, the solstice and equinoctial nodes move through the entire zodiac. It is a coincidence then that in our own time, the winter solstice is placed in the constellation Sagittarius, only about 3° from the galactic center, which, also coincidentally, is within 2° of the ecliptic. Because the winter solstice node is precessing, it is moving closer and closer to the point on the ecliptic where it will eclipse the galactic center. This will occur sometime in the next two hundred years. It is difficult to be more accurate, since the term "galactic center" is ambiguous. A degree covers a large area in space, and the galaxy may be presumed to have a gravitational center, a radio center, and a spatial center. Nevertheless, we suggest that the transition from one zodiacal era of approximately twenty-two hundred years duration to the next may be hinged on the conjunction of the solstice node and the galactic center. It is useful to examine winter solstices on which solar eclipses will occur over the next two hundred years, during which the earth's solstice node will be slowly transiting the area of the galactic center. When this is done the most likely heliacal rising of the galactic center with the solstice sun occurs on December 21, 2012. The eclipse of the galactic center by the solstice sun might be an event unusual enough to signal an onset of concrescence. If a causal connection were shown, it would implicate the galaxy itself as a major formative influence upon the structure of the molecules that maintain and define life. That such a situation would have noticeable effects on life on earth is totally speculative. However, ideas of such an archetypal nature do not arise except upon a basis of biological organization.

The relation of a time of renewal to the conjunction of the solstice nodes and the galactic center has been noted by others:

> Considering the fact that the crossroads of ecliptic and Galaxy
> are crisis-resistant, that is, not concerned with the Precession, the
> reader may want to know why the Mangaians thought they could
> go to heaven only on the two solstitial days. Because, in order

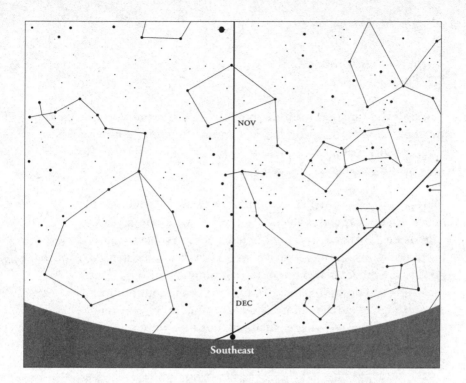

NOV

DEC

Southeast

FIGURE 31

Half an hour before the winter solstice of December 21, 2012, the sun will rise at La Chorrera (73° west, 43' south) in a position that will eclipse the galactic center. The rising sun is caught in the crosshairs of the intersection of the plane of the ecliptic with the ecliptical plane of our galaxy. This illustration was prepared using Voyager 1.0 Desktop Planetarium from Carina Software of San Leandro, California.

to "change trains" comfortably, the constellations that serve as "gates" to the Milky Way must "stand" upon the "earth," meaning that they must rise heliacally either at the equinoxes or at the solstices. The Galaxy is a very broad highway, but even so there must have been some bitter millennia when neither gate was directly available any longer, the one hanging in midair, the other having turned into a submarine entrance.

Sagittarius and Gemini still mark the solstices in the closing years of the Age of Pisces. Next comes Aquarius. The ancients, no doubt, would have considered the troubles of these our times, the overpopulation, the "working iniquity in secret," as an inevitable prelude to a new tilting, a new world-age. (de Santillana and von Dechend 1969, p. 244)

Ideas of the sort that form the philosophical basis of our speculation have reappeared again and again in Chinese thinking. They have been given particularly eloquent expression in the thought of Fu-chih (1619–92), whose mathematical extrapolation of the *I Ching* was familiar to Leibniz:

> His premise is an ordered continuum of existence, which is governed by laws and is all embracing. This continuum "lacks appearance"—that is, it is not immediately accessible to sense perception. But through the dynamism inherent in existence, images are differentiated out of the continuum which by their structure and position partake of the laws of the continuum; they are, in a sense, individuations of this continuum. On the one hand, these images—that is, the sixty-four situations of the Book of Changes—can be perceived and experienced; on the other hand, as embodiments of the law and therefore governed by it, they are open to theoretical speculation. With this they enter into the field of numbers and may be numerically structured and ordered as objects of theory governed by law. Thus each situation can be apprehended in two ways: through theoretical speculation as a consequence of the continuousness of existence and its government by laws. The oracle serves to bring the two aspects into harmony with each other, to co-ordinate a question resulting from immediate, differentiated experience, with the theoretically correct—and the only correct—answer. The questioner thus obtains access to the theoretically established aspect of his own situation, and by reference to the texts set forth under this aspect in the Book of Changes he obtains counsel and guidance from the experience of former generations and the insights of the great masters. Thus the synchronicity disclosed by the oracle is merely the apprehension of two different modes of experiencing the same state of affairs. (H. Wilhelm, in Campbell 1967, p. 219)

The material in the *I Ching* that comprises Book II and is traditionally known as the Ten Wings represents the earliest commentary on the *I Ching* extant. This material strongly indicates that the oracle originally represented a perfected knowledge of the patterns through which change manifests itself. The oldest texts indicate this through references to processes involving the *I Ching* that cannot be construed as simply referring to the traditional yarrow stalk oracle; that is, "The future likewise develops in accordance with the fixed laws, according to calculable numbers. *If these numbers are known, future events can be calculated with perfect accuracy.* This is the thought on which the Book of Changes is based" (R. Wilhelm 1964, p. 323) [italics mine]. Another commentary, which Richard Wilhelm calls "probably very ancient," pursues this theme: ". . . counting that which is going into the past depends on the forward movement. Knowing that which is to come depends on the backward movement. This is why the Book of Changes has backward moving numbers" (1964, p. 285). These statements can become rationally apprehendible only if we assume that the author had in mind construing the order of the hexagrams into some configuration approximate to the configuration that the wave-hierarchy suggests, the configuration suggested by the structure of a hexagram. The whole spirit of the *I Ching* is one pervaded by the atemporal assumption; indeed, the final words of Book I remind us that this is a "book of the future." Like the Adamic speculations of the Iranian light religious, the *I Ching* suggests that its final fulfillment lies in the focus it might be given in a unique personality. In regard to this latter, it is said of the energy in the images: "When it comes upon the right man, one who has inner relationship with this tao, it can forthwith be taken by him and awakened to new life. This is the concept of the supernatural connection between the elect of all ages" (R. Wilhelm 1964, p. 349).

Chapter 14

Evolution and Freedom

Like every major theory, the contemporary theory of evolution and genetics is an intricate combination of fact, hypothesis, and deduction. In the category of established fact belongs evolution as such: that species do change, have emerged in series of changes from ancestral forms, and in their entirety form a branching family system of common descent in which the simple precedes the complex, and transitions are gradual. Also an ascertained fact is the oc-currence of mutations; but not their nature or cause. *Natural selection is a logical deduction from the two premises of competition and of differences in competitors, which themselves are facts.* The chance-character of mutations is a hypothesis: *the inducement of some of them by external forces, such as radiation, is a fact of laboratory experience, but the claim that these are rep-resentative of all of them and for their underlying dynamics is a mere trial with Occam's razor, and the sufficiency of this kind of variability for the emergence of the major plans of organization is, so far, more a metaphysical contention (or, more soberly, a methodological postulate) than a scientific hy-pothesis—if "hypothesis" implies construction of at least a mentally workable model.* [italics ours] (Jonas 1966, p. 44f.)

We have already shown the application of the waveform to short-term as-tronomical movements and the precession of the equinoxes. It seems, therefore, not unreasonable to assume that it is applicable to other phe-nomena of longer duration. In the light of the above, we have examined the history of the fossil record to determine if major evolutionary events are reflected in the quantifications of the modular wave-hierarchy on the 1.3-billion-year scale, for if the wave-hierarchy controls the emergent evo-lutionary properties of life in a given moment, it must do so through the control of mutation. Agreement between the quantified temporal graph and fossil record, if substantially proven, would erode orthodox evolution-ary theory, which leans on the hypothesis of chance mutation. In the fol-lowing quotation from L. L. Whyte (1965), we infer that "low temperature quantum mechanical systems" refers to the temperatures where organism and metabolism are met:

. . . tendency towards the formation of more complex unified patterns does not imply any obscure vitalistic factor, since in appropriate circumstances it can be the direct result of the tendency towards arrangements of minimal potential energy. Thus the potential energy principle can, in complex low temperature quantum mechanical systems, produce a structuring or formative tendency which, under certain conditions, will shape the genetic system towards novel, stable, unified arrangements. Arbitrary changes in the genetic system may thus be reformed into favorable mutations satisfying the Coordinative Conditions. (p. 56)

We have already indicated our belief that the modular wave-hierarchy we have elaborated may be the system that can supply mathematical rigor to the idea of the Coordinative Conditions.

If, as Jonas (1966) says, for an evolutionary doctrine to be a "scientific one it is essential that the dynamics involved do not contain any element of teleology, or preformative disposition, or aspiration toward the higher forms to come but that they 'evolve' those higher forms without their being in any way 'involved' on the initial stage" (p. 43), then this theory, positing as it does preformation and atemporality of life at its own subjective substratum, seeks to reintroduce teleology to contemporary thought at the expense of the satisfying, but logically unfounded, reliance upon the idea of temporal invariance, which is the foundation of science and scientific notions of proof.

Organism is a state wherein matter appears to function, in part, with teleological characteristics associated with the self-experience of mind and banned from the assumptions of causal materialism. Mind, whose self-expectation is satisfied by freedom (the becoming and goal of its teleology), discovers itself in experience, functioning in a situation in part (in *res extensa*) causal. Thus, the teleological completion of mind (freedom in itself), when in interphase with matter, creates the still unresolved philosophical paradox that organic life represents. Having an interior horizon of transcendence (mind) and the causal encumbrances of physical extension no different from that possessed by nonliving matter, the body is a paradoxical union of opposites. However, the self-experienced teleology inherent in mind suggests that the "teleological perspective" may be a primary intuition of emerging concrescence. Perhaps it is not the mechanistic fiat of random mutation and adaptive selection that imparts "apparent teleology" to organic nature, but rather the hierarchical structure of time expressing its structure-goal as the shock wave of being in time. The teleological pattern operates in each organism and is recapitulated in the general character of the evolutionary enterprise. This pattern represents and gives direction to the seeking of itself, which is equivalent to withdrawal from effects in the *res extensa,* and which, as process, the process called life, actually does impart a preformative teleology to an otherwise mechanistic, causal, and entropy-seeking system, the *res extensa.* If the mechanics of mutation were shown to be nonrandom and ordered according to this wave-hierarchy (or any other preformative schema), then the primary role of time in imparting teleology to life—via the modulation of the density of the coincident events that cause mutation—would be clearly indicated.

To gain perspective on the ideas presented in this work and to reduce them to a series of propositions that can be examined independently of each other, we present a tentative minimal description of our experiment and its premises:

1. The tryptamines, primarily 5HT (serotonin), and the beta-carbolines, primarily harmine, offer an informational readout through molecular intercalation into neural nucleic acids and molecular broadcast of the ESR waveform of information hypothetically stored in the neural nucleus. In the case of 5HT, this ESR signal represents the electrochemical basis for consciousness as it is typically experienced. The case of harmine is different. The ESR signal seems to carry more information than does the 5HT ESR of normal serotonin metabolism. The refinement of information output and recall quality that attends the shift of normal 5HT levels in favor of harmine and related compounds marks, we suggest, an adaptative advance of considerable significance. The levels of 5HT and beta-carbolines in human neural tissue may be undergoing a steady shift in the direction of increased beta-carboline secretion and increased inhibition of 5HT. This shift is responsible for the advance of consciousness, consciousness being the self-perceived phenomenon attendant upon the improving ESR resolution of the informational hologram of species' experience stored in DNA. The artificially induced inhibition of MAO and the simultaneous rise in beta-carboline levels in the brain that accompany ingestion of *Banisteriopsis* spp. infusions are thus a means of briefly inducing a state that may anticipate future adaptations of human consciousness, adaptations refined through evolutionary selection working among the various ESR transmitters that intercalate into DNA and RNA. The experience attendant upon harmine intercalation differs from normal consciousness but is experienced superimposed over it. The

harmine-induced ESR modulation registers as a higher cortical experience, intellectually understood as a continuously self-defining totality symbol, represented through time on any of an infinite number of possible symbolic levels.

2. This phenomenon can be entirely stabilized. Stability is achieved through permanently bonding the harmine resonance unit into DNA and is directly maintained through endogenous synthesis. Stability is achieved through techniques using audilely induced ESR harmonic canceling.

3. During the application of these techniques, the owner of the DNA so treated will spontaneously produce ever more complete analogical descriptions of the configuration and interrelations of the energy patterns stored in the structure of DNA, patterns that imbue life with its characteristically preformative, actually atemporal, teleology. The subject feels these ideas to be arising from a source outside the ego, but within her- or himself. The subject experiences the imminent presence of an agency, impersonal and without limitation, that produces these ideas. He or she not only feels this agency to be the more-than-cybernetic matrix of the DNA but also the nonego information source "assures" the subject that this is the case. Further, it offers ever more elaborate models of itself, which are not only descriptions of a static goal that will represent complete concrescence but also, and inherently, these models act predictively relative to when this completion will be achieved. They offer a description of the shifting boundary conditions that will necessarily modify all the temporal moments that separate the present from this completion. These necessary boundary conditions may be mapped through a series of mathematical operations performed on the *I Ching:* the time graph, its quantification, and the quantified modular hierarchy of which it is the basic unit.

We have assumed for some time a predictable moment of concrescence. This idea poses no difficulties for a view seeking to preserve the self-evident phenomenon of free will. The idea of purpose is everywhere in a nature reductionist methods have shown to be nonredundant, and it is a matter of common experience that one may make choices and pursue good or bad influences. Humans, subject to the conditions and conditioning of their environment and nature, neither of which nor both together represent an absolute determinism, are free. Human beings are free as to how they are fulfilled; they freely choose from the possibilities inhering within the imposed boundary conditions of the situations in which they find themselves, and they realize their choices.

That each entity in the universe of a given concrescence *can*, so far as its own nature is concerned, be implicated in that concrescence in one or other of many modes; but *in fact* it is implicated only in *one* mode: that the particular mode of implication is only rendered fully determinate by that concrescence, though it is conditioned by the correlate universe. This indetermination, rendered determinate in the real concrescence, is the meaning of "potentiality." It is a *conditioned* indetermination, and is therefore called a "*real* potentiality." (Whitehead 1969, p. 27)

Humankind is not, however, free to choose the when of its completion. The actual moment of concrescence is a property of the most inclusive epoch. In the modular hierarchy of time, it is an imposed fact. Time must be well used; this is a basis for a possible theory of ethics. But even time well used still hurries us and all beings to its own conclusion. To preserve this perception and the idea of a matter- and history-conditioning atemporal interspecies bio-electronic hologram with a temporally expressed and mathematically describable unfolding, it is necessary to take the following view of humankind's freedom to act and the immutability of the order and rate of novel ingressions. Such ingressions only define boundary conditions. In the unfolding of novel ingressions, there are moments of maximum propitiousness. As the probability of a time of renewal intensifies, who can doubt the possibility that humanity, through an act of free will, may anticipate the new epoch? All philosophy springs from the idea that the human mind is the measure and leading edge of all things. And it is with poetry and philosophy that we must take that measure.

May it not be that the Tao leaves creation unfinished, and humans, who appear according to the will of Tao, are given further levels of creation to weave—the mode of the completion of each level more and more a matter of human decision, of the decisions of visionary humanity? Now the time of rebirth has come upon the world again, and though these years open wide their solstices and eclipses and windows to the ideas, yet, finally, the manner in which we present ourselves in that cumulatively intense final moment may well be a personal decision. Time grows ever more short; in the cosmic year-day of history, dawn is already breaking over Jerusalem.

Epilogue

There can be no certainty at all concerning the outcome of this investigation, nor can a reason be given why this particular idea complex has appropriated our attention. Why does it exist so autonomously if it has no meaning? Yet if it has meaning other than the inevitable transformation that is its message, what might that meaning be? We include this experience in the category of vision such as Blake and Zosimus experienced or, in a different context, such as Wallace or Descartes knew, yet this vision has sought to reveal the mechanics of the phenomenon of vision itself, and by way of making its point, it offers a hierarchical model of time and a new attempt to understand organism and mind. Unlike poetry, and more like science (though teleological structure is unwelcome in scientific speculation), this idea inherently implies its own testability. Indeed, the test is self-imposed by the temporal limits of the idea. If it fails the test, what can possibly have been its *raison d'être*? Would it not then be a rather Mephistophelian comment on the idea that nature does nothing in vain? The *I Ching*, which has been indispensable in the formulation of this theory, says of itself:

> Its principles contain the categories of all that is—literally the
> molds and the scope of all transformations. These categories are
> in the mind of man; everything, all that happens and everything
> that undergoes transformation, must obey the laws prescribed by
> the mind of man . . . fate can be shaped if its laws are known . . .
> reality is always conditioned, and these conditions of time and
> space limit and determine it. The Spirit however is not bound by
> these determinants and can bring them about as its own purpose
> requires. (R. Wilhelm 1964, p. 319)

However,

> A point of reference must be established, and this always requires
> a choice and a decision. It makes possible a system of coordinates
> into which everything else can be fitted . . . The problem, then,
> is to choose one's point of reference so that it coincides with the

point of reference for cosmic events. For only then can the world created by one's decision escape being dashed to pieces against the prepotent systems of relationships with which it would otherwise come into conflict. (R. Wilhelm 1964, p. 302)

Shamanism and the experiment at La Chorrera are not mere theoretical aberrations but are precursors of the ways and means by which conscious-ness will eventually organize its dominants to overthrow the modern on-tology of reductionism and arise reborn in an atemporalized and holistic mode of understanding. The search for a general theory of systems is nothing less than the seeking of an encounter with the divine image con-ceived as understanding. It is the quest par excellence and has always been so. Reality is ever complete in itself and always points beyond itself; the complete resolution of this paradox and the understanding it will bring are now nearer than ever before in the long history of our planet. The Confucian commentary on the Image for hexagram 54, *Kuei Mei*, The Marrying Maiden, hopefully prefigures the deliverance of final time:

In the autumn everything comes to its end. When thunder
is over the lake, the end is near. The eternity of the end is suggested by the trigram Chen, which comes forth in the east
(spring) and reaches the end of its activity in the west (autumn),
in accordance with fixed laws. At that moment the death dealing
power of autumn, which destroys all transient beings, becomes
active. Through knowledge of these laws, one reaches those
regions which are beyond beginning and end, birth and death.
(R. Wilhelm 1964, p. 316)

Let the times fulfill humanity's most ancient hope. We cannot say that it shall not be (fig. 32).

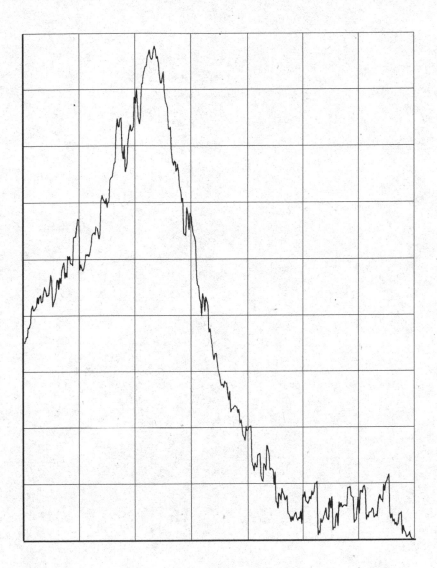

FIGURE 32

History's fractal mountain, the unscaled terminal [$^1/_{64}$] of the wave of novelty on all levels, a snapshot of the movement of the Tao through time at all timescales.

Appendix: The Mathematics of Timewave Zero

by Peter Meyer

1. General mathematical considerations

As usual, let the set of non-negative real numbers be denoted by $[0,\infty)$. Let $v(x)$ be any function $v:(0,\infty) \to (0,\infty)$ such that there exist positive real numbers c and d such that:

(1) for all x, $v(x) < c$, and
(2) for all $x < d$, $v(x) = 0$.

Then the function $f:[0,\infty) \to [0,\infty)$ defined below, where a is a real number greater than 1, is called a "fractal transform" of $v()$.

$$f(x) = \sum_{i=-\infty}^{\infty} \frac{v(x * a^i)}{a^i}$$

Clearly this definition is equivalent to:

$$f(x) = \sum_{i=-\infty}^{\infty} (v(x/a^i) * a^i)$$

To show that $f(x)$ is well defined we must show that $f(x)$ exists for all $x >= 0$.

Let x be any element of $[0,\infty)$. By condition (1), for all i, $v(x*a^i) < c$, so

$$\sum_{i=0}^{\infty} \frac{v(x*a^i)}{a^i} < \sum_{i=0}^{\infty} \frac{c}{a^i} = c * \left[\sum_{i=0}^{\infty} \frac{1}{a^i}\right] = \frac{c*a}{a-1}$$

so the left-most sum exists. Since $a > 1$ there exists an integer n such that $x/a^n < d$, so for all $i > n$, $x/a^i < d$, so by condition (2) for all $i > n$, $v(x/a^i) = 0$.

Thus:

$$\sum_{i=1}^{\infty} (v(x/a^i) * a^i) = \sum_{i=1}^{n} (v(x/a^i) * a^i)$$

which clearly exists. Since

$$\sum_{i=-\infty}^{\infty} \frac{v(x*a^i)}{a^i} = \sum_{i=0}^{\infty} \frac{v(x*a^i)}{a^i} + \sum_{i=1}^{\infty} (v(x/a^i) * a^i)$$

$f(x)$ exists.

As the first theorem of Timewave Zero mathematics we have:

Proposition 1: For all $x >= 0$, $f(a*x) = a*f(x)$.
PROOF: Let $x >= 0$ then

$$f(a*x) = \sum_{i=-\infty}^{\infty} \frac{v(a*x*a^i)}{a^i}$$

$$= \sum_{i=-\infty}^{\infty} a * \left[\frac{v(x*a^{(i+1)})}{a^{(i+1)}} \right]$$

$$= a * \left[\sum_{i=-\infty}^{\infty} \frac{v(x*a^i)}{a^i} \right]$$

$$= a * f(x) \qquad \text{which completes the proof.}$$

2. The mathematical definition of the timewave

The function that represents the timewave is essentially a fractal transform of a saw-tooth function. First we shall define this latter function.

Consider the following set of 384 natural numbers, traditionally known as the *data points* for the timewave:

```
 0,   0,   0,   2,   7,   4,   3,   2,   6,   8,
13,   5,  26,  25,  24,  15,  13,  16,  14,  19,
17,  24,  20,  25,  63,  60,  56,  55,  47,  53,
36,  38,  39,  43,  39,  35,  22,  24,  22,  21,
29,  30,  27,  26,  26,  21,  23,  19,  57,  62,
61,  55,  57,  57,  35,  50,  40,  29,  28,  26,
50,  51,  52,  61,  60,  60,  42,  42,  43,  43,
42,  41,  45,  41,  46,  23,  35,  34,  21,  21,
19,  51,  40,  49,  29,  29,  31,  40,  36,  33,
29,  26,  30,  16,  18,  14,  66,  64,  64,  56,
53,  57,  49,  51,  47,  44,  46,  47,  56,  51,
53,  25,  37,  30,  31,  28,  30,  36,  35,  22,
28,  32,  27,  32,  34,  35,  52,  49,  48,  51,
51,  53,  40,  43,  42,  26,  30,  28,  55,  41,
53,  52,  51,  47,  61,  64,  65,  39,  41,  41,
22,  21,  23,  43,  41,  38,  24,  22,  24,  14,
17,  19,  52,  50,  47,  42,  40,  42,  26,  27,
27,  34,  38,  33,  44,  44,  42,  41,  40,  37,
33,  31,  26,  44,  34,  38,  46,  44,  44,  36,
37,  34,  36,  36,  36,  38,  43,  38,  27,  26,
30,  32,  37,  29,  50,  49,  48,  29,  37,  36,
10,  19,  17,  24,  20,  25,  53,  52,  50,  53,
57,  55,  34,  44,  45,  13,   9,   5,  34,  26,
32,  31,  41,  42,  31,  32,  30,  21,  19,  23,
43,  36,  31,  47,  45,  43,  47,  62,  52,  41,
36,  38,  46,  47,  40,  43,  42,  42,  36,  38,
43,  53,  52,  53,  47,  49,  48,  47,  41,  44,
15,  11,  19,  51,  40,  49,  23,  23,  25,  34,
30,  27,   7,   4,   4,  32,  22,  32,  68,  70,
66,  68,  79,  71,  43,  45,  41,  38,  40,  41,
24,  25,  23,  35,  33,  38,  43,  50,  48,  18,
17,  26,  34,  38,  33,  38,  40,  41,  34,  31,
30,  33,  33,  35,  28,  23,  22,  26,  30,  26,
75,  77,  71,  62,  63,  63,  37,  40,  41,  49,
47,  51,  32,  37,  33,  49,  47,  44,  32,  38,
28,  38,  39,  37,  22,  20,  17,  44,  50,  40,
32,  33,  33,  40,  44,  39,  32,  32,  40,  39,
34,  41,  33,  33,  32,  32,  38,  36,  22,  20,
20,  12,  13,  10
```

These values are derived from certain transformations performed upon a set of 64 numbers, the numbers of lines that change from each hexagram in the King Wen sequence to the next, as explained previously in this book. They provide the basic numerical values used in this mathematical definition of the timewave.

Define w(i) as the ith value of this set, using zero-based indexing. Thus:

$$
\begin{array}{ccccccc}
i & 0 & 1 & 2 & 3 & 4 & \dots \\
w(i) & 0 & 0 & 0 & 2 & 4 & \dots
\end{array}
$$

Extend w to a function wi() such that for any non-negative integer i, wi(i) = wi(i mod 384), where i mod 384 is the remainder upon division of i by 384. Thus, for example, wi(777) = w(777 mod 384) = w(9) = 8. wi() is a discrete function defined only for integers, not for all real numbers.

Now for any non-negative real number x, let v(x) be the value obtained by linear interpolation between the values wi(int(x)) and wi(int(x)+1), where int(x) is the integral part of x. Formally v(x) is defined as

$$
wi(int(x)) + (x - int(x)) * (wi(x+1) - wi(x))
$$

or in expanded form:

$$
v(x) = w(int(x) \bmod 384) + ((x - int(x)) * (w (int(x+1) \bmod 384) - w (int(x) \bmod 384))).
$$

Now consider the fractal transform $f(x)$ of $v(x)$ using $a = 64$, as follows:

$$
f(x) = \sum_{i=-\infty}^{\infty} \frac{v(x*64^{\wedge}i)}{64^{\wedge}i}
$$

or, what is the same thing,

$$
f(x) = \sum_{i=-\infty}^{\infty} (v(x/64^{\wedge}i) * 64^{\wedge}i).
$$

The function $f(x)$ exists because

(1) for all x, $v(x) < 80$, and
(2) for all $x < 3$, $v(x) = 0$.

The fractal function t(x), which represents the timewave, and which is graphed by the software, is a simple transformation of $f(x)$, as follows:

$$t(x) = \frac{f(x)}{64^3}$$

where x = time in days prior to 6 A.M. on the zero date*. The scaling factor of 64^3 is used so as to produce convenient values on the y-axis of the graph.

Thus the value of t() at 6 A.M. on the zero date is

$$t(0) = \frac{f(0)}{64^3} = 0.$$

The value of t() at 6 A.M. on the day before the zero date is

$$t(1) = \frac{f(1)}{64^3} = 0.0000036160151.$$

The value of t() at 6 P.M. on the day ten days before the zero date is

$$t(9.5) = \frac{1}{64^3} * f(9.5) = 0.000047385693$$

and the value at 6 A.M. on the day 1,000,000,000,000 days (about 2,737,888,267 years) before the zero date is 5,192,046.655436.

These values are independent of the actual zero date. The value of the timewave at any point in time is not a function of that temporal location itself but rather of the difference between that time and the time assigned to the zero point of the wave.

---

* The timewave is zero only at one point, when x = 0. For x > 0 the value of the wave is positive. The zero point is the point in time chosen to correspond to the value 0 for x. The usual point used is 6 A.M. on December 21, 2012 (known as the zero date). Thus the timewave has a positive value for all points in time prior to the zero date, is zero only at the zero point, and is undefined after the zero point.

Note that the "direction" of the graph is the opposite of what is usual with Cartesian coordinates. The graph of a function $f(x)$ normally proceeds from left to right along the x-axis for increasing x. In this case the graph proceeds from right to left for increasing x, that is, for increasing number of days *prior* to the zero point.

3. The mathematical basis of resonance

The phenomenon of resonance, whereby regions of the wave at widely separated intervals may have exactly the same shape, is a remarkable feature of the timewave.* The mathematical basis for this phenomenon is as follows:

Consider a point in time x days prior to the zero date, then the value of the wave at that point is $t(x)$, as defined above. Now consider the value, $t(64*x)$, of the wave at the point in time $64*x$ days prior to the zero date. From the result proved at the end of Section 1 above we have that

$$t(64*x) \;=\; \frac{f(64*x)}{64^3} \;=\; \frac{64*f(x)}{64^3} \;=\; 64*t(x).$$

Thus the value of the wave at a point B, 64 times as distant from the zero point as a point A, is 64 times the value of the wave at A. Since this is also true for the points in the neighborhoods of A and B, it is thus clear why a region around B has the same shape as a region around A.

This resonance is called the first higher major resonance, since the region around the point C, 64*64 times as distant from the zero point as the point A, is also resonant with the region around A and constitutes the second higher major resonance of point A. There are an unlimited number of higher major resonances.

Similarly for any point x, $t(x/64) = t(x)/64$, and so the value of the wave at a point B, 64 times closer to the zero point than a point A, is 1/64 the

---

* The phenomenon of resonance is graphically illustrated by means of the software, Timewave Zero, which demonstrates this theory. It is explained in detail in chapter 2 of the manual provided with the software. Timewave Zero, which was designed and coded by the author of this appendix, is available from Dolphin Software, 48 Shattuck Square #147, Berkeley, California 94704; (510-464-3009).

value of the wave at A. Thus the region around B has the same shape as the region around A, and thus constitutes the first lower major resonance of the region around A. As with higher resonances, there are also second, third, fourth, and so on, lower major resonances to any region of the graph. The lower major resonances are compressed geometrically toward the zero point, so that only a few seconds may separate the nth and the (n+1)th major lower resonances for some, not particularly large, value of n.

4. Further mathematical results

The mathematics of Timewave Zero extend considerably beyond the initial proposition proved above.*

Lemma 1: For any natural number x, $v(x) = w(x \bmod 384)$.
PROOF: This follows from the definition of function $v()$, since for a natural number $x = \text{int}(x)$ and so $x - \text{int}(x) = 0$.

Lemma 2: For any natural numbers x and i, $v(x/64^{\wedge}i)*64^{\wedge}i$ is a natural number.
PROOF: By the definition of function $v()$:

$$
\begin{aligned}
v(x/64^{\wedge}i)*64^{\wedge}i = {} & 64^{\wedge}i * w(\text{int}(x/64^{\wedge}i) \bmod 384) \\
& + 64^{\wedge}i * (x/64^{\wedge}i - \text{int}(x/64^{\wedge}i)) \\
& * ((w(\text{int}(x/64^{\wedge}i + 1) \bmod 384) \\
& - w(\text{int}(x/64^{\wedge}i) \bmod 384))
\end{aligned}
$$

$$
\begin{aligned}
= {} & 64^{\wedge}i * w(\text{int}(x/64^{\wedge}i) \bmod 384) \\
& + (x - 64^{\wedge}i*\text{int}(x/64^{\wedge}i)) \\
& * ((w(\text{int}(x/64^{\wedge}i + 1) \bmod 384) \\
& - w(\text{int}(x/64^{\wedge}i) \bmod 384))
\end{aligned}
$$

* The mathematical results presented in the remainder of this appendix are based partly on work done by Klaus Scharff of Bergisch-Gladbach, Germany. Appendix V of the manual for Timewave Zero presents these results in relation to certain trigramatic resonances discovered in the timewave.

Since the values of the function w() are natural numbers, and x is a natural number, the value of this expression is a natural number.

Lemma 3: For any natural number x that is divisible by 3

$$f(x) = \sum_{i=0}^{\infty} v(x/64^\wedge i)*64^\wedge i + w(x*64 \bmod 384)/64.$$

PROOF: Suppose x is a natural number divisible by 3. By the definition of f(x) above:

$$f(x) = \sum_{i=-\infty}^{\infty} v(x/64^\wedge i)*64^\wedge i$$

$$= \sum_{i=0}^{\infty} v(x/64^\wedge i)*64^\wedge i + \sum_{i=1}^{\infty} v(x*64^\wedge i)/64^\wedge i$$

$$= \sum_{i=0}^{\infty} v(x/64^\wedge i)*64^\wedge i + \sum_{i=1}^{\infty} w(x*64^\wedge i \bmod 384)/64^\wedge i$$

by Lemma 1, since x*64^i is integral. Thus f(x) =

$$\sum_{i=0}^{\infty} v(x/64^\wedge i)*64^\wedge i + w(x*64 \bmod 384)/64 + \sum_{i=2}^{\infty} w(x*64^\wedge i \bmod 384)/64^\wedge i.$$

Since x = 3*y for some natural number y

$$\sum_{i=2}^{\infty} w(\text{int}(x*64^\wedge i) \bmod 384)/64^\wedge i = \sum_{i=0}^{\infty} w(3*y*64^\wedge 2*64^\wedge i \bmod 384)/64^\wedge i$$

$$= \sum_{i=0}^{\infty} w(384*y*32*64^\wedge i \bmod 384)/64^\wedge i$$

384*y*32*64^i mod 384 is 0, and w(0) = 0, so each term in this sum is 0.

Thus $f(x) = \sum_{i=0}^{\infty} v(x/64^\wedge i)*64^\wedge i + w(x*64 \bmod 384)/64$. QED

Proposition 2: For any natural number x that is divisible by 3 there is a natural number k such that $f(x) = k/64$.
PROOF: Let x be a natural number divisible by 3 then by Lemma 3

$$f(x) = \sum_{i=0}^{\infty} v(x/64^\wedge i)*64^\wedge i + w(x*64 \bmod 384)/64.$$

By Lemma 2 each term in this sum is an integer, so the sum is an integer, and so is an integral multiple of ⅟64. The second term in the sum is also an integral multiple of 64, and so $f(x)$ is.

On the basis of Proposition 2 we have:
Corollary 1: For any natural number x that is divisible by 3 there is a natural number k such that $t(x) = k/64^\wedge 4$.
PROOF: Since $t(x) = f(x)/64^\wedge 3$.

Proposition 3: For any natural number x that is divisible by 384 there is a natural number k such that $f(x) = 64*k$.
Proof: Let x be a natural number divisible by 384, then x is divisible by 3 so by Lemma 3:

$$f(x) = \sum_{i=0}^{\infty} v(x/64^\wedge i)*64^\wedge i + w(x*64 \bmod 384)/64.$$

Since x is divisible by 384, x*64 mod 384 is 0, so w(x*64 mod 384)/64 = w(0) = 0, so

$$f(x) = \sum_{i=0}^{\infty} v(x/64^\wedge i)*64^\wedge i = v(x) + \sum_{i=1}^{\infty} v(x/64^\wedge i)*64^\wedge i.$$

Now x is integral, so $v(x) = w(x \bmod 384) = w(0) = 0$, so

$$f(x) = \sum_{i=1}^{\infty} v(x/64^{\wedge}i)*64^{\wedge}i.$$

Since x is divisible by 384 there is some natural number k such that $x = 6*64*k$, so

$$f(x) = \sum_{i=1}^{\infty} v(6*64*k/(64*64^{\wedge}(i-1)))*(64*64^{\wedge}(i-1))$$

so

$$f(x) = 64 * \sum_{i=0}^{\infty} v(6*k/64^{\wedge}i)*64^{\wedge}i.$$

Now by Lemma 2 each term in the sum is a natural number, so the sum is, so there is a natural number k such that $f(x) = 64*k$.   QED

The mathematical results presented above are just a beginning. There are no doubt far more profound theorems that await discovery by mathematicians.

Bibliography

Abraham, Ralph. "Hamiltonian Catastrophes," and "Introduction to Morphology." In *Quatrième Rencontre entre Mathematiciens et Physiciens*, 1–114, Lyon, Vol. 4, Fascicule 1, 1972.

Aflven, Hans. *Worlds-Antiworlds*. San Francisco: W. H. Freeman & Co., 1966.

Axelrod, Julius. "Neurotransmitters." *Scientific American* (June 1974): 58–71.

Bigg, Charles. *The Christian Platonists of Alexandria*. Oxford: Clarendon Press, 1913.

Blake, William. *The Complete Writings*. London: Oxford University Press, 1969.

Boisen, Anton. *The Exploration of the Inner World*. New York: Harper, 1936.

———. "The Form and Content of Schizophrenic Thinking." *Psychiatry* 5 (1942).

Brack, A., et al. *Arch. Pharm.* 4(1961): 230.

Cohn, Norman. *The Pursuit of the Millennium*. London: Granada Publishing Ltd., 1970.

De Broglie, Louis. *Matter and Light*. New York: Dover Books, 1970.

———. *Physics and Microphysics*. New York: Pantheon Books, 1955.

De Santillana, G., and H. von Dechend. *Hamlet's Mill*. Boston: Gambit, 1969.

Dicara, L. V. "Learning in the Autonomic Nervous System." *Scientific American* 222 (1970): 30–39.

Drower, E. S. *The Mandaeans of Iraq and Iran*. Leiden: E. J. Brill, 1962.

Dyer, J. R. *Application of Absorption Spectroscopy of Organic Compounds*. New York: Prentice-Hall, 1965.

Eccles, John. *Understanding of the Brain*. New York: McGraw-Hill, 1973.

Eliade, Mircea. *Cosmos and History*. New York: Harper & Row, 1959.

———. *The Sacred and the Profane*. New York: Harper & Row, 1961.

———. *Shamanism: Archaic Techniques of Ecstasy*. New York: Pantheon Books, 1964.

———. *Myths, Dreams, and Mysteries*. New York: Harper & Row, 1967.

———. "Cultural Fashions and History of Religions." *Monday Evening Papers #18*, Center for Advanced Studies, Wesleyan University.

Fung, Yu-Lan. *The Spirit of Chinese Philosophy*. London: Routledge & Kegan Paul Ltd., 1947.

Gamow, George. *A Star Called the Sun*. New York: Viking Press, 1964.

Gardner, Martin. *The Ambidextrous Universe*. Bucks, England: Aylesbury, 1964.

Green, A. M., E. Green, and E. D. Walters. "Voluntary Control of Internal States: Psychological and Physiological." *J. Transpersonal Psychol.* 2 (1970): 1–26.

Grune, Gunther. "Tryptophan Metabolism in Psychoses." In *Amines and Schizophrenia*, edited by H. E. Himwich, S. Kety, and J. R. Smythies. New York: Pergamon Press, 1967.

Harner, Michael. "The Sound of Rushing Water." *Natural History*, July 1968.

Heim, R., and R. G. Wasson. *Les Champignons Hallucinogènes du Mexique.* Paris: Editions du Muséum National d'Histoire Naturelle, 1968.

Hinton, C. H. *What Is the Fourth Dimension?* London: Swan Sonnenschein, Lowrey & Co., 1887.

Hyden, H. "Biological Approaches to Learning and Memory." In *Beyond Reductionism: The Alpbach Symposium,* edited by A. Koestler and J. R. Smythies, 85–117. Boston: Beacon Press, 1969.

Ingram, P. *Biological and Biochemical Applications of Electron Spin Resonance.* London: Adam Hilger Ltd., 1969.

Jonas, Hans. *The Phenomenon of Life.* New York: Dell Publishing Co., 1966.

Jung, Carl G. *Psychology and Alchemy.* New York: Pantheon Books, 1952.

———. *The Practice of Psychotherapy.* New York: Pantheon Books, 1954.

———. *The Archetypes and the Collective Unconscious.* New York: Pantheon Books, 1959.

———. *Mysterium Coniunctionis.* New York: Pantheon Books, 1963.

Kety, S. "New Perspectives in Psychopharmacology." In *Beyond Reductionism: The Alpbach Symposium,* edited by A. Koestler and J. R. Smythies, 334–356. Boston: Beacon Press, 1969.

Knoll, Max. "Transformations of Science in Our Age." In *Man and Time: Papers for the Eranos Yearbooks,* edited by Joseph Campbell, 264–307. Vol. 3. New York: Pantheon Books, 1957.

Lashley, Karl S. "In Search of the Engram." In *Symposium of the Society of Experimental Biology* 4 (1950).

Leibniz, Gottfried Wilhelm von. "Monadology." In *Philosophical Works of Leibniz,* trans. G. Martin Duncan. New Haven: Tuttle, Morehouse, & Taylor, 1890.

Little, W. A. "Superconductivity at Room Temperature." *Scientific American* (February 1965).

Lommel, Andreas. *Shamanism: The Beginnings of Art.* New York: McGraw-Hill, 1967.

Luce, Gay Gaer. *Biological Rhythms in Human and Animal Physiology.* New York: Dover, 1971.

Mandelbrot, Benoit. *The Fractal Geometry of Nature.* San Francisco: Freeman, 1977.

Mandell, Arnold J., and Charles E. Spooner. "Psychochemical Research Studies in Man." *Science* 162(1968): 1442ff.

Morgan, I. G., and L. J. Austin. In *Neurochemistry* 15 (1968): 41–51.

Munn, Henry. "The Mushrooms of Language." In *Hallucinogens and Shamanism,* edited by Michael Harner, 86–122. New York: Oxford Univ. Press, 1973.

Nadel, S. F. "A Study of Shamanism in the Nuba Mountains." *J. Anth. Inst. of Great Britain and Ireland* (1946).

Naranjo, Claudio. "Psychotropic Properties of the Harmala Alkaloids." In *Ethnopharmacologic Search for Psychoactive Drugs,* edited by Donald Efron, Bo Holmstedt, and Nathan S. Kline, 385–391. Public Health Service Publication No. 1645, Washington, D.C., 1967.

———. *The Healing Journey.* New York: Random House, 1973.

Needham, Joseph. *Science and Civilization in China.* 2 vols. Cambridge: Cambridge Univ. Press, 1954.

———. *Time and Eastern Man.* Glasgow: The University Press, 1965.

Newton, B. A. "Chemotherapeutic Compounds Affecting DNA Structure and Function." In *Advances in Pharmacology and Chemotherapy,* edited by S. Garattini, A. Goldin, F. Hacking, and I. J. Kopin, 149–181. Vol. 8. London: Academic Press, 1970.

Nordland, O. "Shamanism as an Experiencing of the Unreal." In *Studies in Shamanism,* edited by Carl-Martin Edsman. Stockholm: Almqvist & Wiksell, 1967.

Pennington, A. "Advances in Holography." *Scientific American* 213 (1968).

Pietsch, Paul. "Shuffle Brain." *Harper's* 244 (1972).

Planz, G., K. Quiring, and D. Palm. "Rates of Recovery of Irreversibly Inhibited Monoamine Oxidases: A Measure of Enzyme Protein Turn-over." *Naunyn-Schmiedeburg's Arch. Pharmacol.* 273 (1972): 27–42.

Polanyi, Michael. "Life's Irreducible Structure." *Science* 160 (1968).

Pribram, Karl. "The Neurophysiology of Remembering." *Scientific American* 22 (1969).

———. "The Brain." *Psychology Today* 5, no. 4 (1971a).

———. *Languages of the Brain.* Englewood Cliffs, NJ: Prentice-Hall, 1971b.

Prigogine, Ilya, Gregoire Nicolis, and Agnes Babloyantz. "Thermodynamics of Evolution." *Physics Today* (November-December 1972).

Quisel, Gilles. "Time and History in Patristic Christianity." In *Man and Time: Papers for the Eranos Yearbooks,* edited by J. Campbell, 85–107. Vol. 3. New York: Pantheon Books, 1967.

Rinder, Irwin D. "New Directions and an Old Problem: The Definition of Normality." *Psychiatry* 27 (1964).

Ritchie-Calder, Lord. *After the Seventh Day.* New York: Simon & Schuster, 1961.

Schrödinger, Edwin. *What Is Life?* Cambridge: Cambridge Univ. Press, 1944.

Schultes, Richard E., and A. Hofmann. *The Botany and Chemistry of Hallucinogens.* Springfield, IL: Charles C. Thomas, 1973.

Sherburne, Donald W., ed. *A Key to Whitehead's "Process and Reality"* Bloomington: Indiana Univ. Press, 1966.

Silverman, Julian. "Shamans and Acute Schizophrenia." *American Anthropologist* 69 (1967).

Sinnot, Edmund W. *Cell and Psyche.* New York: Harper & Bros., 1950.

Smythies, J. R. "A Possible Role for Ribonucleic Acid in Neuronal Membrane." *Communications in Behavioral Biology* 3 (1969): 265.

———. "The Chemical Nature of the Receptor Site." *International Review of Neurobiology* 13 (1970): 181–222.

———. "The Mode of Action of Psychotomimetic Drugs." In *Neurosciences Research Symposium Summaries,* edited by F. O. Schmitt, G. Adelman, T. Melnechuk, and F. G. Worden., vol. 5. Cambridge, MA: The MIT Press, 1971.

Smythies, J. R., and F. Antun. "Binding of Tryptamine and Allied Compounds to Nucleic Acid." *Nature* 223 (1969): 1061.

Snyder, S. H., S. P. Banerjee, H. I. Yamamura, and D. Greenberg. "Drugs, Neuro-transmitters, and Schizophrenia." *Science* (1974): 1243–1253.

Sullivan, H. S. *Conceptions of Modern Psychiatry.* New York: Norton, 1953.

Szent-Gyorgyi, Albert. *Introduction to a Submolecular Biology.* New York: Academic Press, 1960.

Tryon, Edward. "Is the Universe a Vacuum Fluctuation?" *Nature* 246 (1973): 396–397.

Undenfriend, S., B. Witkop, B. Redfield, and H. Weissbach. "Studies with Reversible Inhibitors of Monoamine Oxidase: Harmaline and Related Compounds." *Biochem. Pharmacol.* 1 (1958): 160–165.

Van Der Leeuw, G. "Primordial Time and Final Time." In *Man and Time: Papers for the Eranos Yearbooks,* edited by J. Campbell, 324–352. Vol. 3. New York: Pantheon Books, 1957.

Wallace, Anthony F. C. "On Being Just Complicated Enough." *Proc. of N.A.S.* 47 (1961): 458–464.

Wasson, R. Gordon. *Soma: Divine Mushroom of Immortality.* Italy: Harcourt Brace Jovanovich, 1971.

Whitehead, Alfred North. *The Function of Reason.* Boston: Beacon Press, 1958.

———. *Science and the Modern World.* New York: The Free Press, 1967.

———. *Modes of Thought.* New York: The Free Press, 1968.

———. *Process and Reality.* New York: The Free Press, 1969.

Whyte, Lancelot L. *Internal Factors in Evolution.* New York: George Braziller, 1965.

Whyte, Lancelot L., A. Wilson, and D. Wilson, eds. *Hierarchical Structures.* New York: American Elsevier, 1969.

Wiener, Harry. "External Chemical Messengers." *New York State J. of Med.* (1968).

Wilhelm, Hellmut. "The Concept of Time in the Book of Changes." In *Man and Time: Papers for the Eranos Yearbooks,* edited by J. Campbell, 212–232. Vol. 3. New York: Pantheon Books, 1957.

Wilhelm, Richard. *The I Ching or Book of Changes.* Translated by Cary F. Baines. New York: Princeton Univ. Press, 1964.

Wilson, Albert. "Hierarchical Structure in the Cosmos." In *Hierarchical Structures,* edited by L. L. Whyte, A. Wilson, and D. Wilson, 113–133. New York: American Elsevier, 1969.

Wilson, Donna. "Forms of Hierarchy: A Selected Bibliography." In *Hierarchical Structures,* edited by L. L. Whyte, A. Wilson, and D. Wilson, 287–314. New York: American Elsevier, 1969.

Yielding, K. Lemone, and Helene Sterglanz. "Lysergic Acid Diethylamide (LSD) Binding to Deoxyribonucleic Acid (DNA)." *Proc. Soc. Exp. Biol. Med.* 128 (1968): 1096–1098.

Index

aesthetics, 29
afterlife, 155–156, 185
alchemy, 50–51
Alfven, Hans, 183
Ambidextrous Universe, The (Gardner),
    181–182
amines, 62–63, 69, 90–92, 106, 113. *See also*
    hallucinogens; tryptamines
antimatter. *See* matter/antimatter
Arakawa, 129
archetypes, 12–13, 16–17, 51, 109, 137–138,
    185; *I Ching* and, 121, 123, 140
artist, as shaman, 17–18
astronomy, 127–134
astrophysics, 176–177
audile phenomenon, with tryptamine use,
    95–100, 180
autohypnosis, 24–25
awareness. *See* consciousness
axoplasmic flow, 90
ayahuasca, 95, 104–106, 106

Banisteriopsis, 95, 203. *See also ayahuasca;*
    caapi, 96
behavior, 19; learned, 45–47, 91–92
beta-carbolines. *See* harmine
bioelectronic field phenomenon, 5, 155
Bohr, Niels, 54
Boisen, Anton, 20, 22
Bos indicus (Indian humped cattle), 99, 180
boundary conditions, 41–42, 92–93, 194,
    204; temporal, 139, 146, 189
brain: changes in, 87–88; holographic prin-
    ciples in, 44–49; metabolism in,
    100–101. *See also* mind; mind-body
    connection

calendars, 171: effect of lunar cycles on, 153;
    I Ching as, 123, 127–128, 130–134,
    145–146
Center of the World, 11. *See also* galactic
    center
cerebrum, 46–48
chanting, 180
charge-transfer mechanism, 75–81, 107; in
    ESR signals, 84–86; superconductivity
    of, 101–103, 104–106

China: beliefs of, 146, 167–168, 198; calen-
    dars of, 130–134; culture of, 126–127,
    132–133; *I Ching* in, 121, 145–146
Ching-Chhih, Li, 123
codons, 139–140
collective unconscious, 5; accessing, 12–13,
    27; biological basis of, 51, 106–107,
    176
color, associated with *ayahuasca*, 95
concrescence, 156, 167, 176, 179, 193–194,
    202, 205; final, 185, 187–188, 189; par-
    tial, 168, 185–186; predicting future,
    195–196, 204
consciousness, 50, 175–176, 208; and ESR,
    81, 104, 203; and metabolism, 100–101,
    106–107, 195; and organization, 57, 138,
    139–140; quantum-mechanical basis of,
    80–81
Coordinative Conditions, 135–137
cosmology, 176–179, 194
cultures, 19, 26; concepts of time, 17, 146;
    shamanism in, 12, 27. *See also* China,
    culture of
cycles, 167–168, 189; of time, 126–128, 186,
    190, 195–196

dancing, 15, 180
dawn, importance of, 194–195
death, 10–11, 17, 25
de Broglie, Louis, 181
determinism, 147–150, 170–171, 204–205
divination, 121, 123, 198–199
DNA (deoxyribonucleic acid): DNA-
    harmine, 90–92, 103, 104–107; ESR in,
    112, 203–204; functions of, 137–138, 151;
    intercalation into, 70–74, 76, 88–92;
    structure of, 52, 153, 194
dreams, 22
drug action, 18, 68–75, 78–79, 101. *See also*
    hallucinogens; tryptamines
drumming, 15

ebb and flow, in time, 171–172
Eberhard, W., 123, 130, 132
Eccles, John, 90
ecstasy: shamanic, 6, 10, 11–12, 15, 26; of
    tryptamines, 113

interference patterns, 47, 146
Internal Factors in Evolution (Whyte), 135
intuition, 30, 40
Ionides, 129
isolation, 22, 24

Jívaro Indians, 95
Jonas, Hans, 115, 169, 202
Jung, Carl G., 51, 138
Jupiter, 129–130

Kety, S., 88
King Wen sequence, 121, 138, 140–146, 187, 214
Kraepelin, 20
kua. *See* hexagrams

La Chorrera, 98, 121, 185; experiment at, 104–106, 116–117
language, 115–116, 179–180
Languages of the Brain (Pribram), 49
Lashley, Karl, 45–46
laws of nature. *See* nature, laws of
Lehmann, Heinz, 129
Leibniz, Gottfried Wilhelm von, 52–53, 198
Leidenfrost phenomenon, 182–183
levels of order, 180
liberation, 3–6. *See also* freedom
life-crisis, 24; and mental disorders, 19, 20, 21
light, 95, 193; and pineal gland, 65–67, 195
location, simple vs. quantum, 29, 32, 35–36, 54
Lommel, Andreas, 11, 12, 26–27
low-temperature systems, 180, 201–202
lunations, 126, 127, 153
lysergic acid (LSD), 70

magic, 4, 95
Mandelbrot, Benoit, 172
mass, 31–32
mathematics, of Timewave Zero, 211–220
matter/antimatter, 176, 177, 182–185, 193
Mayans, 171
meaning: lack of, 17; organization of, 180
melatonin, 66–67
memory, 87–88; DNA and, 91–92, 106–107, 137–138; ESR in, 86–87, 203; holographic principles in, 44–47, 48
mental disorders, 129; and shamanism, 12, 13–14, 26–27. *See also* schizophrenia

mescaline, 59, 113
metabolism, 64, 98, 203; and temporal processes, 121, 140, 151
metaphysics, 30, 39–40
methodology, 6, 7, 29–34, 139
Meyer, Peter. *See* Timewave Zero
mind, 6–7, 121, 176, 202, 205; accessing unconscious, 19, 22–23; holographic principles in, 49–55; and organisms, 32–33, 32–34, 36, 39–40, 41–42, 92–93. *See also* mind-body connection
mind-body connection, 4, 41–42, 49–50, 57–58, 101, 138; and unconscious, 5, 51
miracles, 190–191
modular wave-hierarchy: of *I Ching*, 151–152, 181, 204; of time, 146–150, 156–161, 201–203
monads, 50–51, 52–53, 54
monamine oxidase (MAO), 112–113, 203
mutations, in evolution, 201–203
myths, 168–169, 177, 185, 186–188

Nadel, S. F., 14
Naranjo, Claudio, 95
narcotic use, 15
nature, 32–33, 34; laws of, 30–32, 187–188, 190–191; as process, 36–37, 39–40
Needham, Joseph, 123, 126
nerve cells, 44–47, 58–59, 89. *See also* receptor sites; synapses, nerve
nervous system, 62
neurotransmitters, 65; and hallucinogens, 58–65, 67–68; intercalation of, 68–77, 80–81, 85, 90–92
norepinephrine, 61–63
novelty, 29, 176, 180, 195; ingressions of, 140, 150, 156, 187, 190, 205; periods of, 170, 171, 174, 179
nuclear magnetic resonance (NMR), 84–85
nucleic acids: bonding of, 69–74, 79; ESRs of, 81, 85. *See also* DNA; RNA

organisms, 67–68, 136, 139, 195; consciousness of, 37–40, 81, 202. *See also* organization, of organisms
organization, 57; organisms, 41–42, 147, 180; psychic, 19, 20–22, 26; temporal, 146–150, 177
overtones. *See* harmonics

paradisiacal epoch, 17, 185
paranormal powers, 4, 16, 116

Szent-Gyorgyi, Albert, 75–79, 85

Tao, 168, 187, 205
taxonomies, 139–140
teleology, 40, 202–203, 204
telepathy, 16, 110, 116
temporal processes, 101, 121, 153–155. *See also* Coordinative Conditions; time
thought, 22, 29; and brain metabolism, 65–66, 86–87, 100–101, 105–107, 137–138; as holograms, 48, 151
time, 32, 182; cosmology, 176–179; end of, 174–176, 185, 186–188; as experienced by organisms, 37, 50, 101, 138–139, 151–152, 202–203, 205; *I Ching* and, 121, 127, 140; in quantum theory, 34–36; waves, 146–150, 161, 170, 172, 211–220. *See also* space-time; temporal processes; Timewave Zero
Timewave Zero, 161, 170–175, 195–196; mathematics of, 211–220
trances, 10, 25–26, 106, 115
transference, 13, 110, 112
transformation, 161, 174, 186–188; and collective unconscious, 155–156, 176; as theme, 109, 167–168
Tryon, Edward, 177
tryptamines, 59, 78–79; and audile phenomenon, 95–100, 98, 100–101, 104; binding to nucleic acids, 71–74; and evolution, 179–180, 203; at La Chorrera, 98, 104–106; methylated, 101–103, 113; psychological effects of, 4, 109–110, 112, 113–116
tryptophan, 66, 101–103
tryptophan hydroxylase, 66

unconscious, 5, 51; accessing, 6, 17–18, 109, 121; and schizophrenics, 19, 22–23. *See also* collective unconscious
understanding, gaining, 109–110, 112
universe, 176–179, 182–185

vacuum fluctuations, 178, 182
vibration, 35–36, 80–81, 98–100, 168
vocalizations, 104–106; and audile phenomenon, 98–100, 180

Wallace, Anthony F. C., 139–140
Wang Pi, 168
Wasson, R. Gordon, 15
waveforms, 47–48, 105–106. *See also* standing waveforms
wave-hierarchy. *See* modular wave-hierarchy
waves, 98–100, 146, 152–153, 181, 187, 189; mathematics of, 211–220; quantification of, 156–161; of time, 146–150, 172, 195–196
What Is Life? (Schrödinger), 103–104
Whitehead, Alfred North, 7, 30, 53–55, 100, 161, 168, 184, 187–188. *See also* concrescence
Whyte, L. L., 135–137, 201
Wilhelm, Richard, 123, 131, 133, 199
Wilson, Albert, 136

yao, 126, 127, 145–146, 152–153. *See also* hexagrams

zero state, 150, 156, 158, 181, 187; at ends of epochs, 161, 171–172, 188, 189
zodiac, 130–131, 196